Entrepreneurship

D0213933

To Rebecca, who tightens my logic and brightens my life

Entrepreneurship

An Evidence-based Guide

Robert A. Baron

Spears Chair of Entrepreneurship, Spears School of Business, Oklahoma State University, USA

Edward Elgar
Cheltenham, UK • Northampton, MA, USA

Published by
Edward Elgar Publishing Limited
The Lypiatts
15 Lansdown Road
Cheltenham
Glos GL50 2JA
UK

Edward Elgar Publishing, Inc.
William Pratt House
9 Dewey Court
Northampton
Massachusetts 01060
USA

A catalogue record for this book
is available from the British Library

Library of Congress Control Number: 2011942555

ISBN 978 1 78100 037 3 (cased)
ISBN 978 1 78100 039 7 (paperback)

Typeset by Servis Filmsetting Ltd, Stockport, Cheshire
Printed and bound by MPG Books Group, UK

Contents

About the author

● ●

Robert A. Baron (Ph.D., University of Iowa) is the Spears Chair of Entrepreneurship at Oklahoma State University. He has held faculty appointments at several universities, including Rensselaer Polytechnic Institute (where he held the Wellington Chair of Management), Purdue, the universities of Minnesota, Texas, South Carolina, and Washington, Princeton University, and the University of Oxford. From 1979 to 1981 he served as a Program Director at the National Science Foundation. In 2001 he was appointed as a Visiting Senior Research Fellow by the French Ministry of Research (Université de Toulouse and LIRHE). He has also served as a Department Chair (1987–93) and Interim Dean of the Lally School of Management and Technology (2001–03). He is a Fellow of the American Psychological Association and the Society of Industrial and Organizational Psychology, and a Charter Fellow of the Association for Psychological Science. He has published more than 130 articles and 45 chapters, and is the author or co-author of numerous books in management and psychology. He serves on the boards of several journals (the *Academy of Management Journal*, the *Journal of Business Venturing*, and the *Journal of Management*), and is an Associate Editor for the *Strategic Entrepreneurship Journal*. He holds three U.S. patents and was founder and CEO of IEP, Inc. (1993–2000). His current research interests focus on social and cognitive factors in entrepreneurship, and he has published papers on such topics as opportunity recognition, the role of entrepreneurs' social skills in their success, and the role of positive affect in creativity, innovation, and firm-level performance.

Preface: Entrepreneurship's "split personality"—and how to reunite it

· ·

Almost everyone has encountered the term "split personality"; although it has a complex medical meaning, in everyday use it refers to a condition in which a specific person possesses more than one identity or personality—almost as if several "people" inhabit a single body! Although it applies primarily to individuals, in an important sense this term is also relevant to the subject of this book—*entrepreneurship*. In fact, the metaphor of a "split personality" seems to fit entrepreneurship surprisingly well. First, and perhaps most fundamentally, entrepreneurship is both a *business activity* and a recently emerged *academic field*; thus, it has two distinct identities. Further, each of these aspects has its own distinct goals. As a business activity, entrepreneurship seeks to generate *value*—economic (e.g., profits), social (products or services that are beneficial to many people), or both. The academic field of entrepreneurship, in contrast, seeks *basic knowledge*—enhanced understanding of the process of entrepreneurship or how entrepreneurs actually go about converting ideas for something new and better into tangible reality. The ultimate goal of such knowledge, of course, is that of being able to offer better help to entrepreneurs—advice and guidance that will improve their chances of success. But how can such knowledge be acquired? This question highlights yet another basic split—this time *within* the academic field of entrepreneurship.

This division involves the methods used for obtaining increased understanding of entrepreneurship. One approach is very straightforward: *ask experienced entrepreneurs*. They have "been there, done that"—sometimes repeatedly—so their advice and insights should go a long way toward providing the knowledge we seek. Unfortunately, there is a major "fly in this ointment": as we'll see in more detail in Chapter 1, as human beings we are not very good at remembering what we did in the past, why we did it, or even the outcomes that followed. Memory, in short, is far from perfect. In addition, our thinking is subject to many types of error and bias (e.g., a strong tendency to be overoptimistic, and a powerful predilection to ignore information that is inconsistent with our present views). Given these flaws in our cognitive systems, it seems somewhat risky to rely solely on entrepreneurs to provide the information we seek.

Reflecting this idea, a growing number of scholars in the academic field of entrepreneurship have concluded that a different approach is useful and perhaps preferable: one based on systematic research and the *evidence-based knowledge* it yields. What makes this kind of information especially valuable? Perhaps the following example will be helpful. Imagine that we asked 100 famous and highly successful entrepreneurs to describe the true "secrets" of their success—the factors or characteristics that, they believe, propelled them to the heights of achievement. Would they all name the same factors? Probably they would not. Here, by way of illustration, is how two famous entrepreneurs answered when asked to describe the key ingredient in their success: "I do not think there is any other quality so essential to success of any kind as the quality of *perseverance*. It overcomes almost everything, even nature" (John D. Rockefeller); and "The secret of business is to know something that *nobody else knows*" (Aristotle Onassis).

Who is correct? Is it perseverance? Knowledge? Both? Or is success actually due to other factors not mentioned by either of these successful individuals? The history of science suggests that, on the basis of such informal information, we can't really tell. More importantly, it suggests that our chances of knowing will be greatly increased if, instead, we rely primarily on evidence obtained through systematic research. That is a major theme of this book, and is reflected in its subtitle: *An Evidence-based Guide*. Put simply, it suggests that, *whenever possible, we should rely on evidence-based knowledge derived from careful research rather than the personal views of individual entrepreneurs*.

This is no way implies that we should ignore the guidance and insights of entrepreneurs—absolutely *not*! In fact, much systematic research in the field of entrepreneurship relies on information provided by entrepreneurs. But—and this is the crucial point—instead of asking a few entrepreneurs to describe their views in an open-ended, informal manner, we obtain input from hundreds of entrepreneurs who respond to specific questions posed in a highly standardized format (e.g., in printed or online surveys). In addition, systematic research designed to answer important questions about the nature of entrepreneurship often gathers "hard" financial data—information on sales, growth, profits, patents, and so on.

In short, what's recommended throughout this book is a balanced approach in which we draw on several different sources and use many different methods to gather relevant information. Certainly, this includes the comments and advice of experienced entrepreneurs—they are often a fount of invaluable insights. In addition, though, we should obtain the kind of evidence-based knowledge that only systematic research can provide. Overall, *we should use every tool available to add to current knowledge* and so be better able to help entrepreneurs succeed.

I am writing these words in Oklahoma, so it seems only fitting to close with a comment by Will Rogers, the famous cowboy philosopher of this state: "It isn't what we don't know that gives us trouble, it's what we know that *isn't so*." In other words, not having knowledge is not as dangerous as having false information we believe to be true. That is one more reason why, in the pages that follow, evidence-based knowledge rather than entrepreneurs' personal views—no matter how impassioned or ardent—will be our primary guide.

Robert A. Baron
Stillwater, Oklahoma

PART I • THE FOUNDATIONS OF ENTREPRENEURSHIP

1 Making the *possible* real: the core of entrepreneurship

· ·

Chapter outline

Entrepreneurship: Is new venture creation "all there is"?
Entrepreneurship: a search for fortune, fame, personal fulfillment, "doing good," or—perhaps—all of the above?
Can entrepreneurs give us the "secrets of success"—or must we look elsewhere for the answers?
Where, precisely, is "elsewhere?" The benefits of actual data

> If you can dream it, you can do it. (Walt Disney)

> The critical ingredient is . . . doing something. It's as simple as that. A lot of people have ideas, but there are few who decide to do something about them now. . . . The true entrepreneur is a doer, not a dreamer.
> (Nolan Bushnell, founder of Atari and Chuck E. Cheese's)

Entrepreneurship: Is new venture creation "all there is"?

Entrepreneur: the word has an almost mystical ring. For many persons, it triggers mental images of Bill Gates, Steve Jobs, Mark Zuckerberg, Sergey Brin, Larry Page—along with vivid thoughts of the huge fame and vast wealth these famous entrepreneurs have reaped from their efforts. Similarly, the word *entrepreneurship*, which most people interpret as meaning what entrepreneurs *do* (mainly, in the public mind, starting successful new businesses), conjures up images of heroic efforts by entrepreneurs to convert their ideas and visions to reality and so, perhaps, change the lives of countless people—and the world!

Is this enticing view of entrepreneurship accurate? And does it involve, as many people seem to believe, only one major focus: building a new, and preferably high-growth, business? The answer, in most people's minds, is definitely "yes." To paraphrase the words of a song popular back in the 1950s, they believe that, where entrepreneurship is concerned, "That's all there is"—starting and running new ventures is what entrepreneurship is all about.

This is one reason why many courses on entrepreneurship focus heavily on business models and business plans, and seem to assume that these are, and should be, the true heart of the field. In one respect, that idea makes very good sense: entrepreneurship does usually make its home in schools of business or management, and is viewed as being, primarily, a branch of management, where it joins other, more established fields such as marketing, finance, and operations. But in fact entrepreneurship, at its core, involves something more basic. In essence, it involves the application of human creativity, ingenuity, knowledge, skills, and energy to the development of something *new*, *useful*, and better than what currently exists—and that creates some kind of value (social or economic). In other words, it occurs whenever, wherever, and however individuals take concrete action to convert their ideas and dreams about "something better" into reality—whenever and however they try to give them tangible existence in the external world. Reaching this goal certainly does often involve launching and developing a new business; that is certainly a central aspect of entrepreneurship, and will be a key focus of the present book. But it is important to note that this is not the only way in which human creativity can be expressed in efforts to develop something that is both new and useful. In fact, individuals can think and act entrepreneurially without necessarily launching a new venture. What is essential is simply that they *take action to move their ideas from the possible to the real*. (This suggestion is developed in detail in Chapter 9.)

When entrepreneurship is defined in this broader way, the basis for its tremendous popular appeal comes sharply into focus. While many people do not want to start a new venture and spend their time running it, they *do* have ideas for innovations—for ways of doing something better or more efficiently than it is being done at present—and they do want to put these ideas to use. Further, many realize that this can be a road not merely to personal success, but also to improving their own work and lives, and perhaps those of other people too. Ideas that work—that lead to something better than currently exists—can benefit not just the people who originate them, but entire communities and societies, by helping the people in them lead richer, more comfortable, and more fulfilling lives. Consider, for instance, the development of online services for making all kinds of travel arrangements—airline, hotel, and automobile reservations. Certainly, these have made certain aspects of travel easier for hundreds of millions of persons. So yes, indeed, ideas that work do provide important benefits for large numbers of persons.

One more advantage of this broader conception of entrepreneurship is also worth noting: when it is defined as involving the application of human creativity and ingenuity to the creation of something new and useful, the intrinsic excitement often generated by such activities springs

into focus. Seeking something new and doing so under conditions of considerable risk and uncertainty are very challenging experiences—but also
ones that many people find stimulating and enjoyable. In the words of the
Danish philosopher Søren Kierkegaard (slightly paraphrased):

> If I were to wish for anything . . . [it would not be] wealth and power, but . . .
> the passionate sense of the *potential*, for the eye which, forever young . . .
> sees the possible. Pleasure disappoints, possibility never. And what wine is so
> sparkling . . . so fragrant . . . so intoxicating . . . as possibility?

In short, entrepreneurship, with its focus on the *possible*, on transforming
ideas into reality, does indeed offer the promise of a more exciting, stimulating existence than most persons experience much of the time. Little
wonder, then, that it is enticing to so many people and that, around the
world, many millions of new companies are launched each year.

Although the view of entrepreneurship described above may seem
somewhat surprising, it is actually closely aligned with one well-known and
widely accepted definition of the field (Shane and Venkataraman, 2000,
again slightly paraphrased):

> Entrepreneurship, as a field of business, seeks to understand how opportuni-
> ties to create something new (e.g., new products or services, new markets,
> new production processes or raw materials, new ways of organizing existing
> technologies) *arise* and are *discovered* or *created* by *specific persons*, who then
> use various means to *exploit or develop* them, thus producing a wide range of
> *effects*.

In essence, this definition suggests that entrepreneurship does indeed
involve the conversion of ideas (recognized or created opportunities) into
something new and tangible through some kind of overt action. This can
involve starting a new business—absolutely! But entrepreneurship, defined
in this manner, can occur in many other contexts and take many other
forms. For instance, consider a talented teacher who realizes that currently
used techniques for equipping students with basic skills are ineffective. The
teacher, on the basis of her or his experience and talent, develops a new
approach—one that is, in fact, better than the present techniques. This
teacher is thinking and acting entrepreneurially, even if she or he does not
start a new company to develop and promote these new methods.

Similarly, consider a physician working for a government health
agency who notices that a very large proportion of the agency's medical
services (and budget) are being used in a very small number of locations
and to care for a very small number of patients. This may lead the physician to develop effective ways of identifying such persons and of intervening so as to reduce the magnitude of their seemingly endless array of
problems. This would allow the agency to use its resources more effectively

and so, perhaps, to enhance the health of large numbers of persons. Again, the physician is thinking and acting entrepreneurially: she is using her knowledge, ingenuity, and creativity to formulate something new, useful—and better. Starting a new venture is not necessarily involved, although again it might follow if the physician decided to develop programs for identifying these medical "hot spots" that could be sold to other health agencies around the country or the world. (In fact, efforts to identify—and treat—such "hot spots" are currently underway; Gawande, 2011.)

One more point: Are individuals who become franchisees (e.g., someone who opens a new McDonald's restaurant) entrepreneurs? Although they are running a "new" business, the definition offered above suggests that they are not actually entrepreneurs. They are not using their creativity, ingenuity, and so on to create something new and useful. Rather, they are provided with a "turnkey" operation—a detailed plan on how to operate their franchise which franchisors expect them to follow very closely. Little room is left for creativity or autonomy, and franchisees who depart from the rules set up by the franchisor run the very real risk of losing their franchise—and all of their investment. In that sense, then, franchise holders are not entrepreneurs. Of course, many use operating a franchise as a kind of training for opening their own independent business. While they are franchisees, however, their independence and latitude for applying their own creativity are severely limited.

To recapitulate: a central tenet of this book is that entrepreneurship, as an activity, is actually broader in scope than the traditional view which focuses on starting new ventures. To repeat: it occurs whenever, wherever, and however human beings use their own creativity, ingenuity, energy, and talent to develop something new and useful. This will be a basic theme in the remainder of the volume, and, although much attention will certainly be focused on new ventures (this is the source of much of the evidence we will review), this broader perspective will be reintroduced—and restated!—as appropriate.

Having made these points and offered some essential definitions, we turn, in the remainder of this initial chapter, to several basic tasks. First, we will focus on the question of "Why?" Why do individuals become entrepreneurs? Why do they give up regular jobs and, often, relatively high levels of security to attempt to develop something new and useful—to venture beyond the "everyday" or ordinary into relatively uncharted territory? Are they all seeking fame and fortune? Or do other motives play a role? That discussion, in turn, suggests another basic question: "Are entrepreneurs a single, relatively homogeneous group?" It is often assumed that they are, an assumption that affords us the luxury of making statements that take the general form "Entrepreneurs are . . ." or "Entrepreneurs are not . . .," for instance, "risk takers," "rebels," "optimists"—choose your own adjectives.

Given that human beings rarely, if ever, perform complex actions for a single reason or as a result of one all-encompassing motive, the answer seems obvious: entrepreneurs are, by definition, somewhat heterogeneous. They do not all do what they do for the same reasons, and may vary tremendously in terms of skills, talents, and other characteristics. We'll examine this important point and its implications in later chapters.

Next, we'll briefly consider what is truly a central feature of this book: adoption of an *evidence-based* approach. This means that we will use actual findings and data as a basis for discussions and recommendations wherever and whenever possible. Adoption of this approach stems primarily from carefully considering the following key question: "How can we best acquire accurate understanding of the nature of entrepreneurship and the factors that affect it, in order to be better able to assist entrepreneurs to achieve success?" One answer—and a very appealing one—is simply to ask experienced entrepreneurs. After all, they have been through the process (sometimes repeatedly), so it seems reasonable that their observations and insights might provide the information we seek. While this is certainly intuitively appealing, there are strong grounds for questioning its validity. A vast body of evidence in several fields (e.g., cognitive science, social psychology) indicates that, in fact, people are not very good at self-perception—the task of understanding themselves. They cannot accurately remember what they did in the past, why they did it, and how they felt at the time, and they cannot accurately predict how they will feel in the future. They overlook important causes of their own actions, emphasize ones that are relatively trivial, and often focus on factors that did not actually play a key role. We'll review evidence on this issue below, but for now we want to emphasize the fact that, taken as a whole, it offers a compelling case *against* basing the field of entrepreneurship entirely, or even largely, on the reports of entrepreneurs. Yes, we should pay careful attention to what they tell us—they are people who have "been there, done that." But assuming that this is sufficient for reaching accurate conclusions about the nature of entrepreneurship puts us on very risky ground. For this reason, observations, recommendations, and assertions by entrepreneurs should be viewed simply as one potential source of information among several. And among the other potential sources the one that seems most deserving of confidence is evidence gathered through careful, systematic research. This approach has yielded huge dividends in other fields, ranging from physical science to social science, so it seems only reasonable to adopt it as a basic foundation for the field of entrepreneurship. That is why this book is described, in its subtitle, as an "evidence-based guide"—to contrast it with other volumes that adopt an approach that could, perhaps, best be described as "experience-based" or "entrepreneur-based." While such information, too, can certainly be valuable, it will play a secondary role here, and attention will be focused, wherever and whenever possible, on evidence provided by careful research.

Entrepreneurship: a search for fortune, fame, personal fulfillment, "doing good," or—perhaps—all of the above?

Now we turn to a key question that deserves our attention early on: Why do individuals choose to become entrepreneurs? Why do they take the concrete steps needed to convert their ideas or dreams to reality, either by starting new ventures or through other means? The fact that acting entrepreneurially involves high levels of uncertainty and no guarantees of success suggests that this choice must involve strong underlying motives—entrepreneurs are seeking important goals and ends through their actions. But what, precisely, are these? What do entrepreneurs actually seek in their efforts to give their ideas tangible form? Many people believe that the answer to this question is simple: entrepreneurs mainly seek wealth or fame, and see starting a new venture (or other entrepreneurial actions) as useful for attaining these goals. All too often, this is the implicit message in basic courses in entrepreneurship. Instructors often seem to suggest to students, "If you want to be rich and famous, you have come to the right place."

Although that is certainly a key motive for many current or would-be entrepreneurs, it is far from the only one. For instance, some individuals become entrepreneurs largely as an act of "personal survival." They are downsized by their employers or lose their current jobs for other reasons, yet are too young to retire or not ready to do so. If they are over age 50, they may be viewed as relatively undesirable as prospective employees by other companies, so what's left? One option is starting their own business. Still others become entrepreneurs because they are seeking personal fulfillment—or simply to escape from what they perceive to be boring, dead-end jobs. For instance, in recent research Lee, Wong, Foo, and Leung (2011) found that high-tech professionals are especially likely to form the intention of becoming entrepreneurs when they perceive that they cannot act as innovatively as they prefer in their current jobs—their present employers don't encourage or permit such behavior. As a result, they experience low levels of job satisfaction, and formulate plans to "get out"—and run their own businesses.

Similarly, it has recently been proposed (Baron, 2010) that individuals often become entrepreneurs because they are seeking the kind of working conditions identified by research on job design as ones that generate high levels of motivation, satisfaction, and performance (e.g., Baron, 2010; Fried and Jullerat, 2010). In other words, they become entrepreneurs because they are seeking meaningfulness in their work, and this is provided by high levels of autonomy, task significance (tasks being performed seem

important), task identity (entire tasks can be completed, not simply portions of them), and skill variety (many different skills can be exercised and
put to good use). Clearly, the entrepreneurial role provides these conditions, and it may be that individuals who perceive that they can attain such
conditions by starting their own businesses or acting entrepreneurially in
other ways are especially attracted to this role. In essence, they become
entrepreneurs in a quest for "the perfect job or career"—one that will be
closely aligned with their own strong desires for meaningfulness in what
they do and, in this way, will contribute to their personal happiness. For
such persons, the decision to become entrepreneurs is certainly not the
result of strong desires for wealth and fame. Nor are these the key factors
for those individuals who are often known as "lifestyle entrepreneurs."
These are persons who find the idea of being an entrepreneur, with the aura
of being a "free and independent spirit," highly appealing. For instance, I
formerly had the pleasure of team-teaching a course on entrepreneurship with a Nobel Prize winning physicist. He had started a company to
develop his scientific ideas into usable products (e.g., one that could diag-
nose cancer on the basis of the electrical properties of cells). But he took
virtually no steps to obtain adequate financing or build sales. Rather, he
seemed to enjoy "hanging out" in the university's incubator park, where,
as a Nobel scientist, he was always welcome and always treated with great
respect (deservedly so). He was certainly not motivated by a desire for
wealth or fame—he already had as much fame as most people could ever
desire, and was well off financially too. But he did seem to enjoy immensely
the role of "scientist-turned-entrepreneur," and it appeared to contribute
to his sense of personal fulfillment and well-being.

In addition, some persons become entrepreneurs because they want
to "do good"—to enhance human well-being or, at least, the well-being of
people in their own communities, regions, or countries. Such persons are
often described as being social entrepreneurs and, although they realize
that they must make a profit to stay in business and to continue actions
that will be beneficial to many other persons, they are not focused on this
goal. For example, consider the actions of a large group of engineers and
scientists who are working long and hard to develop an improved cooking
stove (Bilger, 2009). Why? Because inefficient cooking stoves that use fires
contribute a huge amount of pollution (they are used by almost 2 billion
people, and the soot and fumes they release exceed that from all factories!);
because such stoves harm the health of the large number of persons who
breathe their fumes; and because such stoves burn and even kill thousands
of children each year. The key goal of this endeavor (which focuses on
a company known as Aprovecho (Spanish for "make use of" or "take
advantage of") is to produce a stove that sells for a very low price (one
people living in poverty or near-poverty can afford), uses 60 percent less

Note: The stove shown here is one that, its designers claim, "may save the world." It uses much less fuel, pollutes much less, and is a far smaller health hazard than traditional stoves. Such stoves are used by more than 1.5 billion people every day to cook their food and stay warm.

Source: Courtesy of StoveTec, Inc.

Figure 1.1   *The stove that will save the world? (Or at least help save it!)*

fuel, pollutes 90 percent less, and greatly reduces the possibility of burns. Are they doing it? Absolutely; the stove shown in Figure 1.1 is one of their latest efforts and, although still not perfect, is truly getting there. As use of this stove spreads, very real benefits will be gained—and, of course, at $10 per stove there is little chance of huge profits; but that is not what these entrepreneurs seek!

Clearly, then, individuals can become entrepreneurs for many reasons. But this still leaves another basic question unanswered: Why do some people, but not others, perceive entrepreneurship as a useful route to satisfying their important motives, whether these are gaining personal wealth, helping others, or simply making a living? There are many other ways of attaining these goals, so why do some people choose entrepreneurship as the route to satisfying these motives? One useful answer is provided by the theory of career choice which suggests that people tend to choose jobs, careers, or occupations that match their personalities, values, needs, and interests (e.g., Kristof-Brown, Zimmerman, and Johnson, 2005). Applying this view to entrepreneurship suggests the following possibility: individuals choose to become entrepreneurs when their personal characteristics fit well with the demands of this role. Strong evidence for this view is provided by research conducted by Zhao, Seibert, and Lumpkin (2010), who analyzed the data of hundreds of previous studies that investigated the relationships between personal characteristics (especially certain key aspects of personality) and entrepreneurial intentions—the intention actually to take entrepreneurial action (e.g., start a new venture).

In their research, Zhao et al. (2010) found that several aspects of personality (several aspects of the "big five" framework; e.g., Costa and McCrae, 1992) are significantly linked to entrepreneurial intentions. In other words, to the extent individuals demonstrate certain personal characteristics, they are more likely to form the intention of becoming entrepreneurs. These characteristics include: (1) *conscientiousness*—the tendency to be high in achievement and work motivation, organization and planning, self-control, and responsibility; (2) *openness to experience*—the tendency to be high in curiosity, imagination, creativity, and seeking out new ideas; and (3) *emotional stability*—the tendency to be calm, stable, even-tempered, and hardy (i.e., resilient). All of these characteristics were positively related to entrepreneurial intentions, which reflect motivation to adopt this role or career. In contrast, another dimension of the "big five" framework, *extraversion* (being outgoing, warm, friendly, energetic, and assertive), was only weakly related to such intentions. And a fifth dimension, *agreeableness*, which involves being trusting, altruistic, cooperative, and modest, was not linked to such intentions. Risk-taking propensity was also positively related to entrepreneurial intentions, so, as has often been proposed, persons who become entrepreneurs are more willing than other persons to enter situations involving high degrees of uncertainty concerning success or failure.

Although the "big five dimensions" and risk-taking propensity play an important role in entrepreneurial motivation, other individual characteristics, too, are relevant. Among these, general *self-efficacy*—individuals' belief that they can successfully accomplish various tasks they undertake (Bandura, 1997)—is perhaps the most important. Research findings indicate a positive relationship between self-efficacy and both the tendency actually to start new ventures (Markman and Baron, 2003; Zhao, Seibert, and Hills, 2005; average correlation = 0.25) and achieving financial success

Note: It is widely assumed that individuals become entrepreneurs mainly because they are seeking wealth and fame. In fact, though, individuals have many different reasons for becoming entrepreneurs, ranging from economic necessity (e.g., they have been "downsized" from their current job) to the desire to help others. In short, people become entrepreneurs for many different reasons, suggesting that entrepreneurs are a heterogeneous rather than homogeneous group.

Figure 1.2   *Why do individuals become entrepreneurs? For many reasons*

through such activities (Chandler and Jansen, 1991). In addition, some findings (Zhao et al., 2005) indicate that self-efficacy fully mediates the impact of several other variables on entrepreneurial intentions—interest in performing various entrepreneurial activities, such as starting a new venture. Specifically, these researchers found that the effects on entrepreneurial intentions of (1) perceived learning from entrepreneurship-related courses, (2) previous entrepreneurial experience, and (3) risk propensity were all fully a function of entrepreneurial self-efficacy.

In sum, it appears that some individuals are indeed more likely than others to choose to become entrepreneurs—those whose personal characteristics, values, and interests match the requirements of this demanding role (see Figure 1.2).

Before we conclude this discussion, it's important to note that, although individual characteristics and preferences are certainly important in the decision to become an entrepreneur, they are definitely not the entire story. External (i.e., societal, social) factors, too, often play a role. For instance, individuals are more likely to pursue entrepreneurial actions vigorously when financial markets are favorable, thus providing ready access to essential financial resources, when government policies favor the founding and operation of new ventures (e.g., through favorable tax policies; Tung, Walls, and Frese, 2006) and when markets for specific new products or services are growing rapidly (Shane, 2008). These factors, too, are important, because individuals do not choose to pursue their dreams through entrepreneurial activity in isolation from social and economic conditions. Trying to understand entrepreneurship without considering these factors is like trying to prepare a complex recipe without a full list of the key ingredients.

If entrepreneurs seek different goals and differ greatly in terms of basic characteristics that make them more or less suited to this role, can we generalize about them? Can we assume, for instance, that entrepreneurs are "tolerant of risk," or "passionately committed to their idea and companies," or "generally optimistic"? Existing evidence suggests that a degree of caution should be exercised with respect to such assumptions. On the other hand, it is clear that there *is* something that unites all entrepreneurs and makes them, to an extent, distinct from many other persons. While they differ greatly in motives, skill, interests, values, and countless other ways, they are all individuals who have decided to take overt action to convert their ideas into reality. As Locke and Baum (2007, p. 93) put it, "A person may have sufficient technical skill and money to start a business, but without motivation [to do so] nothing happens." So, as the second quotation at the start of this chapter suggests, one central characteristic that unites entrepreneurs is that they are indeed all *doers* rather than merely dreamers—and the difference between these categories is not only real, but is central to what follows next.

Can entrepreneurs give us the "secrets of success"—or must we look elsewhere for the answers?

At one popular internet site (Growthink Blog), the following advice is offered by Tom Zeleznock, a popular freelance writer: "There is no simple formula for creating a successful business. Luckily, there is an easy way to improve your chances. And that's by listening to the wisdom of those who have done it already."

Certainly, this sounds reasonable: Why *not* listen to people who have been successful in starting new businesses—"stars" in the entrepreneurial firmament? In fact, we started this chapter with quotations from two such persons, so clearly the present author is not opposed to such advice and recognizes that it can be of considerable value. On the other hand, as a psychologist, I know only too well the limitations of our abilities to accurately remember, describe, and interpret our own past actions, motives, and feelings. In fact, a wealth of evidence indicates that we are actually quite poor at these tasks. Memory is fallible and easily distorted. Our understanding of why we have done what we did in the past is uncertain and prone to error. And we are not even good at accurately distinguishing between the factors and conditions that actually do influence (or have influenced) our thoughts and actions, and ones that do not (or have not) exert(ed) such effects. (We'll return to this topic in Chapter 8, where we examine the factors that actually influence venture capitalists' decisions about funding new ventures—and note that these are different, in important ways, from the factors they *think* influence these decisions.) We are also often unsuccessful at guessing how we will feel in the future if specific events occur (e.g., Gilbert, Lieberman, Morewedge, and Wilson, 2004).

These are very general statements, so it's important to back them up with specific examples and findings. Let's start with memory. Is it accurate? Can we remember information we want to recall with a high degree of accuracy? Or does it often fail? Anyone who has tried to recall specific information only to find that they cannot already realizes that memory is far from infallible. Often, the information we seek is still present, but simply can't be found—the "retrieval problem," as cognitive scientists who study memory would suggest (Neath and Surprenant, 2003). In addition—and this is considerably more disturbing—when we do retrieve information from memory the mere act of doing so often changes it. Moreover, this is especially likely to occur when we remember the general meaning or gist of information rather than specific content (Koutstaal and Cavendish, 2005). So, remembering that we paid a particular price for a used car is less likely to distort our memory for such information than remembering the situation in which we bought it—for instance, that we bargained with the past owner, took the car to our mechanic, and so on. Each time we recall this information and then re-enter it in memory, it may be slightly different. Here's an example from my own life.

Many times, I am asked: "Why did you start your company?" (People who pose this question are usually referring to the one I started in 1992 and ran until 2000—Innovative Environmental Products.) As I have retrieved this information over and over again over several years, these memories have almost certainly changed. Further, research findings indicate that they have probably been changed in ways to make them more consistent and more reasonable, so that, in a sense, they tell a better story. At the time I started this company, I had no very clear idea about *why* I wanted to do

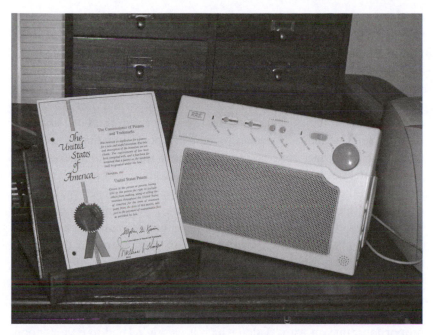

Note: Looking back, the author can offer a plausible explanation of why and how he came up with the idea for this product, for which he obtained two U.S. patents. (It was later sold in stores, on the internet, and even through in-flight magazines.) But are these memories accurate? There is no way of knowing for certain, but research on our ability to understand and explain our own actions suggests the need for a healthy dose of skepticism.

Figure 1.3   *Why and how did the author invent this product—does he really know?*

this. I already had a career as a professor and, as an author of several text-books, more than enough to keep me busy. And I was already earning a substantial income from these two sources. So why did I decide to become an entrepreneur? No one will ever know for sure, but now, after trying to reconstruct this situation many times, a "story" along the following lines emerges. (1) I had been doing research on how the physical environment affects performance. (2) My daughter was in college, and complained about dusty air, bad smells, and lack of privacy in the dorms. (3) This led me to come up with the idea of a device that would filter the air, introduce pleasant fragrances, and include a noise-cancellation feature. The result: patent applications, several patents—and a profitable company (see Figure 1.3).

Was it really that straightforward? Research on memory and on memory distortion suggests that this is almost certainly an oversimplification—one in which details have been omitted, others have been added, and the overall "gist" has been smoothed and enhanced. The same would be true for anyone asked to recall events that happened in the past and that have been retrieved from memory on countless occasions. This is one reason why it is somewhat risky to accept the statements of famous entrepreneurs as providing accurate information about how and why they started their companies: the same processes described above almost certainly operate, and probably operate even more strongly, since these individuals are asked for such information over and over again.

But the fallibility and ready distortion of information stored in memory are not the only reason to be wary of entrepreneurs' interpretations of their own actions and the factors that led to their success. Unfortunately, other evidence indicates that we are simply not very good at recognizing the variables or conditions that actually influence our behavior or distinguishing them from ones that do not. A vivid illustration of this fact is provided by a now famous study conducted years ago by Nisbett and Wilson (1977). These researchers asked participants in their study (college students) to memorize a list of word pairs. Some of these (e.g., ocean–moon) were designed to generate mental associations that would lead to certain outcomes—certain words closely related to the word pairs. For instance, participants were asked to name a detergent. A very large proportion came up with "Tide," which is clearly related to ocean–moon. But when asked if the word pair had influenced their answer, participants vehemently denied this; instead, they insisted that they had come up with "Tide" because they liked it best or used it all the time or because it was the most famous brand on the market. Was this true? Evidence indicates it was not, and that the word pairs had indeed affected their behavior; but the participants didn't, or couldn't, recognize this fact.

Here's another example, very different in context, but highly similar in meaning. Participants in another study (Maddux et al., 2010) were shown a coffee mug and then arbitrarily told to assume either that they were sellers of this mug (they already owned it and could either sell it or take it home with them) or that they were buyers (they did not own a mug, but could buy one from a seller). Both groups were shown a list of prices ranging from $0.00 to $10.00 in 50 cent increments, and asked whether, for each price, they would buy the mug (if they were buyers) or sell it (if they were sellers). Presumably the mug had an intrinsic value, so buyers and sellers should have come up with similar prices. Can you guess the results? In fact, buyers demanded $4.83 before they would sell the mug, but sellers offered only $2.34 to buy one. Why? Because of what is known as the *endowment effect*—a strong tendency to overvalue whatever belongs to us. Similarly, we tend to overvalue our own views, whatever they are, believing that they are much more accurate and useful than those of other people. Entrepreneurs are not immune to such effects—far from it (Baron, 2007). So, when they offer explanations for their own success, we should wonder: Is this information accurate? Perhaps. But the general principle is that we should accept it only with care and, if possible, rely more heavily on the findings of systematic research.

Just as icing on the cake, here are some other ways in which we are not very good at understanding our own actions or using them as a guide for advice to others:

- We are very bad at reporting accurately on the frequency of various events.
- We are inaccurate in reporting how much change we have experienced.
- When we think about our past actions, we tend to remember options we chose as being better than ones we rejected.
- We often remember information relating to ourselves better than information relating to others.
- We tend to evaluate ideas we generate ourselves as better than ideas generated by other persons.

The bottom line of all this is that *often we don't know why we have acted as we did, why events turned out as they did, or what factors played a key role* (Wilson, 2009). To the extent that's true—and a great deal of evidence indicates that it is (e.g., Klauer, Voss, and Stahl, 2008; Wilson, 2009)—it is clear that we often think we know more than we really do, and believe that we understand our own actions, motives, and feelings, and the factors that influence us, much better than we actually do. The take-away principle, then, is this: because human self-perception or self-knowledge is so imperfect, we really can't build a field of entrepreneurship solely, or even largely, on what entrepreneurs tell us about their own experiences, why they succeeded (or failed), and what factors played a key role in this complex process. That, in essence, is why, throughout this book, we will rely, as much as possible, on the findings of systematic research. It's not that we don't think entrepreneurs have a lot to tell us—on the contrary, they *do*! But if they, like the rest of us, don't fully understand their own motives, can't accurately identify the factors that actually played a role in their thought and behavior, and don't know when their memories are accurate and when they are inaccurate, we should proceed cautiously—more cautiously, in fact, than the field of entrepreneurship has sometimes done in the past.

Where, precisely, is "elsewhere?" The benefits of actual data

Having explained why we can't rely solely on the memories, opinions, and reflections of entrepreneurs—even highly experienced and successful ones—we return, now, to the "elsewhere" mentioned above. If we can't rely solely on the memories and advice of entrepreneurs, what should be the foundation of our efforts to understand the nature of the complex process of entrepreneurship? A compelling—and straightforward—answer is provided by hundreds of years of progress in all fields of science and in important fields that rest on science to a large extent, such as engineering and medicine. In all of these fields, major progress occurred only as actual evidence—data about the processes or events of interest—was obtained. Prior to the availability of such evidence, experts in various fields offered many interpretations about why the world was the way it was or why certain events or processes occurred, but these views were rarely accurate. For instance, in medicine, famous physicians, highly regarded in their field, proposed many "explanations" for diseases that killed millions of persons (e.g., the infamous plague that wiped out one-third or more of the world's population in the fourteenth century). They attributed such illnesses, and their rapid spread, to harmful vapors, a lack of balance in the "humors" of the body, evil spirits, or other sources. But no real progress was made in treating these diseases, or preventing their spread, until sufficient data concerning the real causes of disease (microorganisms, often spread through contaminated drinking water or faulty sewer systems) were gathered and interpreted.

Another example is very vivid in the author's memory, because in college he flirted briefly with the idea of being a geology major. In one course in this field, the professor noted that fossils of dinosaurs had been found in Antarctica and also called attention to the fact that the coastlines of major continents seemed to fit together much better than chance alone would predict (e.g., Africa and South America). But, when pressed by members of the class, he could offer no compelling explanation for these diverse facts. Such an explanation emerged years later, as data from deep drilling of mid-oceanic trenches became available, and indicated that the continents were in constant motion, drifting over the face of the earth's molten interior. So dinosaurs lived in Antarctica because it was much closer to the equator, and the coastlines of South America and Africa fit together because, in fact, they were once joined.

In short, across many different fields, a compelling case exists for relying on *data*—actual evidence, carefully collected—as a key foundation for enhanced knowledge and understanding. This basic principle is adopted in the present volume. Wherever and whenever possible, we will rely on the findings of actual research to gain insights into the nature of entrepreneurship and the factors that affect it. Are entrepreneurs truly risk takers? Should new ventures locate in geographic areas where similar companies are operating, or strike out on their own? How can entrepreneurs determine whether a given opportunity is worth pursuing, or just a "false alarm" that will drain their resources and energies with little chance of success? To answer these and countless other questions, we'll focus on actual data—the findings reported in published research. This in no way suggests that we will ignore the experiences, recommendations, or insights offered by entrepreneurs—far from it. We have already noted that these, too, can be valuable. But whenever possible we will assign extra weight to actual evidence rather than personal observations and reflections.

This raises another basic question: How can research on entrepreneurship be conducted so as to yield the kind of data we seek? Researchers in this field can't collect the kind of physical measurements obtained in many scientific fields, and can't use microscopes to identify entrepreneurs' motives, intentions, or skills. Does this mean that we must rely on asking entrepreneurs what they have done, why they have done it, and what results they experienced? While such subjective reports can provide one useful source of information, we have already seen that they can be very unreliable. What other sources of evidence can we use? Fortunately, many exist. For instance, the financial results of many companies, even young ones, are often available, and relationships between these data and various actions by entrepreneurs or their companies can be examined. Similarly, information on industries, market share, competitors, patents, and many other outcomes can be gathered independently of entrepreneurs. The key point is that, in such research, we don't have to rely solely on what entrepreneurs tell us: other sources of useful information exist.

Perhaps, at this point, a specific example of research in entrepreneurship will be helpful, so let's consider a recent study by the present author and colleagues (Baron, Tang, and Hmieleski, 2011). This research addressed the following question: it is widely assumed that entrepreneurs are very "upbeat" individuals—they are enthusiastic, cheerful, and optimistic. Is this always a "plus" in terms of their success and the success of their companies? Or can there be "too much of a good thing" where the tendency to be "up" much of the time (i.e., to experience positive moods and feelings) is concerned? To find out, the researchers asked a large number of entrepreneurs (several hundred) to complete a short questionnaire designed to measure their tendencies to experience positive moods and emotions in many situations, and often. The same entrepreneurs also provided information on the number of innovative products introduced by their companies. In addition, information concerning the rate of growth in sales was obtained for each company from an independent source. On the basis of previous research, it was predicted that the relationship between entrepreneurs' tendencies to be "up" and both product innovation and sales growth would be curvilinear: up to a specific point, the more "upbeat" the entrepreneurs were, the higher would be product innovation and sales growth. But, beyond some point, these measures would decrease because very high levels of positive affect can interfere with effective decision making, choosing appropriate business strategies, paying close attention to negative information (which might reduce entrepreneurs' positive

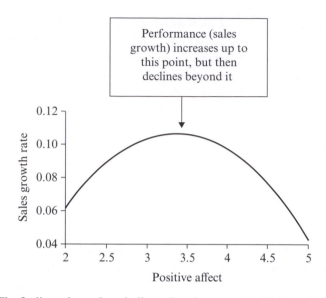

Note: The findings shown here indicate that the answer to this question is "Yes." The more "up" entrepreneurs are (the higher their tendency to experience positive feelings and emotions), the better the performance of their companies (as measured by sales growth), but only up to a point. Beyond that level, firm performance declines as entrepreneurs' tendencies to experience positive affect increase further. Several factors, including a growing tendency to ignore negative information, contribute to this pattern.

Source: Based on data from Baron, Tang, and Hmieleski (2011).

Figure 1.4 *Can there be "too much of a good thing" where entrepreneurial enthusiasm is concerned?*

moods), and other important processes or actions. Results offered strong support for these predictions. As shown in Figure 1.4, which illustrates results for sales growth, the function was indeed curvilinear in form— taking the shape of an upside-down letter *U*. Additional findings indicated that, in general, the entrepreneurs in the sample were high in positive moods or emotions, so the view they tend to be very positive people was also confirmed. This research, and the data it yielded, has an important message for entrepreneurs: beware of your own enthusiasm; although it is often beneficial, if it is extreme it can get you into serious trouble!

Note that this research was not based solely on reports and statements by entrepreneurs; financial data were also collected. In addition, it was not based on the subjective statements of one or a few entrepreneurs; rather, the data involved several hundred entrepreneurs and many different companies. That's a key point: of course we can, and often do, rely on data based on what entrepreneurs tell us. But that doesn't mean posing our questions to a small number of entrepreneurs we happen to know and basing our conclusions on their informal conversations with us. Rather, it means asking large numbers of entrepreneurs specific questions in a standardized format, and then searching (often statistically) for clear themes in their replies. Such qualitative methods of research can be just as informative and valuable as research based on financial records or other "hard" data. The study reported above combined financial data with entrepreneurs' answers to a widely used questionnaire specifically designed to measure their tendency to experience positive affect—to experience positive moods or feelings. So, yes, we certainly *do* listen to what entrepreneurs tell us, but we attempt to do so in a careful and systematic way.

To conclude: On what kind of information would *you* prefer to rely? The memories, reflections, and subjective impressions reported by entrepreneurs? Or data such as those described above? If your answer is "Give me the data!" you have come to the right place, because that will be an important foundation for the rest of our discussions. But if you prefer the guidance offered by entrepreneurs, don't despair: we'll include that too. What we'll seek, first and foremost, is a balance—but in that balance we'll do our best, whenever possible, to give more weight to actual evidence.

Summary of key points

Entrepreneurship is not restricted to starting new ventures. In fact, it has a broader meaning: the application of human creativity, ingenuity, knowledge, skills, and energy to the development of something *new* and *useful*. This implies that people can think and act entrepreneurially in a wide range of contexts—not solely when they launch new ventures to develop business opportunities. Although it is widely assumed that individuals become entrepreneurs in order to gain wealth and fame, they do so for many other reasons too. For instance, some persons become entrepreneurs because they are seeking personal fulfillment and meaningful work. Others adopt this role in order to do social good—for instance, developing a stove that greatly reduces air pollution and the danger of accidental burns for the two billion persons who cook with such stoves. Personal characteristics, too, play a role in intentions to become entrepreneurs (e.g., several aspects of personality, such as conscientiousness and openness to experience).

Advice and guidance from experienced entrepreneurs can be very informative, but people are not very accurate in remembering what they did in the past, explaining why they did it, or predicting what they will feel or experience in the future. For instance, each time information concerning past events or experiences is retrieved from memory it is changed, so that it becomes more consistent and, overall, "tells a better story" about these events. Further, we are subject to many forms of cognitive bias such as the endowment effect (overvaluing items we own or our own ideas) and excessive optimism. As a result, it is essential for the field of entrepreneurship to base its own conclusions and recommendations to entrepreneurs on data gathered in systematic research whenever, and to the extent that, this is possible.

References

Bandura, A. (1997). *Self-efficacy: The exercise of control*. New York: W.H. Freeman.

Baron, R.A. (2007). Behavioral and cognitive factors in entrepreneurship: Entrepreneurs as the active element in new venture creation. *Strategic Entrepreneurship Journal, 1*, 167–182.

Baron, R.A. (2010). Job design and entrepreneurship: Why closer connections = mutual gains. *Journal of Organizational Behavior, 30*, 1–10.

Baron, R.A., Tang, J., and Hmieleski, K.M. (2011). Entrepreneurs' dispositional positive affect and firm performance: When there can be "too much of a good thing." *Strategic Entrepreneurship Journal, 5*, 111–119.

Bilger, B. (2009). Hearth surgery: The quest for a stove that can save the world. *New Yorker*, December 21.

Chandler, G.N., and Jansen, E. (1991). The founder's self-assessed competence and venture performance. *Journal of Business Venturing, 7*, 223–236.

Costa, P.T., Jr., and McCrae, R.R. (1992). *NEO PI-R professional manual*. Odessa, FL: Psychological Assessment Resources.

Fried, Y., and Jullerat, T. (2010). Work matters: Job design in classic and contemporary perspectives. In S. Zedeck (Ed.), *Handbook of industrial and organizational psychology*. Washington, DC: American Psychological Association.

Gawande, A. (2011). The hot spotters: Can we lower medical costs by giving the neediest patients better care? *New Yorker Magazine*, January 24.

Gilbert, D.T., Lieberman, M.D., Morewedge, C.K., and Wilson, T.D. (2004). The peculiar longevity of things not so bad. *Psychological Science, 15*, 14–19.

Klauer, K.C., Voss, A., and Stahl, C. (2008). *Cognitive methods in social psychology*. New York: Guilford Press.

Koutstaal, W., and Cavendish, M. (2005). Using what we know: Consequences of intentionally retrieving gist versus item-specific information. *Journal of Experimental Psychology: Learning, Memory, and Cognition, 32*, 778–791.

Kristof-Brown, A.L., Zimmerman, R.D., and Johnson, E.C. (2005). Consequences of individuals' fit at work: A meta-analysis of person–job, person–organization, person–group, and person–supervisor fit. *Personnel Psychology, 58*, 281–342.

Lee, L., Wong, P.K., Foo, M.D., and Leung, A. (2011). Entrepreneurial intentions: The influence of organizational and individual factors. *Journal of Business Venturing, 26*, 124–136.

Locke, E.A., and Baum, J.R. (2007). Entrepreneurial motivation. In J.R. Baum, M. Frese, and R.A. Baron (eds), *The psychology of entrepreneurship* (pp. 91–112). Mahwah, NJ: Erlbaum.

Maddux, W.W., Yang, H., Falk, C., Adam, J., Adair, W., Endo, Y., Carmon, Z., and Haine, S.J. (2010). For whom is parting with possessions more painful? Cultural differences in the endowment effect. *Psychological Science, 21*, 1910–1917.

Markman, G.D., and Baron, R.A. (2003). Person–entrepreneurship fit: Why some persons are more successful as entrepreneurs than others. *Human Resource Management Review, 13*, 281–302.

Neath, I., and Surprenant, A.M. (2003). *Human memory: An introduction to research, data, and theory*, 2nd edition. Belmont, CA: Wadsworth.

Nisbett, R.E., and Wilson, T.D. (1977). Telling more than we can know: Verbal reports on mental processes. *Psychological Review, 84*, 231–259.

Shane, S. (2008). *The illusions of entrepreneurship: The costly myths that entrepreneurs, investors, and policy makers live by*. New Haven, CT: Yale University Press.

Shane, S., and Venkataraman, S. (2000). The promise of entrepreneurship as a field of research. *Academy of Management Review, 25*, 217–226.

Tung, R.L., Walls, H.J., and Frese, M. (2006). Cross-cultural entrepreneurship: The case of China. In R. Baum, M. Frese, and R.A. Baron (eds), *The psychology of entrepreneurship* (pp. 265–286). Mahwah, NJ: Erlbaum.

Wilson, T.D. (2009). Know thyself. *Perspectives on Psychological Science, 4*, 384–389.

Zhao, H., Seibert, S.E., and Hills, G.E. (2005). The mediating role of self-efficacy in the development of entrepreneurial intentions. *Journal of Applied Psychology, 90*, 1265–1272.

Zhao, H., Seibert, S.E., and Lumpkin, G.T. (2010). The relationship of personality to entrepreneurial intentions and performance: A meta-analytic review. *Journal of Management, 36*, 381–404.

2 Cognitive foundations of entrepreneurship: the origins of ideas, creativity, and innovations

. . . .

Chapter outline

Human cognition: our systems for making sense of the external world
Systems for storing and retrieving information: three kinds of memory
Limited processing capacity: a "bottleneck" in memory
Cognitive errors and biases
Creativity: generating the *new*
Concepts: mental categories that sometimes enhance, and sometimes block, creativity
Human intelligence: a foundation for creativity and innovation
Entrepreneurial cognition: the mind of the entrepreneur
Do entrepreneurs really think differently from other persons?
Increasing creativity: the confluence approach

> Creativity is seeing something that doesn't exist already. (Michele Shea)

> Creative things have to sell to get acknowledged as such. (Steve Jobs)

Many years ago, I moved from the Midwest, where toll roads were rare, to New York, where they were much more common. As a result, I often drove on one such road when traveling from my home to my university office. The toll was trivial—20 cents each way. But the wait at the toll gates was truly annoying. Sometimes, it would be only a few minutes, but other times—especially at rush hour or on holiday weekends when traffic was especially busy—it could be 10 or 15 minutes. Often I found myself thinking: "What a waste of time—and fuel. Isn't there some other way to pay without these delays?" Of course, the answer to these prayers did emerge, but only years later, when technology caught up with the situation. Now, all toll roads, including the ones on which I drive at present, have equipment that automatically reads account numbers as motorists zip by. In New York, the process is still relatively slow—drivers must slow down to five miles per hour; but in other states, the traffic can move along at normal speeds, so no delays occur.

Clearly I didn't have the expertise—or interest—to develop the equipment that made this change possible. But I did have the idea for it in mind; I simply didn't know how to move forward with it in any way. Fortunately, others did—and life for me and millions of other drivers is much better because of their efforts.

Why do I start with this example? Because it illustrates a basic fact about entrepreneurship: essentially, the process starts in the minds of specific persons. These individuals notice that some need is not being met (or is being met poorly), or are "bugged" by something in their lives that seems unnecessarily annoying (such as long waits at toll gates). As a result, they begin thinking about possible ways to change this situation. In other words, as we noted in Chapter 1, entrepreneurship involves ideas (thoughts about or mental images of something—almost anything) that can, potentially, lead to overt actions that help to move these ideas from the "possible" to the real. But, as was the case with me and toll roads, if the persons who have such ideas do not possess the skills, knowledge, or motivation to do anything concrete about them that is the end of the story: the ideas do not result in action, and entrepreneurship does not begin—at least not then, and not for these persons.

Regardless of which path unfolds, it is clear that entrepreneurship, defined as the application of human creativity, ingenuity, energy, and knowledge to developing something *new* and *useful* rests on important foundations in human cognition—our continuing efforts to make sense out of the external world by noticing, storing, processing, retrieving, and using information (e.g., Solso, Maclin, and Maclin, 2009). In a sense, cognition provides the "raw materials" from which creativity, ingenuity, innovations, and—ultimately—entrepreneurship flow. Cognition also plays a key role in opportunity recognition—a central aspect of the entrepreneurial process and one we'll examine in detail in Chapter 3 (e.g., Grégoire, Barr, and Shepherd, 2010). Here, though, we will focus on the basic cognitive foundations of entrepreneurship, thus setting the stage for later discussions of its important role. Specifically, the present chapter will proceed as follows.

First, we'll examine the nature of our basic cognitive systems, the equipment we possess as human beings that allows us to accomplish the tasks listed above—to store, retrieve, process, and use information. As we'll soon see, these systems are truly amazing in some respects, but they are severely limited in others—a fact with important implications for decision making, planning, and many other processes central to entrepreneurship (e.g., Baron, 2004). Overall, these limitations and potential "weaknesses" in our cognitive systems, and the errors and "tilts" they generate, are so important that we'll pause to examine several that are especially powerful. Next, we'll consider the nature and origins of creativity—the capacity to create something truly new that has not, perhaps, existed before. Third, we'll turn to the role of human intelligence in entrepreneurship, focusing especially on evidence concerning the important role of certain aspects of intelligence that are known, together, as *successful intelligence* (Baum and Bird, 2010). Finally, we'll address the topic of *entrepreneurial cognition*, which centers around the questions "How do entrepreneurs think, reason, plan, and decide?" and "Do they differ, in these respects, from other persons?" Together, these discussions will pave the way for understanding the role of cognition in many central aspects of entrepreneurship—and for topics we will examine in later chapters.

Human cognition: our systems for making sense of the external world

Are you reading and understanding these words? Can you remember what you ate for dinner last night? What you did on your last birthday? Can you conjure up images of your mother, your grandfather, or your favorite aunt, and recall how they looked long ago when they were much younger? Can you read or speak more than one language? Play a musical instrument? Do you know how to bowl, play golf, or play tennis? What are your intentions and plans for the future? For instance, do you plan to start a new company sometime soon? All of these experiences and activities derive from, and involve, our basic cognitive systems. Without these basic tools, we could not make decisions, remember information, reason, plan, talk, think, or perform any skilled activity. Clearly, then, they are crucial for almost everything we do; and, as we'll soon see, they are also the source of ideas, creativity, and ingenuity—key foundations of entrepreneurship. To understand the important role of these systems in entrepreneurship, we'll first briefly describe their basic nature and then examine their relative strengths and weaknesses, as well as some of the errors that seem in some ways to be inherent in these basic features (e.g., Ariely, 2009).

Systems for storing and retrieving information: three kinds of memory

In order to process information—to use it to make decisions, develop business strategies, or solve problems—it must somehow be retained. In other words, we must be able to store it for future use. The cognitive systems that permit this function to occur are known, collectively, as *memory*, and are an essential aspect of cognition. We say "collectively" because, in fact, several such systems exist. One, working memory, holds a limited amount of information for brief periods of time—perhaps up to a few seconds. If you look up a phone number and then try to remember it just long enough to dial it, you are using working memory. In a sense, working memory is where our current consciousness exists: it is the system that holds information we are processing or using now.

Another, and very different, system is known as *long-term memory*. This system allows us to retain truly vast amounts of information for long periods of time. In fact, research findings indicate that there may be no limits to how much long-term memory can hold or how long it can retain information. So we can continue to acquire new knowledge and new skills throughout life: there is no apparent limit to these processes, at least where memory is concerned. Long-term memory, like other biological systems, does decline somewhat with age, but the rate is very slow and, barring serious illness, memory can function very well throughout the lifespan.

Long-term memory can hold many kinds of information, including factual knowledge (e.g., the price of a competitor's product, or the number of people now using Facebook). It also contains personal knowledge about events we have experienced in our own lives (e.g., what are known as *autobiographical memories*).

Another kind of information retained in long-term memory is much harder to express in words. For instance, a skilled tennis player can't easily describe to others how she or he generates such devastating serves, and a champion home-run hitter in major league baseball can't readily explain how he hits so many out of the park. Highly experienced entrepreneurs often remark that they can tell a potentially valuable opportunity from one that is probably unlikely to succeed very quickly—and without being able to readily describe how they make this judgment. This is related to expertise, a topic we'll consider in more detail below, but here we should note that one effect of developing expertise in almost any field is that it provides the persons who gain it with amazingly rapid access to information stored in long-term memory. Remember: that system can hold a vast amount of information, so a key problem is finding relevant information when it is needed. Being able to do that very quickly—and accurately—may be one of the reasons why experts in a given field perform at such amazingly high levels: their expertise permits them to use the information stored in memory much more efficiently than is true of other persons. This kind of memory—memory for information that can't be readily put into words—is known as *procedural memory*. It is a kind of long-term memory, because information stored in it can be retrieved years, or even decades, later. For example, if you learn to ride a bicycle as a child you can probably do so many years later, even if you have had no chance to ride one during the intervening time.

It's both important and interesting to note that our decisions, goals, and plans are often strongly influenced by information stored in procedural memory or in other aspects of memory that are outside conscious awareness. We can't describe such information and often are only dimly aware of its presence, but it influences important aspects of our cognition nevertheless. Such information is the basis for intuition, which is sometimes described as "offline processing" because it involves processing of information that does indeed occur outside our normal stream of conscious experience. It is also reflected in tacit knowledge, knowledge that involves what is often described as "know-how"—knowing how to perform various actions (e.g., complex mathematical computations, or speaking another language)—rather than "know-what" (knowledge of specific information). Because tacit knowledge is represented in procedural memory, it is often difficult to share with others, who must learn from observing what we do, rather than listening to what we say about some activity.

Limited processing capacity: a "bottleneck" in memory

Although long-term memory can seemingly store a virtually unlimited amount of information, it does suffer from one major drawback: there is a bottleneck in terms of getting information into this system. This occurs primarily in working memory, which can handle only a small amount of information at any given time. As a result, when we encounter lots of new information only a portion can be stored in memory; the rest may be lost unless it is repeated. How limited is working memory? Research findings indicate that it can handle only seven to nine items of information at a given time—one reason why phone numbers with 7, 10, or more digits are hard to remember. Information can be combined in these items, so that the number "7" doesn't necessarily mean seven different facts, numbers, or anything else. For instance, the letters ATT, IBM, and GE refer to well-known companies. Short-term memory could hold seven to nine combinations of this type, not simply seven to nine individual letters. So working memory is somewhat greater, in its capacity, than might be assumed. Still, unless information passes through this "filter," it will not enter long-term memory and may quickly be lost. This is why truly excellent speakers, whether politicians, professors, attorneys, or anyone else, often try to limit the amount of information they present in a given period of time: they realize that only if they do will the information they present "stick"—be retained by members of their audience. This is an important point for entrepreneurs to keep in mind when they give presentations to venture capitalists or other potential sources of funds: in such settings, too much information can be a dangerous thing!

Cognitive errors and biases

A few years ago, a book entitled *Predictably Irrational* became a best seller (Ariely, 2009). The basic theme of this book was that, because of built-in limitations in our cognitive systems, our thinking is often far from totally rational; on the contrary, it is strongly influenced by emotions, assumptions, unfounded beliefs, and many factors that should not, in principle, influence our thinking—or our decisions. This theme is echoed in a very large body of evidence on what are sometimes known as *cognitive errors* or biases—tendencies in cognition that can, and often do, lead to serious errors. We describe several of these here because they are highly relevant to entrepreneurship and, if permitted to operate unchecked, can prevent entrepreneurs from succeeding in their efforts to convert even very promising ideas into useful products, services, or other beneficial outcomes:

- *The confirmation bias.* If we were totally rational processors of information, we would be especially sensitive to information that is inconsistent with our current beliefs or views. Such information would be very helpful in terms of allowing us to examine these beliefs and to determine if they are in fact accurate. Unfortunately, we show precisely the opposite tendency. Most people, most of the time, have a strong preference to notice, process, and store only information that confirms their existing beliefs; they filter out or discount the rest, and do not let it remain in working memory and then pass through to long-term memory. As a result, people become locked into what have been termed "inferential prisons"—external information that is inconsistent with their current thinking tends to be ignored rather than change their thinking.

- *Heuristics: quick and simple—but inaccurate—rules for making judgments and decisions.* Often we encounter more information than we can possibly process at a given time. This leads to a strong tendency to use heuristics—quick (and sometimes "dirty") rules for making complex judgments and decisions. Several exist, but two that are especially powerful should be briefly mentioned. The first, known as the *availability heuristic or rule,* suggests that whatever we can bring to mind most easily tends to be viewed as most important or accurate. So, if we can remember information easily, it has a powerful impact on our current thinking. Unfortunately, such information is sometimes easy to recall because it is vivid or unusual, not because it is particularly useful or revealing. That's why the cartoon gecko used by GEICO has been effective in increasing sales for this insurance company. Many people find this cartoon character amusing, and so can readily bring it to mind—along with the message the company wishes to promote: "You can save lots of money by insuring with GEICO." Another heuristic—and one that is especially important to entrepreneurs—is the *anchor-and-adjustment heuristic*. This refers to our powerful tendency to accept an opening price or position as an anchor from which adjustments can be made. In fact, such initial offers or positions may have little relationship to reality, yet they strongly influence our judgments. This is why realtors try to set the price at an ideal point: high enough to influence buyers to pay more, but not so high that they discount the initial price entirely and walk away. If you have ever watched the popular television show *Pawn Stars*, you have seen the anchor-and-adjustment heuristic in operation. In this show, the owners of a large pawn shop attempt to negotiate the price of various items people bring to them to sell. Usually, the owners ask the would-be sellers to name a starting price—mainly so they can indicate, immediately, that this is completely unreasonable. (The phrase one of them uses says it all very succinctly: "No way that's going to happen"—meaning that there is no way he will pay the asking price.) After this, the owners name a price of their own, and the sellers—who are far less experienced as negotiators—usually adopt this as an anchor and then try to make small adjustments to it (in their favor, of course). The outcome is almost always the same: the pawn shop owners (the experts) buy the items for a very favorable price. The moral: beware of the anchor-and-adjustment heuristic, because it can prove very costly in negotiations—a process of major importance for entrepreneurs.

- *The self-serving bias.* Another strong tendency in our thinking is to attribute favorable outcomes to our own effort or talent, while negative outcomes are attributed to external factors beyond our control. The result is that individuals do not learn from their errors—because they don't see them as errors; instead, they perceive negative outcomes as "not their fault," and so discount them instead of examining them very carefully. This bias can also lead to considerable friction between partners (e.g., founders of a new company), since each assumes that she or he is primarily responsible for positive outcomes, while the partners are responsible for negative ones.

- *Optimistic bias and planning fallacy.* People are, by and large, very optimistic: they tend to believe that things will turn out well, even if there is no rational basis for such beliefs. Closely related is the tendency to underestimate the amount of time needed to complete a given task, or to assume that more can be completed in a given period of time than is feasible. Together, these cognitive biases can lead to serious errors in planning, formation of strategy, and many other activities. Moreover, growing evidence indicates that they are truly a basic aspect of human thought—tendencies "built in" to the structure and function of our minds and brains (e.g., Sharot, 2011). Recent research indicates that the optimistic bias is directly relevant to entrepreneurship and in ways that seem to contradict widespread beliefs: the more optimistic entrepreneurs are, the *poorer* the performance of their companies (Hmieleski and Baron, 2009). Why? Apparently because high levels of optimism interfere with setting appropriate goals and with effective processing of relevant information, thus interfering with effective decision making.

- *Delay discounting: later payoffs are worth less than immediate ones.* Entrepreneurs, by definition, must be able to delay gratification—to refrain from seeking short-term gains now in order to reap larger rewards later. Yet research findings indicate that we suffer from a powerful "delay discounting" bias. We tend to discount rewards that will be obtained later relative to ones that are available now. This works strongly against the capacity to delay gratification to later times—and can be a serious problem for entrepreneurs.

- *Affect infusion: how feelings shape thought.* If we were totally rational beings, our feelings and emotions would not influence our decision or judgments. Do they? Of course! A large body of research evidence indicates that feelings, and even mild and subtle shifts in moods, often exert powerful effects on our thinking. For instance, when we are in a good mood, we tend to recall mostly positive information; when we are in a bad one, we tend to remember mostly negative information. Clearly, what we recall can strongly influence our decisions, so affect infusion—the tendency for our current feelings to influence key aspects of our cognition—is another potentially important source of cognitive errors. (We'll consider the role of emotions and feelings in entrepreneurship in detail in Chapter 4, where we discuss such topics as entrepreneurial passion and the question of whether entrepreneurs can sometimes be *too* positive or enthusiastic.)

- *Sunk costs: getting trapped in bad decisions.* Have you ever repaired a used car only to have it break down again very soon? What do you do then? Rationally, at some point, you should "walk away" and write off the money you have already spent on the car as wasted. But in fact most people find it very difficult to do this. Instead, they feel psychologically committed to their previous decisions, and *can't* walk away. They get trapped in what are called *sunk costs*—the resources they have already invested in a failing course of action. This is a very powerful tendency, and can badly distort the thinking and actions of individuals who become its victim.

- *Affective forecasting: the perils of predicting our future feelings.* Can you predict how various events will make you feel? Rationally, this should be possible: you have experienced similar outcomes in the past, so generalizing from these should not be a problem. Unfortunately, it is, and in fact people are not very good at knowing how future events will make them feel. They tend to overestimate both the positive and the negative feelings they'll experience, and this can strongly influence their current decisions and judgments.

Table 2.1 *Cognitive errors that can be especially costly for entrepreneurs*

Cognitive error	Description	Relevance for entrepreneurship
Confirmation bias	Tendency to notice, process, and store only information consistent with current beliefs.	Reduces capacity to be flexible in the face of changing conditions, and capacity to respond to negative information.
Heuristics	Rules of thumb for making decisions and judgments quickly.	Efficient in terms of reducing cognitive effort, but can lead to serious errors when more systematic and detailed analysis is required.
Self-serving bias	Tendency to attribute positive outcomes to one's own talent, effort, etc., but negative outcomes to external factors beyond one's control.	Reduces capacity to learn, since negative outcomes are perceived as generated by external agencies or factors.
Optimistic bias	Tendency to expect more positive outcomes than is rationally justified.	Leads to unrealistically high goals and aspirations, and to underestimating the amount of time or effort needed to complete various tasks.
Delay discounting	Tendency to discount the value of future rewards.	Reduces capacity to delay gratification until more advantageous times.
Affect infusion	Powerful influence of emotions and feelings on key aspects of cognition (e.g., decision making, evaluation of various objects or alternatives).	Can seriously distort judgments and decisions by entrepreneurs in a wide range of contexts.
Sunk costs	Tendency to get trapped in bad decisions or failing course of action.	Can prevent entrepreneurs from "cutting their losses" by walking away from poor decisions or strategies.
Forecasting errors	Inability to predict reactions to future events accurately.	Can lead to avoidance of strategies or courses of action expected (falsely) to generate strong negative reactions.

Note: All of the errors listed here can interfere with entrepreneurs' capacities to make accurate decisions and judgments, as well as other important aspects of cognition.

We could continue, because many other cognitive errors and biases exist as well; for example, we briefly examined the endowment effect—the tendency to overvalue whatever belongs to us—in Chapter 1. By now, though, the main point should be clear. Partly because of the limitations of our own cognitive systems, we are far from totally rational as information processors. Instead, we are susceptible to many errors and forms of bias, which together often interfere with our capacity to make accurate and effective decisions, judgments, and choices. These and other potential cognitive errors are important in themselves, in a general sense, but as noted in Table 2.1 they are highly relevant to many key aspects of entrepreneurship, and to efforts by entrepreneurs to transform their ideas for something new and better into actuality.

Before concluding, we should briefly address one more issue—a very important one. Can the impact of these potential forms of error be reduced? Given that they seem to be very basic aspects of our cognitive systems, it is easy to conclude that they are irresistible and unavoidable. However, scholars who have studied these processes in detail remain optimistic (perhaps because of the optimistic bias?). For instance, Ariely (2009, p. 244) states:

> although irrationality is commonplace, it does not necessarily mean that we are helpless. Once we understand when and where we may make erroneous decisions, we can try to be more vigilant, force ourselves to think differently . . . or use technology to overcome our inherent shortcomings.

Similarly, Sharot (2011) notes: "Once we are made aware of our optimistic illusions, we can act to protect ourselves." In essence, both authors—who are also active researchers—suggest that in this case, as in many others, enhanced self-knowledge may be one basis for mitigating the impact of our built-in proclivities for such errors. Only future research will reveal whether, and to what extent, that is the case, but it is consistent with other evidence suggesting that "to be forewarned is, often, to be forearmed" (e.g., Baron and Branscombe, 2012).

Creativity: generating the *new*

Have you ever encountered a new idea, new product, or new service, and immediately thought "Wow—this is great!"? Such experiences indicate that, when we come across something truly new and useful, we often recognize its worth immediately—although, of course, not always. For instance, about 10 years ago I was visiting my brother and saw him use a kitchen tool I had never seen before: a new kind of grater. He used it to quickly grate the skin of several lemons—a task that often results in raw fingers and torn fingernails. Then he used it to grate some spices. "Stop," I almost shouted. "What *is* that . . . and where can I get one?" What my brother was using was a Microplane, a kitchen tool that is now standard equipment for chefs on all popular television shows—and for tens of millions of cooks around the world. It is so superior to what existed before that almost everyone recognizes this fact immediately (see Figure 2.1), and sales of this product have zoomed.

This new kind of grater is a good example of a useful innovation—an application of the ideas generated by creativity to something concrete that is better than what existed before and generates value (economic or

Note: The device shown here—a Microplane—is a new type of grater that developed out of the idea of using an ancient tool (wood rasps) in food preparation. The idea behind this invention reflects creativity, while actual use of this idea involves innovation.

Source: Courtesy Robert A. Baron.

Figure 2.1 *From creativity to innovation*

social). As we hope you'll recall, that is the essence of entrepreneurship. One leading expert on creativity and innovation puts it this way (Amabile, 1996, p. 143): "All innovation begins with creative ideas . . . creativity by individuals and teams is a starting point for innovation." In other words, the products of creativity—new ideas, principles, or concepts—serve as the "raw materials" for innovation. Thus creativity is often a necessary condition for subsequent innovations, although not a sufficient one, since many ideas generated by creativity are not commercially feasible or cannot be developed by the persons who generated them (e.g., Baron and Ward, 2004; McMullen and Shepherd, 2006). Recent findings indicate that creativity does indeed enhance innovations by new ventures (Baron and Tang, 2011), although this relationship is stronger in highly dynamic environments (i.e., ones that are rapidly changing) than in more stable environments.

It is interesting to note that the United States Patent Office applies the same criteria to patent applications: to qualify for a patent, an idea must be *new* (not obvious to anyone familiar with similar ideas or products that already exist) and *useful* (in the sense that it can actually be produced or put to use). Ideas that can't be translated into real products or devices cannot be patented. So creativity is truly a building block of entrepreneurship: it provides the foundation from which innovations develop. But how does this process actually unfold? How, and why, do specific individuals come up with ideas for something new that is also useful? Since creativity is clearly a result of human cognition—ideas originate in the minds of specific persons—it's useful, once again, to consider what basic knowledge of cognition tells us; and, as we'll now see, it tells us quite a bit!

Concepts: mental categories that sometimes enhance, and sometimes block, creativity

As we noted earlier, the capacity of long-term memory is vast—perhaps virtually without limit. This means that information entered into memory can easily get lost, like a computer file without a distinctive name or one that is saved to the wrong folder or sub-folder. To reduce this problem, information in memory is organized in various ways—it is grouped together in internal frameworks that enhance its ease of recall. Several types of mental frameworks exist and are useful, but the ones most relevant to creativity are known as *concepts*. Concepts are categories for objects or events that are somehow similar to each other in certain respects. Consider, for instance, the words *automobile*, *airplane*, and *boat*. All are included in the concept *vehicle*, because all share certain key features: they move people from place to place, and have controls to start and stop them, and to change their direction. Similarly, consider the words *shirt*, *jeans*, and *shoes*. All fit within the concept *clothing*, because all share key features: they are worn by people, can be put on or removed, cover various parts of the body, and so on. A key feature of concepts—and one closely related to their role in creativity—is that they all get "fuzzy" around the edges. Consider the concept of *vehicle* once again: automobile, airplane, and boat are all very close to the core of this concept. But what about elevator? It carries people and can start and stop, but does not ordinarily change direction. And what about escalator? Roller skates? Similarly, think about the concept *clothing*. Shirts, jeans, and shoes are at the core of this concept; but what about a wig? It might qualify as clothing, but just barely.

And what about tattoos? They cover parts of the body, but do not fit well within the concept *clothing*.

The fact that concepts get fuzzy at the edges is closely related to their role in creativity. Briefly, concepts can encourage creativity when they are expanded or combined in various ways. The fact that they get fuzzy at the edges can greatly facilitate these processes. First, let's see how concepts can be combined to generate something very new. Do you use a smart phone? If so, you know that such phones combine many concepts into a single new product: they are phones, GPS devices, cameras, music systems, tools for finding the prices of various products in nearby stores, or for gaining access to the internet, and many other purposes—the list goes on and on and is limited only by the number of "apps" owners obtain and use. (Unfortunately, though, as recent news stories suggest, smart phones, useful as they are, can also be used to find *you*—to reveal to others where you are located physically.) Smart phones represent a combination of several (or many) concepts, and this combination is so useful to many people that they can no longer imagine life without these phones. In instances like this, creativity is greatly enhanced through the combination of several initially separate concepts.

Another route to the same goal is concept expansion. This happens when new products emerge and quickly develop into something even better. The first railroad cars looked very much like the horse-drawn carriages they replaced. The concept of "carriage" had been expanded to include a vehicle for moving people, but what resulted was very similar to the original concept in appearance, if not means of propulsion. Similarly, early television sets were often placed in beautiful wooden cabinets because they were seen as a form of furniture—another type of home entertainment device like radios and phonographs, and that's how *those* inventions had been presented to consumers. Sometimes, however, concepts are so clearly defined in a given culture or context that what seem to be straightforward logical expansions of them fail to occur. For instance, when the Spanish conquistadors first encountered the Inca civilization they observed the children playing with wheeled toys such as miniature carts. Yet the Inca never expanded this concept from "toys" to useful devices such as wagons for transporting various products.

A third way in which concepts can be changed or expanded is through analogy. Analogies involve perceiving similarities between objects or events that are otherwise dissimilar. The history of science, technology, and the arts is filled with examples of creativity and innovation emerging from analogies, but perhaps de Mestral's invention of Velcro is an especially good example. After examining how burrs clung to his clothing with minute hooks, he reasoned "Why can't we use the same system to attach things to each other?" The result was Velcro—a material we now take for granted (see Figure 2.2).

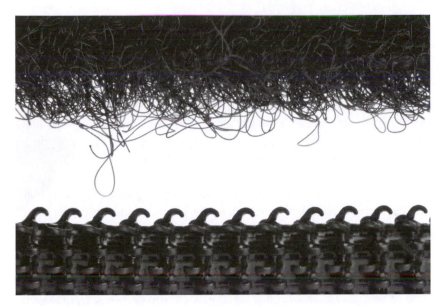

Note: When Swiss inventor George de Mestral put plant seeds and burrs under a microscope and noticed that many clung to clothing or skin by means of tiny hooks, he reasoned that this would work for attaching almost anything—and Velcro was born.

Figure 2.2   *Creativity as a result of analogy*

Clearly, then, the existence of mental categories in our minds—concepts—can be a major "plus" in terms of enhanced creativity. But, as noted briefly above in connection with the Inca's failure to use the wheel to transport various items, there is an important downside to this story. If they are very strong and clear, concepts can lock us into traditional ways of thinking—what I often describe as "mental ruts." Unfortunately, these "mental ruts" can be very deep. For instance, consider this amazing—but totally true—series of events. In the 1970s, engineers and scientists at Sony Corporation were charged with the task of developing music CDs. They made great progress, but ultimately gave up for the following reason: the CDs they produced stored fully 18 hours of music, and that was viewed as being too large to be marketable. Why did the CDs they developed hold so much? Because the engineers made them the same size and shape as existing LP records! Although they were brilliant scientists and engineers, they simply could not escape from the "mental ruts" created by their past experience to realize that the new CDs could be any size they wished.

In sum, concepts can either encourage or restrict human creativity; the key task is to use them as a basis for creative ideas, while avoiding the mental ruts into which they sometimes direct our thinking.

Human intelligence: a foundation for creativity and innovation

The cognitive systems that allow us to think, speak, plan, remember, solve problems, be creative, and perform countless other functions are part of our human inheritance. This means that they are shared by all members of our species—they are part of what it means to be "human." This does not imply, however, that these systems operate identically in all persons. On the contrary, large individual differences exist in the capacity to process information. These differences are often referred to by the term *intelligence*, which in its most general meaning refers to individuals' abilities to understand complex ideas, to adapt effectively to the world around them, to learn from experience, to engage in various forms of reasoning, and to overcome a wide range of obstacles (e.g., Sternberg, 2001). Is intelligence related to creativity, innovation, and entrepreneurship? A few studies suggest that it is; persons who found new ventures tend to be higher in intelligence than persons who do not (e.g., managers; Shane, 2003). Moreover, entrepreneurs have been found to be higher in intelligence than other persons matched for age and work experience, even when intelligence was measured many years in the past—when they were, on average, 12 years old (van Praag and Cramer, 2001)! But, in a key sense, the question "Is intelligence related to key aspects of entrepreneurship" is far too general to be answered. Although individuals do certainly differ in something we describe as "intelligence," this dimension is far from unitary in nature. On the contrary, intelligence is similar to a sparkling jewel, one that shows many different facets. A given individual can be high in some of these, but lower in others. For instance, Nobel Prize winning scientists are high in what is often described as *analytic intelligence*—the aspect of intelligence measured by traditional IQ tests: the abilities to learn, remember, retrieve, and process information—especially complex information—both quickly and effectively. In contrast, consider world-famous athletes. Such persons may not be highly adept at mastering many kinds of complex verbal or mathematical information, but are exceptional in the ability to perform incredibly controlled and precise body movements far beyond the capacity of most persons.

Taking note of this fact, one expert on human intelligence—Robert Sternberg (2004)—has suggested that, to be successful, entrepreneurs do not necessarily need to be high in analytic intelligence, but rather high in practical intelligence and creative intelligence. Practical intelligence refers to what is known as a "street smarts"—being able to use a wide array of skills and tacit knowledge (knowledge that can't be readily put into words) to solve everyday problems. Persons with practical intelligence are adaptable and flexible, and adept at dealing with rapidly changing situations.

Creative intelligence, in contrast, refers to the ability to generate high-quality ideas for something new—new approaches to solving problems. Overall, Sternberg (2004) suggests that individuals will be most likely to succeed in the complex, ever-changing world faced by entrepreneurs if they are high in all three of these aspects of intelligence: practical, creative, and analytic. Such persons, he suggests, will learn quickly (analytic intelligence), be proficient at applying a wide range of practical skills, and be very good at devising new and useful ideas and strategies. Recent research (Baum and Bird, 2010) provides strong evidence for Sternberg's (2004) views.

In this research, information was obtained on the practical, analytic, and creative intelligence of a large number of CEOs who had been involved in starting new ventures. In addition, measures of growth by the companies headed by these CEOs were also obtained. The researchers predicted that all three aspects of intelligence would be related to firm performance, but that successful intelligence—the combination of all three—would show a stronger relationship to growth than any single aspect of intelligence. This is precisely what was found. In addition, other findings indicated how the combination of analytic, practical, and creative intelligence produced these effects. Apparently, CEOs high in this combination of successful intelligence take swifter action to deal with problems and new situations as they arise, and are more likely to engage in multiple efforts to improve their companies' products and services. In short, they put their cognitive skills and capacities to use strongly and effectively—and so helped their companies succeed (see Figure 2.3).

So, does intelligence matter in entrepreneurship? On the basis of existing evidence, the answer seems to be "yes"—but it is a special kind of intelligence rather than simply the aspect measured by IQ tests (primarily, analytic intelligence). Successful entrepreneurs *do* possess strong cognitive capacities, and overall, it is a combination of "street smarts," creativity, *and* strong capacity to learn that seems to allow them to move their ideas from the real of the possible, to that of actuality.

Entrepreneurial cognition: the mind of the entrepreneur

> Capital isn't that important in business. Experience isn't that important. You can get both of these things. What *is* important is *ideas*. (Harvey Firestone, founder of Firestone Tire and Rubber Co.)

Famous entrepreneurs, whether from the past or present, often attribute their success to the ways in which they think—their ideas, creativity, and ability to differentiate between bona fide opportunities and false alarms. As we noted in Chapter 1, we can't assume that these entrepreneurs are correct in their assertions or beliefs, but in this instance so many refer

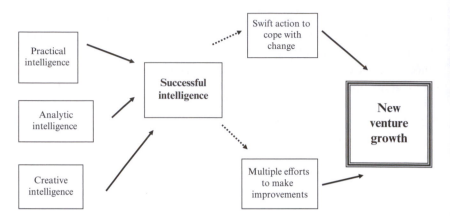

Note: Researchers (Baum and Bird, 2010) have recently obtained evidence indicating that successful intelligence—a blend of analytic, creative, and practical intelligence—is positively related to new venture performance. Successful intelligence produces these beneficial effects because it encourages entrepreneurs to take swift action in response to changing conditions and to engage in multiple efforts to improve firm performance.

Source: Based on data from Baum and Bird (2010).

Figure 2.3   *The role of successful intelligence in entrepreneurship—and new venture success*

to their own cognition, and so much additional evidence supports their views, that it seems reasonable to conclude that cognition does indeed play a key role in entrepreneurship, and in entrepreneurs' success. Further, growing evidence indicates that entrepreneurs *do* think differently from other people in certain respects, and that these differences play an important role in their efforts to transform ideas into reality. Increasing recognition of this fact has led, in recent years, to a rising volume of research on what is known as *entrepreneurial cognition*—an area of theory and research focused primarily on how entrepreneurs think, reason, plan, and act with respect to the central task of entrepreneurship—creating value (something new and better) by recognizing and developing opportunities (e.g., Mitchell et al., 2007). Implicit in this approach is the idea that entrepreneurs' cognitive processes may be different, in important ways, from those of other persons. Are they? That is an intriguing question, and the one to which we'll turn next.

Do entrepreneurs really think differently from other persons?

Cognitive scientists—scholars in several different fields who investigate all aspects of human cognition—generally make the assumption that the basic processes that allow us to notice, store, retrieve, and process information are much the same for all human beings. For instance, consider memory: they assume that it operates very much the same for all persons, in all cultures, and has done so since the appearance of human beings as a unique species. In other words, everywhere, regardless of geographic location, memory—which emerges from a complex interplay between many parts of the brain—operates to provide a mechanism for noticing, storing, and later retrieving information. Yes, serious illness, injury, poor nutrition, or other biological factors can interfere with its operation, and people do differ greatly with respect to key aspects of memory—some can perform amazing feats of memory, while others can't even recall a few phone numbers. Overall, though, memory itself is a process about which we can hope to obtain general, enduring knowledge, just as—for instance—physicians seek to obtain general knowledge about the factors that influence human health.

If that's true—if memory and other cognitive systems operate in basically the same ways among all human beings—the following question arises: How can entrepreneurial cognition differ from cognition in general? How can entrepreneurs think, plan, make decisions, reason, or perform any other cognitive activity in ways that set them apart from other persons? The most reasonable answer, we believe, is that although the basic processes are much the same (i.e., memory functions in the same basic ways in entrepreneurs and other persons), the environments in which entrepreneurs operate are so distinct and so exceptional that they virtually require certain shifts in modes of thought and other aspects of cognition. In other words, the conditions faced by entrepreneurs are so unusual that entrepreneurs' cognitive processes are shifted in certain ways or into certain paths.

What are the crucial conditions that generate such effects? Several are important. First, entrepreneurs often operate in highly complex situations in which they must process large amounts of unfamiliar information; this incoming information may be so voluminous and so varied in nature that entrepreneurs soon face "information overload"—the volume of information exceeds the limits or capacity of their cognitive systems. Second, they must process this wealth of information under what often amounts to "emergency" conditions—ones involving very high time pressures that allow little, if any, time for careful reflection. Third, entrepreneurs frequently face conditions of extreme uncertainty; not only is vital information unavailable, but it actually can't be obtained because, for instance, it doesn't yet exist. What will competitors do when the entrepreneur launches a new product? Predictions can be made, but, until events unfold, certain forms of information are simply not available. Together, these unusual conditions have important effects on entrepreneurs' cognition, shifting it into patterns and approaches not commonly observed among other groups of individuals.

First, research findings indicate that entrepreneurs may be more likely to depend on heuristic thinking than other persons—thinking that relies heavily on quick "rules of thumb" for making decisions and planning future actions (e.g., the availability heuristic). Why do entrepreneurs rely so heavily on heuristic thinking? Because such thinking is almost a necessity under conditions of high information overload and high uncertainty (e.g., Baron, 1998). Research findings indicate that entrepreneurs do tend to engage in heuristic thought more frequently than persons in other fields (e.g., Busenitz and Barney, 1997), so this is an important way in which entrepreneurs' cognition differs from that of other persons. Note that it is a difference of degree, not kind, and that is generally true of all the differences we will examine. One more point should be noted: heuristic thought is often highly efficient and allows entrepreneurs (and others) to "get the job done" quickly. But it does not always yield the best—that is, most accurate or effective—outcomes. Sometimes, these can be obtained only through slower, but more detailed and systematic, thought. In short, heuristic thinking is something of a mixed blessing in which individuals trade accuracy for speed and efficiency—a classic trade-off in many spheres of life.

A second way in which entrepreneurs' cognitive processes may differ from those of other persons relates to the fact that they often possess or develop expertise in the fields in which they work. As noted by McMullen and Shepherd (2006), entrepreneurs usually move ahead with efforts to develop ideas only in areas (industries, fields, etc.) they know well. In a sense, then, they are often experts in these fields. Once they decide to proceed, of course, they devote many hours to running their businesses, and to increasing their knowledge and skills with respect to various tasks they must perform. As a result, they may develop considerable expertise in areas related to their work. A large literature on the nature and impact of expertise (or *expert performance*, as it is often termed; e.g., Ericsson, Nandagopal, and Roring, 2009) suggests that, as it develops, expertise is related to profound shifts in cognitive systems. For instance, experts in a given field or domain gain amazingly rapid access to information stored in memory—they can retrieve it in an almost instantaneous manner.

In addition, they learn to "zero in" on the factors that are most important in relevant situations, giving these the bulk of their attention. And, perhaps most intriguing of all, they gain increased understanding of what they know and what they do not know—what is known as *metacognitive knowledge* (Haynie, Shepherd, Mosakowski, and Earley, 2010). Such gains in self-knowledge allow them to set more realistic—and attainable—goals, and may also assist them in choosing the most appropriate strategies for attaining these goals (e.g., Baron and Henry, 2010; Carver and Scheier, 2010). In sum, the fact that many entrepreneurs become expert in fields or domains relevant to their activities can result in the emergence of patterns of cognition or actual enhancements to cognitive processes that are different from those shown by other persons.

Third, growing evidence indicates that entrepreneurs often think about the task of converting their ideas into something real in highly distinctive ways. According to Sarasvathy (2008), a key proponent of this view, entrepreneurs often do not adopt standard cause-and-effect logic; they do not focus on trying to predict the future and on attaining specific ends. Rather, they use a very different approach in which they recognize that, if they can shape or control future events, they do not need to predict them; rather, they can focus on *means*—the resources they currently have available or can readily secure—as the starting point, and move ahead from there. These ideas are consistent with the following statement by Peter Drucker, who once noted: "The best way to predict the future is to create it." In addition, according to this view (known as effectuance theory), entrepreneurs tend to focus on affordable losses (what they can afford to lose) rather than on expected gains, and view surprises (unanticipated changes in the external world) as a source of opportunity and a basis for change—for shifting their goals and strategies. In contrast, individuals using standard cause-and-effect logic generally focus on predicting the future (what scientists seek to accomplish), on the goals they wish to reach rather than currently available means, on projected gains, and on avoiding surprises rather than benefiting from them. Growing evidence suggests that entrepreneurs—especially highly successful ones—do tend to adopt this alternative kind of logic (e.g., Wiltbank, Dew, Read, and Sarasvathy, 2009a, 2009b). However, some of this research has been called into question, so the overall picture is still somewhat uncertain. (e.g., Baron, 2009). In any case, effectuation does call attention to additional and important ways in which entrepreneurs' cognition differs from that of other persons, and so is well worthy of further study.

Finally, entrepreneurs seem to focus, to a greater extent than other persons, on searching for connections between various events or trends in the external world—on attempting to recognize patterns that link seemingly unrelated events. While everyone engages in this kind of activity from time to time, research findings indicate that entrepreneurs tend to engage in it more frequently (Baron and Ensley, 2006), and build it into their normal activities, so that they are constantly searching for patterns others have not discovered (e.g., Tang, Kacmar, and Busenitz, in press). Such patterns, when they emerge, may constitute an important source of ideas that can be used to create value—a core task of entrepreneurship. (We'll return to this process, opportunity recognition, in more detail in Chapter 3.)

In sum, although basic cognitive processes operate in much the same manner in all human beings, there are indeed grounds for suggesting that entrepreneurs think, reason, make decisions, plan, and set goals in quite distinctive ways. In a sense, they develop a mindset (way of thinking) that assists them in applying their creativity to making constructive changes in their work, their communities, or their entire society. Understanding this basic fact offers important insights into the mind of the entrepreneur— and that is an important step on the road to understanding the complex process through which entrepreneurs create something new and useful from ingredients that have sometimes been described as "nothing," but are, in fact, very close to the essence of the human spirit: creativity, ingenuity, energy, and passionate commitment.

Increasing creativity: the confluence approach

"Creativity" is another word—like "entrepreneurship"—with a definite positive aura: individuals, companies, schools of business, venture capitalists, and in fact almost everyone views it as a positive attribute or outcome. There is much less agreement, however, on how it can be encouraged. Many consulting firms offer programs designed to increase creativity, but the outcomes of such programs—like creativity itself—are difficult to measure. Perhaps a better approach—and one consistent with the perspective adopted in this book—is to see what existing evidence gathered in systematic research tells us. Fortunately, such evidence seems to converge on basic procedures that, although they can't *guarantee* a high level of creativity, can at least provide the central ingredients which encourage its occurrence. In this regard, Sternberg (2001)—perhaps the leading expert on creativity in the field of psychology—has crafted the following list of key components that may be especially helpful in enhancing creativity:

- *Obtaining a broad knowledge base.* Creativity does not emerge in an information vacuum; rather, to come up with something truly new (and potentially useful), a broad array of relevant knowledge is generally required. In the absence of such information, individuals run the real risk of "reinventing the wheel"—proposing ideas that already exist but of which they are unaware. So knowledge is generally a key ingredient in creativity, and acquiring it is a key step on the road to this process.
- *Key aspects of intelligence.* Earlier, we noted that creativity is closely related to successful intelligence—a combination of practical, creative (synthetic), and analytic intelligence. Together, these three basic capabilities pave the way for creativity, and it is often the combination of all three that is crucial. Here's an example: imagine an executive who loves his job, but hates his boss. What should he do? His first approach

might be to visit a "head-hunter" to find another position. But, after considering the situation carefully, he realizes that another solution is also possible—one that involves redefining the problem. This solution? Hire the head-hunter to get his *boss* a job! That is a better solution than leaving a company and job he loves, and illustrates the role of basic aspects of intelligence in devising creative solutions.

- *Adopting an appropriate thinking style.* Creativity is often encouraged by what is known as an *inventing* style of thought—one that seeks new and better ways of doing things. This is in contrast to an *implementing* style, which involves execution of existing ideas and methods. To the extent individuals show a preference for inventive thinking, and an ability to "see the big picture," they can escape from mental ruts which are the antithesis of creativity.
- *Personal attributes.* Creativity also involves such characteristics as willingness to take risks and to tolerate ambiguity; these tendencies help individuals to consider ideas and solutions others may overlook. It's important to note that such attributes are not inherited or "set in stone"—they can be changed, so that ones conducive to creativity are encouraged.
- *High levels of motivation.* Even if people possess high levels of successful intelligence and creativity-enhancing styles of thought and characteristics, nothing is likely to happen unless they also have high levels of intrinsic, task-focused motivation. They must want to generate something new and better, so motivation, too, is a key ingredient.
- *An environment that encourages creative ideas.* Finally, creativity is enhanced by environments that encourage it. What are these like? Basically, they are ones that do not impose uniformity of thought but rather help individuals overcome their basic reluctance to seek or implement change. One way of accomplishing this is to emphasize the fact that maintaining the status quo involves definite losses—things are not being done as efficiently or effectively as possible. A focus on losses, in turn, tends to enhance people's willingness to accept risk by taking a chance on something new; in contrast, a focus on real or potential gains tends to make people risk-averse—and less likely to seek or accept change.

Overall, the approach to creativity recommended by Sternberg and his colleagues (e.g., Sternberg, O'Hara, and Lubart, 1997) suggests that creativity will emerge among individuals and in companies to the extent that conditions promoting its occurrence exist. A key task for entrepreneurs, then, is that of ensuring that such conditions exist in their own companies, or in any environment where they seek to develop something new and better than currently exists.

Summary of key points

Our basic cognitive systems permit us to make sense out of the world in which we live. Central among these is memory, several systems that, together, allow us to notice, store, retrieve, process, and later use information. Working memory holds small amounts of information for brief periods of time and is the place where information we are currently processing is held. Long-term memory can retain seemingly unlimited amounts of information, but there is a bottleneck in terms of getting information from working memory into long-term memory. Since the amount of information in long-term memory is vast, problems often occur in terms of finding information once it has been stored. This and other limitations in memory and our other cognitive systems lead to important errors in our processing of information. These take many different forms, but among the most important are the confirmation bias, overreliance on heuristics, the self-serving bias, and—perhaps most powerful of all—the optimistic bias.

Creativity involves generating something new from existing information or knowledge. It is both facilitated and impeded by concepts—mental categories for organizing information in memory. Concepts can be expanded, combined, or stretched through analogies—processes that aid creativity—but they sometimes serve as a barrier to creativity by preventing individuals from thinking in new ways.

Human intelligence is related to creativity and to entrepreneurship. Intelligence is not unitary; rather, it consists of several different forms. Recent evidence indicates that most relevant to entrepreneurship is successful intelligence, which involves analytic intelligence, creative intelligence, and practical intelligence.

Growing evidence suggests that, although basic cognitive processes operate similarly in all human beings, the unique environments faced by entrepreneurs tend to shift their cognition into patterns and pathways somewhat different from those of most other persons. Entrepreneurs rely more heavily on heuristic thought, experience gains in cognitive capacities as a result of growing expertise, use effectual rather than cause-and-effect logic, and are more adept at noticing patterns that link seemingly unrelated trends of events.

Research on creativity suggests ways in which it can be increased, basically by providing key ingredients in its development. These include obtaining a broad array of knowledge in a field or domain, possessing or developing certain intellectual abilities, adopting an inventive, open-minded thinking style, possessing or developing certain personality characteristics (e.g., a high tolerance for ambiguity), having high levels of motivation, and working in environments that encourage creativity.

Bibliography

Amabile, T.M. (1996). *Creativity in context*. Boulder, CO: Westview Press.

Ariely, D. (2009). *Predictably irrational*. New York: HarperCollins.

Baron, R.A. (1998). Cognitive mechanisms in entrepreneurship: Why, and when, entrepreneurs think differently than other persons. *Journal of Business Venturing, 13*, 275–294.

Baron, R.A. (2004). The cognitive perspective: A valuable tool for answering entrepreneurship's basic "why?" questions. *Journal of Business Venturing, 19*, 221–240.

Baron, R.A. (2009). Effectual versus predictive logics in entrepreneurial decision making: Differences between experts and novices: Does experience in starting new ventures change the way entrepreneurs think? Perhaps, but for now, "caution" is essential. *Journal of Business Venturing, 24*, 310–315.

Baron, R.A., and Branscombe, N. (2012). *Social psychology*, 13th edition. Boston, MA: Allyn & Bacon.

Baron, R.A., and Ensley, M.D. (2006). Opportunity recognition as the detection of meaningful patterns: Evidence from comparisons of novice and experienced entrepreneurs. *Management Science, 52*, 1331–1344.

Baron, R.A., and Henry, R.A. (2010). How entrepreneurs acquire the capacity to excel: Insights from basic research on expert performance. *Strategic Entrepreneurship Journal, 4*, 49–65.

Baron, R.A., and Tang, J. (2011). The role of entrepreneurs in firm-level innovation: Joint effects of positive affect, creativity, and environmental dynamism. *Journal of Business Venturing, 26*, 49–60.

Baron, R.A., and Ward, T. (2004). Expanding entrepreneurial cognition's toolbox: Potential contributions from the field of cognitive science. *Entrepreneurship Theory and Practice, 28*, 553–573.

Baum, J.R., and Bird, B.J. (2010). The successful intelligence of high-growth entrepreneurs: Links to new venture growth. *Organizational Science, 21*, 397–412.

Busenitz, L.W., and Barney, J.B. (1997). Differences between entrepreneurs and managers in large organizations: Biases and heuristics in strategic decision-making. *Journal of Business Venturing, 1*, 9–30.

Carver, C.S., and Scheier, M.F. (2010). Self-regulation of affect and action. In K.D. Vohs and R.F. Baumeister (eds), *Handbook of self-regulation: Research, theory, and applications* (pp. 3–23). New York: Guilford Press.

Ericsson, K.A., Nandagopal, K., and Roring, R.W. (2009). Toward a science of exceptional achievement: Attaining superior performance through deliberate practice. *Annals of New York Academy of Science, 1172*, 199–217.

Grégoire, D.A., Barr, P.S., and Shepherd, D.A. (2010). Cognitive processes of opportunity recognition. *Organizational Science, 21*, 413–431.

Haynie, J.M., Shepherd, D.A., Mosakowski, E., and Earley, C. (2010). Cognitive adaptability: Metacognition and the "entrepreneurial mindset." *Journal of Business Venturing*, *25*, 217–229.

Hmieleski, K., and Baron, R.A. (2009). Entrepreneurs' optimism and new venture performance: A social cognitive perspective. *Academy of Management Journal*, *52*, 473–488.

McMullen, J.S., and Shepherd, D.A. (2006). Entrepreneurial action and the role of uncertainty in the theory of the entrepreneur. *Academy of Management Review*, *31*(1), 132–152.

Mitchell, R.K., Busenitz, L.W., Bird, B., Gaglio, C.M., McMullen, J.S., Morse, E.A., and Smith, B. (2007). The central question in entrepreneurship cognition research. *Entrepreneurship Theory and Practice*, *31*(1), 1–27.

Sarasvathy, S.D. (2008). *Effectuation: Elements of entrepreneurial expertise*. Cheltenham, UK and Northampton, MA, USA: Edward Elgar Publishing.

Shane, S. (2003). *A general theory of entrepreneurship: The individual–opportunity nexus*. Cheltenham, UK and Northampton, MA, USA: Edward Elgar Publishing.

Sharot, T. (2011). *The optimism bias*. New York: Random House.

Solso, R.L., Maclin, O.H., and Maclin, M.K. (2009). *Cognitive psychology*, 8th edition. New York: Pearson.

Sternberg, R.J. (1997). *Successful intelligence*. New York: Plume.

Sternberg, R.J. (2001). What is the common thread of creativity? Its dialectical relation to intelligence and wisdom. *American Psychologist*, *56*, 360–362.

Sternberg, R.J. (2004). Successful intelligence as a basis for entrepreneurship. *Journal of Business Venturing*, *19*, 189–202.

Sternberg, R.J., O'Hara, L.A., and Lubart, T.L. (1997). Creativity as investment. *California Management Review*, *40*, 8–21.

Tang, J., Kacmar, K.M., and Busenitz, L. (in press). Entrepreneurial alertness in the pursuit of new opportunities. *Journal of Business Venturing*.

van Praag, C., and Cramer, J. (2001). The roots of entrepreneurship and labour demand: Individual ability and low risk aversion. *Economica*, *68*, 45–62.

Wiltbank, R., Dew, N., Read, S., and Sarasvathy, S. (2009a). Marketing under uncertainty: A knock on the door. *Journal of Marketing*, *73*, 1–18.

Wiltbank, R., Dew, N., Read, S., and Sarasvathy, S. (2009b). Logical frames in entrepreneurial decision making: Differences between experts and novices. *Journal of Business Venturing*, *24*(4), 287–309.

3 Opportunity recognition: where entrepreneurship begins

• •

Chapter outline

> There is a tide in the affairs of men which, taken at the flood, leads on to fortune; Omitted, all the voyage of their life is bound in shallows and in miseries.
> (William Shakespeare)

> Luck is a matter of preparation meeting opportunity. (Oprah Winfrey)

Many years ago, I spent a summer on Cape Cod, in the town of Sandwich, MA. One thing I noticed immediately was that ice cream was amazingly popular there. Local businesses—mainly located in stands along the highways—sold every imaginable flavor, and all of it was good! My favorite place had a very clever name: the Ice Cream Sandwich (after the town in which it operated), and I went there so often that I soon became friendly with the owner. I explained to him that I was a professor at a large Midwestern university, and was visiting that summer to work on a book. He asked me how many local ice cream parlors there were near my university, and I realized that in fact there were none, despite the fact that the university had more than 35 000 students—all of them hungry much of the time! Soon an idea took shape in my mind: Why not learn about the ice cream business while on Cape Cod, and then—perhaps with the help of the owner of the Ice Cream Sandwich—open an ice cream business when I returned home? (I was on the faculty of Purdue University at the time.) I felt that there would be a huge market for really good ice cream among students, faculty, and town residents. In short, I perceived what seemed to be an excellent business opportunity that was not currently being exploited.

I'm still convinced that this opportunity existed at the time—and continues to do so even now!—but sadly I never acted on it, so it simply remained an idea, a possibility that I never converted to reality. Why not? Perhaps because I was so busy with other aspects of my life or perhaps because the owner of the Ice Cream Sandwich wanted what seemed like excessive compensation for training me in the business and then helping me start my own ice cream operation (which would involve his assistance in purchasing lots of equipment, used if possible, to save costs). Whatever the reason, I never took action to give my vision tangible form. Interestingly, neither did anyone else, and even today, so far as I know, there is no local ice cream parlor near that major university. That's somewhat surprising, because it is widely assumed that most opportunities have a short "half-life"—they appear, and then disappear, as the "window of opportunity" in which they exist closes. While this may well be true in certain fields or industries where progress is extremely rapid (e.g., high-tech, information-based industries), it is not the case in many other contexts, where opportunities can exist for months, years, or even decades without being developed. For instance, although Chester Carlson came up with the basic idea and technology for a copier that could reproduce images on regular paper in the 1930s, the first Xerox machine did not appear until 1949, so this major breakthrough product was not developed for many years (see Figure 3.1).

Whatever their duration, opportunities are clearly often the starting point for entrepreneurship. It is only when entrepreneurs recognize the existence of opportunities, and then take action to convert them to reality, that entrepreneurship begins. Understanding the nature of this process—how opportunities come into existence, are recognized, and are then developed—is, therefore, a central task for the field of entrepreneurship, and one that has received growing attention in recent years. To provide an accurate overview of what we now know about opportunities and opportunity recognition, we'll proceed as follows. First, we'll focus on the basic nature of opportunities and opportunity recognition. Many definitions

Note: Although it is widely assumed that most opportunities exist in short "windows" of time, history is filled with examples of important new products or services that were not developed until years or even decades after the idea for them existed. For instance, Chester Carlson developed all the technology needed for a plain-paper copier at least 10 years before this product was actually developed and sold.

Source: Xerox Corporation.

Figure 3.1   *Do opportunities exist only for brief windows of time?*

of the term *opportunity* have been proposed, and many perspectives on its nature have been adopted (e.g., Bhave, 1994; Herron and Sapienza, 1992; Kirzner, 1979; Shane, 2003), but here we'll adopt one that is closely related to a cognitive perspective on these topics (e.g., Grégoire, Barr, and Shepherd, 2010; see below).

Next, we'll examine some of the basic factors that have been found to play a role in opportunity recognition—factors such as access to and effective use of information. After that, we'll address the question of whether entrepreneurs differ in the capacity to recognize opportunities by focusing on individual differences in alertness—the ability to identify opportunities that are overlooked by others (Kirzner, 1979). As we'll soon see, recent research has helped clarify the precise nature of alertness, and its role in opportunity recognition (e.g., Tang, Kacmar, and Busenitz, in press). Next, we'll examine basic cognitive processes that appear to play a key role in opportunity recognition: pattern recognition (Baron, 2006) and structural alignment—a sophisticated search for basic similarities between new information and information already present in the memory (Grégoire et al., 2010). We'll then turn to the question of whether opportunities are recognized or created, and will conclude with a brief description of how entrepreneurs can become expert in this important task.

Opportunities and opportunity recognition: their basic nature

Many definitions of the term *opportunity* have been proposed (e.g., Bhave, 1994; Herron and Sapienza, 1992; Kirzner, 1979; Shane, 2003), but careful examination of these proposals suggests that most include reference to three central characteristics (1) *potential value* (i.e., the potential to generate profit or other benefits); (2) *newness* (i.e., some product, service, technology, etc. that did not exist previously); and (3) *perceived desirability* (e.g., the moral and legal acceptability of the new product or service in society; e.g., Webb, Tihanyi, Ireland, and Sirmon, 2009). For purposes of the present discussion, therefore, *opportunity* is defined as *perceived means of generating value (i.e., profit or other benefits) that are not currently being exploited and are perceived, in a given society, as desirable or, at least, socially acceptable.* We'll return to this last point below, since it is one that has often been overlooked in the past.

If *opportunity* is defined in this manner, then within the present discussion *opportunity recognition* refers to the cognitive process (or processes) through which individuals conclude that they have identified a bona fide opportunity. It is important to note at this point that, as emphasized by Ardichvili, Cardozo, and Ray (2003) and McMullen and Shepherd (2006), opportunity recognition is only the initial step in a continuing process. To result in entrepreneurial action it must be followed by careful evaluation of the feasibility and potential economic value of identified opportunities and then by overt actions designed to develop them. In my ice cream example above, I recognized what seemed to be a potentially valuable opportunity, but did not follow through with efforts to develop it.

The social desirability of opportunities: entrepreneurship in the formal, informal, and renegade economies

Opportunities, by definition, offer the potential to create economic or social value. Not all opportunities that meet these criteria, however, would also be viewed as socially acceptable or desirable in a given society. As noted by Webb et al. (2009), opportunities—and the entrepreneurial activity they stimulate—can, and often do, differ in terms of their location along several key dimensions involving the extent to which the means used in their development and the ends they generate are legal or illegal, legitimate or illegitimate. If both the means and the ends are illegal, the opportunities fall into what is known as the *renegade economy*—activities that are essentially banned in a given society. For instance, trafficking in illegal, harmful drugs falls under this heading: neither the means used nor the ends generated are legal and, moreover, both would be viewed as illegitimate by most persons. Actions in the renegade economy are generally crimes, punishable by law.

There are other activities, however, that fall into what is termed the *informal economy*. Here, either the means or the ends employed may be viewed by many persons as legitimate. For instance, consider companies that manufacture and sell drugs in a country where these drugs are illegal, although they are legal in other countries, where they are viewed as medically beneficial. Many people would view such activities as at least relatively legitimate, since the ends produced—supplying beneficial medicines to people who could not otherwise obtain them—are acceptable. Similarly, consider a company that hires illegal aliens to manufacture its products. The illegal residents may work for lower wages and without fringe benefits, but the work they do may be of good quality and the products manufactured are identical to ones made by documented, legal employees. In such situations, many persons would view the activities as legitimate, even if not entirely legal (see Figure 3.2).

To recap, for purposes of the present discussion, the term *opportunity* will be defined as involving three criteria: potential value or profitability, newness, and social desirability in a given society; and opportunity recognition is the cognitive process (or processes) through which individuals conclude that they have identified an opportunity.

Opportunity recognition: the role of information, experience, and social networks

A key question that has emerged and re-emerged in efforts to understand opportunity recognition is this: "Why are some people and not others able to recognize specific opportunities?" If we can understand why certain people recognize opportunities that others overlook, this may potentially provide key insights into how this process takes place—and how, perhaps, it can be enhanced. A focus on information, both access to it and its effective use, provides important insights into this question, so this basic perspective will now be briefly reviewed.

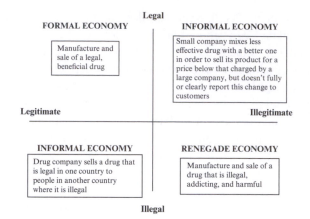

Legal

FORMAL ECONOMY	INFORMAL ECONOMY
Manufacture and sale of a legal, beneficial drug	Small company mixes less effective drug with a better one in order to sell its product for a price below that charged by a large company, but doesn't fully or clearly report this change to customers

Legitimate ———————————————— **Illegitimate**

INFORMAL ECONOMY	RENEGADE ECONOMY
Drug company sells a drug that is legal in one country to people in another country where it is illegal	Manufacture and sale of a drug that is illegal, addicting, and harmful

Illegal

Note: Business opportunities can be evaluated as legal or illegal, and legitimate or illegitimate in terms of their means and ends. Opportunities that are illegal in both respects (means and ends) are part of the renegade economy (e.g., illegal production and sale of dangerous drugs). Others, which are legal and legitimate with respect to both their means and their ends, are part of the formal economy. Opportunities that are illegal but perceived as legitimate by at least some persons are part of the informal economy (e.g., supplying drugs that have beneficial effects to people in a society where these drugs are illegal). In many societies, the informal economy is very large and is accepted, if not approved, by many persons.

Source: Based on suggestions by Webb, Tihanyi, Ireland, and Sirmon (2009).

Figure 3.2   *Business opportunities in the formal, informal, and renegade economies*

Access to information and its effective use as the basis for opportunity recognition

It has often been suggested (and confirmed in many studies) that specific persons gain an advantage with respect to opportunity recognition by having enhanced access to relevant information. They can acquire such access in several ways. For example, they may have jobs that provide them with information on the "cutting edge" that is not widely available to others. Jobs in research and development or marketing appear to be especially valuable in this respect. Similarly, entrepreneurs often gain enhanced access to information through a large social network (Ozgen and Baron, 2007). Other people often serve as a valuable source of information, and frequently the information they provide cannot be acquired easily in any other way.

Greater access to information is only the beginning of the process, however. Entrepreneurs who recognize opportunities do not merely have greater access to information than other persons: they are also better at using such information. In other words, cognitive skills or abilities too enter the picture. As a result of having greater access to information, some persons have richer and better-integrated stores of knowledge than other persons—for instance, more information (retained in memory) about markets and how to serve them. This, in turn, enhances their ability to interpret and use new information, because not only do they have more information at their disposal, but it is better organized too.

Other aspects of cognition relating to the effective utilization of information also play a role. For instance, persons who found new ventures tend to be higher in intelligence than persons who do not, but, as noted in Chapter 2, such intelligence is broader in scope than the analytic intelligence measured by standard IQ tests—it involves practical and creative intelligence as well (e.g., Baum and Bird, 2010). Additional evidence suggests that entrepreneurs are especially likely to be higher than other persons in *successful* intelligence—the combination of analytic, practical, and creative intelligence discussed in Chapter 2 (Baum and Bird, 2010). Finally, entrepreneurs are higher in creativity than other persons (Baron and Shane, 2008). In other words, they are more adept at combining the information at their disposal into something new. In sum, it seems clear that a key component in opportunity recognition is information—greater access to it, and possession of better cognitive tools (e.g., successful intelligence) for putting it to use.

The role of prior knowledge and social networks in opportunity recognition

A third factor that plays an important role in theoretical perspective on opportunity recognition that emphasizes the impact of information is prior knowledge of a market or industry. Much evidence offers support for this view, indicating that information gathered through rich and varied life experience (especially through varied business and work experience) can be a major "plus" for entrepreneurs in terms of recognizing potentially profitable opportunities. For example, it has been found that prior knowledge of customer needs and ways to meet them greatly enhances entrepreneurs' ability to provide innovative solutions to these problems—in other words, to identify potentially valuable business opportunities (Shane, 2000).

Finally, the breadth of entrepreneurs' social networks, too, is a key variable in theoretical frameworks emphasizing the importance of information in opportunity recognition. Specifically, the broader entrepreneurs' social networks (the more people they know and with whom they have relationships), and the more conferences and professional meetings they attend, the more opportunities they would be expected to identify, and this proposal has been confirmed by many studies (e.g., Aldrich and Kim, 2007; Ozgen and Baron, 2007). Social networks are an important source of information for entrepreneurs and, as such, often provide the "raw materials" on which opportunity recognition rests.

In sum, considerable evidence confirms the importance of information—access to it, its effective use, its presence in prior experience, and its acquisition through social networks and other sources—in effective opportunity recognition. In short, what entrepreneurs know and how they use this knowledge are important building blocks in their capacity to identify potentially valuable, socially acceptable opportunities (e.g., Webb et al., 2009).

As useful as a perspective emphasizing the role of information in opportunity recognition is, however, it largely ignores one central question: How does opportunity recognition actually occur? What cognitive processes underlie the emergence, in the minds of specific entrepreneurs, of ideas for new products or services, or—more generally—for something new, useful, and better? This question, in turn, reflects the basic assumption that recognition of specific opportunities is an event that occurs primarily in the minds of individual entrepreneurs. While information can be—and often is—shared or exchanged, and various events and trends in markets, technology, and government policies can be readily observed by many persons, it is often just one or a few individuals who move from these external conditions and changes to the formulation of specific opportunities. If these events do indeed occur within the minds of specific entrepreneurs, then the following, and potentially valuable, approach to enriching our understanding of opportunity recognition is suggested: Why not adapt existing, and often well-validated, theories of human cognition to the task of understanding opportunity recognition? This has been a basic theme in recent efforts to understand the essential nature of opportunity recognition and its key role in entrepreneurship. To fully represent this recent research and its important implications, we'll focus on three major topics: the nature and impact of alertness—individual differences in the capacity to recognize opportunities (e.g., Tang et al., in press); and the role of two basic cognitive processes in this activity—pattern recognition (e.g., Baron, 2006) and structural alignment (Grégoire et al., 2010).

Individual differences in opportunity recognition: the nature and impact of alertness

Are some people better at recognizing opportunities for entrepreneurial action than others? Interestingly, although economists are not typically concerned with differences between individuals, it was a well-known economist—Israel Kirzner—who first emphasized this possibility. In fact, Kirzner (1979) suggested that some individuals—and some entrepreneurs— are simply very good at this task: they are able to recognize opportunities that most other persons overlook. Kirzner described such persons as high on a dimension of alertness, and added that, since noticing opportunities is a crucial first step to deciding to pursue them, alertness is a crucial variable in entrepreneurship. People do indeed differ in a seemingly countless number of ways, so on the face of it this was a very reasonable suggestion. But Kirzner simply called attention to this variable and, being an economist, went no further in trying to understand its origins and nature. Why, in other words, are some persons more alert to opportunities than others? Is it something about their past experience that equips them with this enhanced capacity, something about the ways in which they search for opportunities in the external world, a particular skill they have acquired, or something else? Kirzner did not address these basic issues, with the result that, for many years, it was widely accepted that something like alertness does indeed play a role in opportunity recognition, but the essential nature of this variable remained somewhat vague. Recently, however, this situation has changed, largely because of efforts to understand the basic cognitive nature of alertness (e.g., Alvarez and Barney, 2001; Gaglio and Katz, 2001; McMullen and Shepherd, 2006). The results of this research now provide a much more complete and useful picture of the nature of alertness and how it operates.

The most informative work to date on these issues is that reported recently by Tang et al. (in press). These researchers have conducted the systematic studies necessary to clarify the nature of alertness and its role in opportunity recognition. After carefully reviewing existing evidence and theory concerning alertness, Tang et al. (in press) proposed that it involves three basic dimensions: (1) *alert scanning and search*—continuing efforts by actual or potential entrepreneurs to identify opportunities for doing something better; (2) *alert association and connection*—continuing efforts to connect or integrate various sources of information, and to perceive links between them and use these as a basis for creating something new and useful; and (3) *evaluation and judgment*—efforts to distinguish between high- and low-potential opportunities and being able to choose the best opportunities out of several identified opportunities. To measure individual differences in these three aspects of alertness, Tang et al. (in press) developed a questionnaire and then tested it extensively to determine if this questionnaire did indeed measure the core nature of alertness, and to determine if it is related to other aspects of entrepreneurship in ways that make sense and would be predicted on the basis of the three components described above, which the scale is designed to measure. Results indicated that three clear factors reflecting these dimensions did indeed emerge in responses by a large group of CEOs; thus alertness does indeed seem to consist of these three basic factors.

Additional research using this questionnaire was then conducted with large samples of entrepreneurs to see if the three components of alertness were related to other aspects of entrepreneurship. For instance, it was predicted that alertness (all of the three basic dimensions) would be related to innovation in new ventures and to research and development expenditures in these companies. These predictions were confirmed. Further, it was predicted that the more "upbeat" entrepreneurs were (i.e., the higher they were in dispositional positive affect), the higher they would score in terms of alertness, since positive affect is related to broadened perceptions of the external world (e.g., Baron, 2008). Overall, findings were consistent with these and other predictions, so it appears that the framework offered by Tang et al. (in press) does clarify the basic nature of alertness and confirms its important role in opportunity recognition. As Kirzner (1979) suggested, people do indeed differ in their capacity to recognize opportunities, and this reflects differences in their tendencies to engage in careful, continuous scanning of the environment (an active search for opportunities), their capacity to perceive connections between seemingly unrelated information and events they encounter, and their ability to evaluate the potential of the various opportunities they identify. All of these components can be strengthened with practice and effort, so the upshot of this recent and highly sophisticated research on alertness is highly encouraging. Alertness, it appears, represents a cluster of skills that can be acquired or enhanced, so strengthening alertness may be one important step actual or would-be entrepreneurs can take to tip the odds of attaining success in their favor.

Cognitive foundations of opportunity recognition: pattern recognition and structural alignment

In discussing alertness, Tang et al. (in press) note that association and connection play important roles. Entrepreneurs search for connections in information they acquire, seeking to use these perceived connections as a basis on which to formulate ideas for something new and useful—the core of opportunities. How does this search actually proceed? Basic research in the field of cognitive science offers important insights. To describe the implications of this research for understanding opportunity recognition, we'll now focus on the role of two basic processes—pattern recognition and structural alignment. Both involve a search for similarities and patterns in available information, but they take somewhat different forms.

Pattern recognition: opportunities as complex, discernible patterns

The term *perception* as used in cognitive science and cognitive psychology refers to the complex process through which we interpret information brought to us by our senses and integrate it with information already stored in memory (e.g., Baddeley, Eysenck, and Anderson, 2009). If some opportunities, at least, exist in the external world as complex patterns of observable events or stimuli, then perception must, logically, play a role in opportunity recognition. Basically, there is a pattern of observable events or stimuli in the external world that entrepreneurs can perceive, and whether this pattern is or is not recognized is, in a sense, a central question in opportunity recognition. Basic research on perception refers to this task as *pattern recognition* (e.g., Matlin, 2004), and it involves a process through which specific persons perceive complex and seemingly unrelated events or stimuli as forming identifiable patterns. As applied to opportunity recognition, then, pattern recognition involves instances in which specific individuals notice or mentally construct these links (Alvarez and Barney, 2001). The patterns they perceive then become the basis for identifying new business opportunities. For instance, consider an entrepreneur who noticed the following seemingly unrelated events: (1) the number of college-educated parents has risen dramatically in recent years; (2) these parents have relatively high levels of income; and (3) because of their education, they tend to believe, very strongly, that early mental stimulation will increase their children's cognitive abilities. Combining these disparate facts suggests to the entrepreneur that parents might be willing to pay high prices for products that promise to provide their children with mental stimulation, so the entrepreneur starts a new venture to develop this perceived opportunity—this perceived pattern among several diverse trends. In fact, such a company was started by Julie Aigner-Clark, a former teacher who—like millions of other college-educated parents—believed ardently in early mental stimulation for her children. The company she founded produced a large array of products designed to have such effects (see Figure 3.3), and went on to attain very large sales (hundreds of millions of dollars each year). Ultimately, the company was sold to the Walt Disney Company. Currently, there is considerable uncertainty about whether its products are truly beneficial to toddlers as claimed, but, regardless of this controversy, the idea for the company clearly arose out of its founder's perception of a pattern of trends that together constituted a potentially valuable business opportunity.

Evidence that pattern recognition plays a role in opportunity identification

Several lines of evidence suggest that pattern recognition may indeed play a key role in opportunity recognition. First, as noted at the start of this chapter, it is clear that many opportunities exist for years before they are noticed and developed. For instance, consider wheeled luggage of the type that is now used by a large majority of all air travelers. Such luggage was used for decades by air flight crews before it was introduced into the market for general sale. Why? Perhaps because no one "connected the dots"

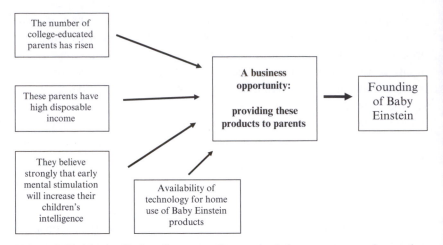

Note: Julie Aigner-Clark, a former teacher, noticed the convergence of several trends: the number of college-educated parents had risen sharply, these parents had high levels of disposable income, they believed—fervently—that providing their children with early mental stimulation would enhance the children's cognitive growth, and technology for presenting such materials to babies at home existed. To develop this perceived opportunity, Aigner-Clark founded Baby Einstein, a company that soon attained hundreds of millions of dollars in sales. Ultimately, Aigner-Clark sold the company to the Walt Disney Company for a very large sum. Currently, there is considerable uncertainty about whether its products are truly beneficial, but the idea for the company clearly arose out of its founder's perception of a pattern that connected several seemingly unrelated trends.

Figure 3.3 *Pattern recognition as a basis for opportunity recognition*

between several seemingly unrelated, but pertinent, trends: a large increase in the number of passengers, growing problems with checked luggage, expansion in the size of airports, and so on. Once these trends were linked into a unified pattern within the minds of several different entrepreneurs, a product that would help meet the needs of a large and growing market was suggested. As soon as such luggage appeared, it came to dominate the market and drove earlier models to extinction.

Second, there is a large body of evidence in cognitive science suggesting that pattern recognition is a basic aspect of our efforts to understand the world around us. That is, we do indeed expend considerable effort searching for patterns among various events or trends in the external world. To the extent that opportunity recognition also involves perceiving links or connections between seemingly independent events or trends, it may be closely related to this basic perceptual process. Third, there is empirical evidence indicating that predictions derived from models of pattern recognition are accurate and that, therefore, such models offer important insights into the nature of this process (e.g. Baron and Ensley, 2006). In this research, participants were first-time entrepreneurs and highly experienced entrepreneurs (ones who had started several different companies). It was expected that the highly experienced entrepreneurs would have richer and more fully developed mental frameworks for business opportunities than the novice entrepreneurs. (In this case, these frameworks would involve mental representations of the most typical member of a category or concept—what is known as a prototype.)

To compare these mental frameworks—frameworks that would be helpful in "connecting the dots" between seemingly divergent trends or information—both groups were asked to respond to two open-ended questions: "Describe the idea on which your new venture was based" and "Why did you feel this was a good idea—one worth pursuing?" Replies to these items were then content-analyzed, and the results of these analyses provided the primary data for identifying the content of the opportunity prototypes of novice and experienced entrepreneurs, and for comparing these prototypes. It was predicted that the opportunity prototypes of experienced entrepreneurs would be more clearly defined, would be richer in content, and—most importantly—would be more directly related to key aspects of starting and running a new venture than the business opportunity prototypes of first-time entrepreneurs. In other words, as a result of having started on average 2.6 companies, the experienced entrepreneurs would have a clearer mental picture of what constituted a bona fide business opportunity than the novice entrepreneurs. Results offered strong support for this general prediction. The business opportunity prototypes of experienced entrepreneurs were more clearly defined and richer in content than those of novice entrepreneurs. Perhaps most importantly, these prototypes were also much more clearly focused on important aspects of starting and running a new business. For instance, experienced entrepreneurs focused more than novice entrepreneurs on solving a customer's problems, the ability to generate positive cash flow, manageable risk, and having people in their networks with whom to develop the venture. In contrast, novice entrepreneurs focused more heavily on the novelty of an idea, the extent to which it was based on new technology, and their own intuition or "gut-level feelings" (see Table 3.1).

Overall, these findings indicate that one important thing entrepreneurs learn from repeated experience in starting and running new ventures—from engaging in overt efforts to convert ideas into real products, services, or other benefits—is how to determine whether an array of seemingly unrelated trends, events, or changes constitutes a bona fide opportunity. In a sense, then, their growing experience equips entrepreneurs with cognitive frameworks useful in determining where and how to search for the opportunities they seek.

Table 3.1 *Key features of business opportunity prototypes of novice and experienced entrepreneurs*

Factors important for novice entrepreneurs	*Factors important for repeat entrepreneurs*
How novel the idea is	Solving a customer's problems
Extent to which idea is based on new technology	Ability to generate positive cash flow
Superiority of product or service	Speed of revenue generation
Potential to change the industry	Manageable risk
Intuition or gut feel	Others in their network with whom to develop the venture

Note: As shown here, experienced entrepreneurs, as compared to novice entrepreneurs, assign greater importance, in their evaluations of potential business opportunities, to factors directly related to starting and running a new venture. In other words, they focus more on factors affecting the likelihood that these opportunities can (or cannot) be successfully developed.

Source: Based on findings reported by Baron and Ensley (2006).

Structural alignment: coordinating markets and technologies in the quest for opportunities

Pattern recognition is a very basic cognitive process and appears to play a role in many important activities, including opportunity recognition (e.g., Baron, 2006). However, it is not the only cognitive process that underlies the identification of potentially valuable business opportunities. Another is what is known as *structural alignment* (Grégoire et al., 2010). Basically, this refers to the cognitive processes through which individuals attempt to identify similarities between new information and information currently present in memory. This can occur at several different levels: at a superficial level, specific attributes or features are considered. For instance, with respect to a new technology, this could involve a focus on the basic elements of the new technology, who developed it, or its major parts. With respect to markets, it might involve the products or services currently available, the individuals who make up the market, and similar features. More important than these comparisons of superficial features or attributes, however, is higher-level comparisons which focus on aligning features of the new technology and features of the potential markets. For instance, the benefits and advantages of the new technology could be considered in relationship to the problems they will solve in specific markets.

Recent research (Grégoire et al., 2010) indicates that the search for higher-level structural alignment may underlie the identification of many opportunities. To obtain information on these complex processes, the researchers asked senior executives who had previously founded new ventures to "think aloud" as they tried to imagine opportunities that could be based on two new technologies and the markets they would serve. Careful analysis of their comments was then used to identify the executive's thoughts about structural alignment between the technologies and potential market uses. Results indicated that, in many cases, the participants in the research did formulate opportunities on the basis of efforts to align these two important factors. In other words, when they encountered new technologies, the executives (former or current entrepreneurs) searched actively for ways in which these technological advances could meet important market needs, and used this as the basis for identifying opportunities that could be developed with these technologies.

These findings, in contrast to those of earlier research (e.g., Baron and Ensley, 2006), were based on what and how entrepreneurs (or senior executives) actually thought as they attempted to identify opportunities, rather than on their memories of such cognitive activity in the past. Thus it provides information on how this process actually occurs, rather than reports of how it occurred in the past. In short, in trying to identify opportunities, individuals do consider similarities between new information and information already present in memory and how they can be aligned, as well as how this new information and its contexts might prove useful. As Grégoire et al. (2010, p. 425) put it:

> we found that in their efforts to recognize opportunities, participants considered the alignment between how a technology operates and the cause-and-effect principles explaining the benefits and advantages of a technology, with what individuals in a market do, why they do it, and . . . the unsatisfied needs and problems in that market.

The search for opportunities, in short, is anything but simple, and often involves deep and complex thought on the part of the persons engaged in this quest. Given the stakes involved in identifying truly valuable opportunities, however, this appears to be effort that is well worthwhile.

Opportunities: discovered, created, or both?

A key assumption of this discussion so far has been that opportunities exist in the external world and are recognized or discovered by entrepreneurs who have the cognitive equipment (i.e., the experience-based cognitive frameworks, alertness, etc.) needed to accomplish this task. Although existing theories differ on the mechanisms that play a role in this process, many agree that it is a process of discovery or identification. However, a sharply contrasting view also exists. Several scholars (e.g., Alvarez and Barney, 2005, 2007) have proposed that opportunities are not so much discovered as created. They contend that entrepreneurs, by their actions, "build the mountains"—create the opportunities they then exploit rather than simply discover them. In other words, opportunities do not exist independently of entrepreneurs (as, for instance, mountains exist independently of people who perceive them); rather they emerge as entrepreneurs begin to act on, and within, their environments.

This perspective certainly has considerable appeal; growing evidence indicates that only rarely do entrepreneurs discover an opportunity and proceed to develop or exploit it in the ways they initially planned. Rather, the process is often one that evolves as the nature of the opportunities in question becomes clear, and sometimes changes radically over time (as a result of the actions of competitors, shifts in markets, demographics, technology, etc; Sarasvathy, 2008). Recognizing this fact, many entrepreneurs report that they do truly "make it up as they go along." Although they begin with relatively clear ideas about what they want to accomplish and the kind of products or services they wish to bring to market, they soon change their goals, business models, and strategies in response to an ever-changing and always complex environment.

The fact that these changes occur does not, however, by itself, provide a compelling case for the view that opportunities are created rather than discovered. In most instances, entrepreneurs do not begin the process until they have some idea of the products or services they believe to be new, useful, and potentially profitable. Certainly, their ideas about the nature of these new products and services do change, and the ventures they launch, too, are often transformed as entrepreneurs adapt to ever-changing circumstances. But still, it appears that there is at least some initial act of discovery or identification that underlies or initiates the process.

Overall, the most reasonable approach may be to suggest that, where opportunities are concerned, there is not a strong or clear-cut line between "discovery" and "creation." After all, even if many opportunities exist in the external world as something to be discovered (e.g., a potential, emergent pattern), they do not actually take form until one or more persons perceive their existence—until one or more entrepreneurs perceive links between seemingly disparate and unrelated events that suggest new products or services. In essence, then, opportunities both are discovered, to the extent that the potential for them is generated by changes in the external environment, and are created, since it is only when these trends and changes coalesce within the minds of individual entrepreneurs that ideas worthy of overt, entrepreneurial action develop. A basic conclusion, then, is that opportunities are both discovered and created, and that there is not a basic inconsistency between these views (e.g., Vaghley and Julien, 2010).

How entrepreneurs can become skilled at recognizing opportunities: applying basic principles of expert performance

It has long been observed that some entrepreneurs are much better than others at identifying potentially profitable opportunities. One source of such differences may lie in the fact that some have "better" (i.e., broader, more fully developed, more interconnected) cognitive frameworks than others, and so are more successful at "connecting the dots"—noticing patterns that suggest new products or services (Baron, 2006). Similarly, recent research on alertness (Tang et al., in press) suggests that important individual differences also exist with respect to active search, and the capacity to notice connections and to evaluate various opportunities, and may play a key role in opportunity recognition. This raises an intriguing question: Can these findings help entrepreneurs to develop their capacity to identify excellent opportunities? A large literature on the nature of expertise and expert performance suggests that they may. This research indicates that in many different fields (e.g., sports, music, science, medicine, chess, financial forecasting, creative writing) some individuals are able to rise above ordinary or "average" levels of performance largely as a result of engaging in a special kind of practice—practice that is highly focused, very effortful, and specifically designed to improve their performance. As result of engaging in such practice (generally known as *deliberate practice*), they obtain consistently superior levels of performance on tasks that are representative of a particular domain or activity (e.g., Ericsson, 2006). Interestingly—and contrary to what common sense suggests—attaining such performance does not derive primarily from high levels of innate talent or sheer amount of time spent engaging in a specific activity. On the contrary, in many fields, most people do not continue to show improved performance as their time in that field increases. Rather, most reach a plateau within the "ordinary" range, and only a few individuals surpass this level and demonstrate truly exceptional performance—and they do so only as a result of engaging in long periods of deliberate practice. As Michael Jordan, the star basketball player, once remarked: "I'm not out here sweating for four hours every day because I like to sweat." Clearly, he understood very well that it was only his participation in vigorous deliberate practice that generated his exceptional performance.

Deliberate practice has been found to be a key ingredient in the development of exceptional performance in many different fields (e.g., Ericsson, Krampe, and Tesch-Römer, 1993). Moreover, even if individuals possess unusually high levels of talent, deliberate practice is still required to translate this talent into high levels of performance. Thus, as Malcolm Gladwell (2008) suggests in his best-selling book *Outliers*, talent is less important in generating exceptional levels of performance than high levels of effort and a favorable environment—one that encourages the development of such performance.

How does deliberate practice generate exceptional levels of performance—the kind shown by famous athletes, world-class musicians, or amazingly skilled surgeons? Apparently, by enhancing basic cognitive systems in several ways. First, persons who engage in deliberate practice gain increased amounts of domain-specific information and enhanced cognitive frameworks for storing and processing such information. The value of such information has been well documented in past research on entrepreneurship, where many studies indicate that the greater entrepreneurs' knowledge of a given field or industry, the greater the likelihood that the new ventures they launch will be successful (e.g., Fiet, 1996; Fiet and Patel, 2007). Second, deliberate practice provides individuals who engage in it with enhanced self-regulatory and metacognitive skills. Self-regulatory mechanisms—skills we'll examine in more detail in Chapter 5—are aspects of cognition that assist individuals in monitoring, regulating, and enhancing their own performance. These skills are useful in a wide range of contexts, including that of becoming truly excellent in performing various tasks. Third, and perhaps most dramatic, deliberate practice provides individuals with actual enhancements to basic cognitive processes. For example, persons who engage in focused, effortful cognitive activity in a given domain may develop improved perceptual skills in that domain: they can often make finer discriminations than novices, notice more in such situations, and are generally superior at recognizing complex patterns than novices (e.g., Baron, 2006; Ericsson, 2004). Further, persons who engage in extensive deliberate practice may also experience changes in working memory, the memory system where, as we noted in Chapter 2, information currently being considered is held and processed (e.g., Ericsson, 2005). Although working memory has severely limited capacity, engaging in deliberate practice can effectively increase this capacity by strengthening links between working memory and long-term memory. As a result, developing experts in almost any field acquire enhanced capacity to locate and retrieve information stored in long-term memory. This enhanced access, in turn, can greatly improve performance by permitting experts in a given domain to use this information to guide their current performance and to better anticipate future events. The end result is that individuals who have developed expertise in a particular field through deliberate practice can make more rapid and accurate judgments than other persons because they essentially have greater access to vast stores of useful information held in long-term memory.

How do these benefits operate with respect to opportunity recognition? The words of a famous and highly successful entrepreneur known to the present author are revealing. At one point, I asked this entrepreneur how he managed to identify one highly profitable business opportunity after another. The entrepreneur replied: "I just know. When I consider an opportunity, I can see hundreds or thousands of others in my mind's eye. . . . And when I see how this idea compares with *those*, I know instantly whether it will work." These words are consistent with the findings of basic research suggesting that experts in many fields acquire enhanced working memory, a cognitive capacity that provides them with augmented access to vast stores of information acquired through past experience.

Together, the benefits provided by deliberate practice may enhance entrepreneurs' ability to recognize opportunities, to accomplish this task quickly and efficiently, and to choose, from among many opportunities, those that offer the greatest economic potential. Of course, entrepreneurs cannot ordinarily engage in deliberate practice in the same way that it occurs in many other domains (Baron and Henry, 2010)—they cannot practice the same piece of music or a special kind of tennis serve over and over again. They can, however, focus attention and effort on engaging in active scanning and search for opportunities, identifying connections between trends, events, and changes in the external world, and on accurately evaluating noticed opportunities. Moreover, they can also gain some of the advantages of deliberate practice by engaging in it in a vicarious, rather than direct, manner—that is, by careful study of the experiences of other entrepreneurs. This all leads to an encouraging conclusion: current or future entrepreneurs can enhance their own capacities to identify valuable opportunities by engaging in vigorous efforts to develop the basic skills on which successful opportunity recognition rests.

One more point should be noted: cognitive processes that contribute to expertise in many other fields may also be relevant in entrepreneurship. Specifically, entrepreneurs who, perhaps because of highly developed self-regulatory skills (e.g., high levels of self-control; Vohs and Baumeister, 2010; see Chapter 5), are able to engage in deliberate practice with respect to key components of opportunity recognition may be the ones who become especially skilled at this task. And that, in turn, may give them a crucial "edge" in their efforts to convert their ideas or visions for something new and better from enticing possibilities into concrete, and potentially profitable, realities.

Summary of key points

Entrepreneurial opportunities possess three basic characteristics: (1) *potential value* (i.e., the potential to generate profit or other benefits); (2) *newness* (i.e., some product, service, technology, etc. that did not exist previously); and (3) *perceived desirability* (e.g., moral and legal acceptability of the new product or service in society. *Opportunity recognition* refers to the cognitive process (or processes) through which individuals conclude that they have identified a bona fide opportunity. Opportunities vary considerably in terms of their legality and their perceived legitimacy or illegitimacy in a given society. Access to information and its effective utilization are important aspects of opportunity recognition. In addition, social networks play a key role in this process.

Individuals differ considerably in their ability to recognize opportunities; that is, they differ with respect to alertness. This variable involves three basic components: (1) *alert scanning and search*—continuing efforts by actual or potential entrepreneurs to identify opportunities for doing something better; (2) *alert association and connection*—continuing efforts to connect or integrate various sources of information, and to perceive links between them and use these as a basis for creating something new and useful; and (3) *evaluation and judgment*—efforts to distinguish between high- and low-potential opportunities and being able to choose the best opportunities out of several identified opportunities. Basic cognitive processes, too, play an important role in opportunity recognition. These include pattern recognition and structural alignment. Pattern recognition involves identifying emergent patterns in seemingly disparate information. Structural alignment, in contrast, involves efforts to relate new technologies to market needs, a process that results in identification of opportunities that can be developed with these technologies.

Entrepreneurs can acquire enhanced skill at opportunity recognition by applying the principles of deliberate practice to this task—by practicing active scanning and search, searching for and identifying patterns in existing events and trends, and similar steps. Such practice increases their cognitive capacities (e.g., their access to information stored in long-term memory), sharpens their perceptual skills, and generally equips them with skills helpful in identifying potentially valuable opportunities.

Bibliography

Aldrich, H., and Kim, P.H. (2007). Small worlds, infinite possibilities? How social networks affect entrepreneurial team formation and search. *Strategic Entrepreneurship Journal*, *1*, 147–166.

Alvarez, S.A., and Barney, J.B. (2001). How entrepreneurial firms can benefit from alliances with large partners. *Academy of Management Executive*, *15*, 139–148.

Alvarez, S.A., and Barney, J.B. (2005). How entrepreneurs organize firms under conditions of uncertainty. *Journal of Management, 31*, 776–793.

Alvarez, S.A., and Barney, J.B. (2007). Discovery and creation: Alternative theories of entrepreneurial action. *Strategic Entrepreneurship Journal, 1*, 11–26.

Ardichvili, A., Cardozo, R., and Ray, S. (2003). A theory of entrepreneurial opportunity identification and development. *Journal of Business Venturing, 18*, 105–124.

Baddeley, A., Eysenck, M.W., and Anderson, M.C. (2009). *Memory*. Hove: Psychology Press.

Baron, R.A. (2006). Opportunity recognition as pattern recognition: How entrepreneurs "connect the dots" to identify new business opportunities. *Academy of Management Perspectives, 20*, 104–119.

Baron, R.A. (2008). The role of affect in the entrepreneurial process. *Academy of Management Review, 33*, 328–340.

Baron, R.A., and Ensley, M.D. (2006). Opportunity recognition as the detection of meaningful patterns: Evidence from comparisons of novice and experienced entrepreneurs. *Management Science, 52*, 1331–1344.

Baron, R.A., and Henry, R.A. (2010). How entrepreneurs acquire the capacity to excel: Insights from basic research on expert performance. *Strategic Entrepreneurship Journal, 4*, 49–65.

Baron, R.A., and Shane, S.A. (2008). *Entrepreneurship: A process perspective*, 2nd edition. Cincinnati, OH: Thomson South-Western.

Baum, J.R., and Bird, B.H.J. (2010). The successful intelligence of high-growth entrepreneurs: Links to new venture growth. *Organizational Science, 21*, 397–412.

Bhave, M.P. (1994). A process model of entrepreneurial venture creation. *Journal of Business Venturing, 9*, 223–242.

Ericsson, K.A. (2004). Deliberate practice and the acquisition and maintenance of expert performance in medicine and related domains. *Academic Medicine, 79*, S70–S81.

Ericsson, K.A. (2005). Recent advances in expertise research: A commentary on the contributions to the special issues. *Applied Cognitive Psychology, 19*, 233–241.

Ericsson, K.A. (2006). The influence of experience and deliberate practice on the development of superior expert performance. In K.A. Ericsson, N. Charness, P.J. Feltovich, and R.R. Hoffman (eds), *The Cambridge handbook of expertise and expert performance* (pp. 683–703). New York: Cambridge University Press.

Ericsson, K.A., Charness, N., Feltovich, P.J., and Hoffman, R. (eds) (2006). *The Cambridge handbook of expertise and expert performance* (pp. 41–67). New York: Cambridge University Press.

Ericsson, K.A., Krampe, R.T., and Tesch-Römer, C. (1993). The role of deliberate practice in the acquisition of expert performance. *Psychological Review*, *100*, 363–406.

Fiet, J.O. (1996). The informational basis of entrepreneurial discovery. *Small Business Economics*, *8*, 419–430.

Fiet, J.O. and Patel, P.C. (2007). Evaluating the wealth creating potential of business plans. *Journal of Private Equity*, *10*, 18–32.

Gaglio, C.M., and Katz, J. (2001). The psychological basis of opportunity identification: Entrepreneurial alertness. *Small Business Economics*, *16*, 95–111.

Gladwell, M. (2008). *Outliers*. New York: Little, Brown.

Grégoire, D.A., Barr, P.S., and Shepherd, D.A. (2010). Cognitive processes of opportunity recognition: The role of structural alignment. *Organizational Science*, *21*, 413–431.

Herron, L., and Sapienza, H.J. (1992). The entrepreneur and the initiation of new venture launch activities. *Entrepreneurship Theory and Practice*, *16*, 49–55.

Kirzner, I.M. (1979). *Perception, opportunity, and profit*. Chicago: University of Chicago Press.

Matlin, M.W. (2004). *Cognition*, 6th edition. Fort Worth, TX: Harcourt College Publishers.

McMullen, J.S., and Shepherd, D.A. (2006). Entrepreneurial action and the role of uncertainty in the theory of the entrepreneur. *Academy of Management Review*, *31*, 132–152.

Ozgen, E., and Baron, R.A. (2007). Social sources of information in opportunity recognition: Effects of mentors, industry networks, and professional forums. *Journal of Business Venturing*, *22*, 174–192.

Sarasvathy, S.D. (2008). *Effectuation: Elements of entrepreneurial expertise*. Cheltenham, UK and Northampton, MA, USA: Edward Elgar Publishing.

Shane, S. (2000). Prior knowledge and the discovery of entrepreneurial opportunities. *Organization Science*, *11*, 448–469.

Shane, S. (2003). *A general theory of entrepreneurship: The individual–opportunity nexus*. Cheltenham, UK and Northampton, MA, USA: Edward Elgar Publishing.

Sternberg, R.J. (2004). Successful intelligence as a basis for entrepreneurship. *Journal of Business Venturing*, *19*, 189–202.

Tang, J., Kacmar, K.M., and Busenitz, L. (in press). Entrepreneurial alertness in the pursuit of new opportunities. *Journal of Business Venturing*.

Vaghley, I.P., and Julien, P.A. (2010). Are opportunities recognized or constructed? An information perspective on entrepreneurial opportunity identification. *Journal of Business Venturing*, *25*, 73–86.

Vohs, K.D., and Baumeister, R.D. (eds) (2010). *Handbook of self-regulation*, 2nd edition. New York: Guilford Press.

Webb, J.W., Tihanyi, L., Ireland, R.D., and Sirmon, D.G. (2009). You say illegal, I say legitimate: Entrepreneurship in the informal economy. *Academy of Management Review, 34*, 492–510.

4 The "ups" and "downs" of an entrepreneurial life: affect, passion, and coping with failure

· ·

Chapter outline

The basic nature of affect—and its interface with cognition
The benefits—and potential costs—of positive affect
Entrepreneurial passion: doing what you love and loving what you do
How entrepreneurs cope with failure—and rebound to try again
    Is confidence a plus? Why highly confident entrepreneurs are more likely to
        bounce back from failure
    Emotional intelligence: a key attribute for entrepreneurs?

> There can be no knowledge without emotion. We may be aware of a truth,
> yet until we have felt its force, it is not ours. To the cognition of the brain
> must be added the experience of the soul. (Arnold Bennett)

> We were young, but we had good advice and good ideas and lots of *enthusiasm*.
> (Bill Gates)

Memory; creativity; innovation; successful intelligence; pattern recognition; structural alignment; so far, *cognition*—how we think about and seek to make sense out of the external world—has been the center of our attention. As the quotations above suggest, however, cognition is far from the entire story where human existence is concerned. There is a "feeling" side of life too, and it is just as important and central as cognition. In fact, scientists in several different fields (neuroscience, psychology, cognitive science) agree that, in some respects, this "feeling" or emotional side of life is more basic than, and pre-dates (in an evolutionary sense), cognition. Structures and systems within our brains that appear to be intimately linked to feelings and emotions are ones we share with many other species and that have been present in life on earth for many millions of years; in contrast, structures and systems that are more central to what are sometimes known as *higher mental processes* (reasoning, decision making, planning, etc.) are ones we do not share with other species and that, apparently, developed or expanded much more recently in the course of evolution.

But why focus on feelings, emotions, and related concepts in a book on entrepreneurship? Is the "feeling side of life" really relevant to efforts to create something new and useful? In fact, there are several reasons for replying with an emphatic "Yes!" First, it is clear that entrepreneurs often lead an incredibly rich emotional life. Typically, they show intense commitment to and enthusiasm for the ideas they generate. Further, they are known for high levels of optimism, enthusiasm, energy, and perseverance in the face of adversity—reactions with strong emotional components (e.g., Baron, 2008).

Research findings offer support for these informal observations, indicating that entrepreneurs do indeed frequently experience strong emotions or feelings and that these are highly relevant to their efforts to create something new and useful. For example, several studies indicate that passion—entrepreneurs' powerful commitment to their ideas, visions, and ventures—plays an important role in their success (e.g., Baum and Locke, 2005; Baum, Locke, and Smith, 2001; Cardon, Wincent, Singh, and Drnovsek, 2009). Specifically, passion influences entrepreneurs' goals and self-efficacy (their beliefs that they can accomplish whatever they set out to accomplish); these factors, in turn, strongly affect new venture growth. Similarly, many studies confirm the view that entrepreneurs are indeed higher than other persons in optimism—the belief that events will generate positive outcomes (e.g., Hmieleski and Baron, 2009). Since optimism is often closely linked to positive feelings and emotions, these findings suggest that entrepreneurs are indeed individuals who frequently experience very strong feelings—and especially positive moods and emotions.

Other findings point to the same general conclusion. For instance, the results of several studies indicate that entrepreneurs are somewhat higher than other persons in extraversion—a tendency to be outgoing, expressive, and sociable (e.g., Ciavarella, Buchholtz, Riordan, Gatewood, and Stokes, 2004). Similarly, entrepreneurs tend to be relatively high in expressiveness, the propensity to communicate their feelings and emotions in outward, visible ways (e.g., Baron and Markman, 2003; Baron and Tang, 2009). Research comparing entrepreneurs with managers and small business owners also indicates that entrepreneurs, more than these other groups, do indeed show characteristics associated with relatively intense levels of emotion—characteristics such as high levels of energy and powerful motivation to convert their beliefs and their vision into reality.

Finally, entrepreneurs—in contrast to other groups such as managers—tend to truly ride an emotional roller-coaster. Their "highs" are higher and their "lows" lower than those experienced by many other persons. For instance, consider the devastating emotional effects of starting a business and investing one's heart and soul in it, only to see it fail. Clearly, the emotional impact of such experiences—which are all too common for entrepreneurs—is intense (e.g., Shepherd, 2009; Shepherd, Wiklund, and Haynie, 2009). How do entrepreneurs cope with such events and manage to "rise from the ashes" to try once again? Clearly, this involves their ability to manage their own emotions (e.g., Baumeister, Zell, and Tice, 2007), one key component of emotional intelligence (e.g., Salovey and Grewal, 2005), which includes the capacities to recognize emotions accurately (in others and ourselves), to use them to advance important activities and goals, and to manage one's own emotions effectively. An example: the capacity to refrain from losing one's temper at times when this is inappropriate and could have important negative consequences.

In sum, there are strong grounds for suggesting that the "feeling side of life" is highly relevant to entrepreneurship. To examine this relationship in detail, the present chapter proceeds as follows. First, a basic framework for understanding the nature of *affect*—a term that includes many aspects of the "feeling side of life"—will be presented, along with a brief consideration of the important fact that affect and cognition are intimately and continuously interrelated so that one cannot really be understood in isolation from the other. Next, the benefits and potential costs for entrepreneurs of positive affect—positive moods, feelings, and emotions—will be examined. This is an important topic because, as we'll soon see, entrepreneurs as a group tend to be very high in terms of such feelings. Following that, attention will be turned to entrepreneurial passion, the powerful positive feelings and deep commitment entrepreneurs feel with respect to their ideas for something new and useful (Cardon et al., 2009). Finally, the emotional effects of failure, and how entrepreneurs attempt to cope with it, will be considered.

The basic nature of affect—and its interface with cognition

The most general term used to refer to the "feeling side of life" is *affect*—a term that includes a wide range of feeling states. Affect encompasses both moods, which are often relatively long-lasting reactions but are not clearly focused on specific events or objects (e.g., cheerfulness, depression), and emotions, which are generally shorter in duration but more specifically directed toward a particular object (e.g., a person, event, object), and include reactions such as anger, sorrow, and joy; Frijda, 1993). Several models of the basic nature of affect exist (Feldman-Barrett and Gross, 2001; Feldman-Barrett and Russell, 1999), but most converge on the view that it involves two basic dimensions: activation (low–high) and valence (pleasant–unpleasant). Research findings indicate that both dimensions are important for a full understanding of the nature of affect and its impact (e.g., Baas, De Dreu, and Nijstad, 2008). Yet most research on the impact of affect has tended to focus primarily on the valence dimension and, especially, on the benefits of positive affect (e.g., Lyubomirsky, King, and Diener, 2005). We'll briefly review this evidence and its important implications for entrepreneurship below. Before doing so, however, it is important to emphasize the following basic point: regardless of the specific nature of affect (positive or negative, low or high in activation), it interacts continuously and intimately with cognition (e.g., Forgas, 2000; Isen and Labroo, 2003). In fact, existing evidence strongly suggests that the relationship between affect and cognition is very much a two-way street: emotions and moods strongly influence several aspects of cognition, and cognition, in turn, exerts strong effects on our emotions and moods. Here are a few examples of some of the most well-documented effects of this type: (1) current moods strongly influence perceptions of the external world, so that these are more favorable in the presence of positive affect than negative affect (the world through "rose-colored glasses" effect); (2) current moods influence memory, so that information consistent with current feelings is more likely to be recalled than information inconsistent with such moods; (3) current moods influence creativity, with positive moods generally enhancing the volume of creative ideas, while negative moods sometimes enhance the quality of new ideas; (4) expectations (an aspect of cognition) often strongly influence the emotions and feelings we experience—when we expect positive reactions, we are much more likely to have them than when we expect negative ones; (5) we use several cognitive techniques to regulate our emotions and feelings—for instance, people often expose themselves to distracters (e.g., pleasant stimuli or activities) to reduce negative moods or feelings; (6) often our internal feelings or emotions are subtle, so in order to interpret them we often rely on information from the external world—for instance, if we feel highly activated and are in the presence of a very attractive person, we may conclude that we are attracted to that person, but if, on the other hand, we feel highly activated in the presence of a dangerous-looking person we may conclude that we are experiencing fear (Baron and Branscombe, 2012).

Many forms of evidence point to the conclusion that affect and cognition are intimately linked, but some of the most dramatic findings in this regard are those provided by neuroscience research using modern techniques for scanning brain activity as individuals work on various tasks. Taken together, this research suggests that there are actually two distinct systems for processing information within the human brain (e.g., Cohen, 2005). One system is concerned with what might be termed "reason"—logical, careful, systematic thought—while the other system deals primarily with affect or emotion. These two systems, although distinct in certain respects, interact in complex ways as individuals engage in such important tasks as problem solving, decision making, and planning.

A truly intriguing illustration of the intimate links between affect and cognition is provided by research employing what is known as the *ultimatum paradigm*. In this situation, two persons are told that they can divide a given sum (e.g., $10) between them. One person can suggest an initial division, and the second can accept or reject it. If the second person rejects the division proposed by the first, neither receives any money. Since *any* division provides the second person with positive outcomes, total rationality (and classic economic theory) suggests that the second person should accept whatever the first proposes; after all, this is the only way in which she or he can receive any gains. Is that what happens? Absolutely not! In reality, most people reject divisions that offer them less than $3, and many reject divisions that offer them less than $5. Scans of activity in the brains of people performing this task (magnetic resonance imaging—MRI) reveal that, when people receive offers they view as unfair (i.e., ones below half of the available $10), regions of the brain related both to reasoning (e.g., the dorsolateral prefrontal cortex) and to emotion (e.g., the limbic system) are activated. Further, the greater the amount of activity in the emotion-processing regions, the greater the likelihood that individuals will reject the offers they receive (e.g., Sanfey, Rilling, Aronson, Nystrom, and Cohen, 2003). In other words, emotional reactions appear to overrule logic, and such reactions are visible in actual patterns of brain activity. These findings provide evidence for the existence of two distinct systems within our brains—one concerned primarily with reason and one concerned primarily with emotion. Further, they also indicate that these two relatively distinct systems interact in complex ways during decision making and other cognitive processes.

Additional research indicates that the neural system for emotion tends to be impulsive, preferring immediate rewards, while the system for reason is more forward-looking and accepting of delays that ultimately yield larger rewards. For instance, when offered the choice between an immediate gain (a $15 Amazon.com gift card now) and a larger one in two weeks (a $25 gift voucher), activity again occurs in both emotion- and reason-processing regions of the brain. The immediate option, however, induces greater activity in the emotion-related regions than the delayed option (e.g., the limbic system; McClure, Laibson, Lowenstein, and Cohen, 2004).

Overall, then, evidence from neuroscience research indicates that affect plays a fundamental role in human thought, and that trying to understand cognitive processes such as decision making, planning, and problem solving in isolation from affect and emotion is unlikely to yield the full, comprehensive information we seek. Thoughts do indeed influence feelings, and feelings influence thought, and both play a key role in everything we do, including efforts to convert our ideas, dreams, and visions from the realm of the possible to the realm of the real—the core of entrepreneurship.

The benefits—and potential costs—of positive affect

There is a powerful and general belief that being "positive"—experiencing and expressing positive feelings—is an important "plus" in life. For instance, Winston Churchill put it this way: "For myself I am an optimist—it does not seem to be much use being anything else." Similarly, in words that seem directly related to the essence of entrepreneurship William James, one of the founders of modern psychology, commented: "Your hopes, dreams, and aspirations . . . are trying to take you airborne, above the clouds, above the storms, if you only let them." Scores of other observers of human existence have offered similar sentiments, so positive affect has indeed long been viewed as beneficial.

Although "common sense" or the "wisdom of the ages" is frequently wrong (dead wrong!), in this case it appears to be accurate: a very large body of evidence gathered in several different fields (e.g., social and cognitive psychology, human resource management, organizational behavior) indicates that the tendency to experience and express positive affect is strongly associated with many desirable outcomes (Ashby, Isen, and Turken, 1999; Kaplan, Bradley, Luchman, and Haynes, 2009; Lyubomirsky et al., 2005; Weiss and Cropanzano, 1996). Among the most consistently reported beneficial effects are the following: (1) increased energy, (2) enhanced cognitive flexibility, (3) increased generation of new ideas, (4) greater confidence and self-efficacy, (5) adoption of efficient decision-making strategies (e.g., satisficing), (6) increased use of heuristics that can reduce cognitive effort, and (7) improved ability to cope with stress and adversity (Ashby et al., 1999; Baron, 2008; Fredrickson, 2001). In addition, and more generally, high levels of positive affect have been found to be related to improved performance on a wide range of cognitive and work-related tasks (Kaplan et al., 2009), increased career success, the formation of more extensive and higher-quality personal relationships (Baas et al., 2008; Lyubomirsky et al., 2005), and even enhanced personal health, both physical and psychological.

Given the magnitude and generality of these effects, there appear to be strong grounds for concluding that positive affect either produces or is associated with a wide range of beneficial effects. Indeed, on the basis of an extensive review of extant literature, Lyubomirsky et al. (2005, p. 804) conclude: "People who experience a preponderance of positive emotions tend to be successful and accomplished across multiple life domains . . . not merely because success leads to happiness, *but because positive affect engenders success.*" Similarly, Fredrickson and Branigan (2005, p. 314) note that "Positive emotions . . . broaden individuals' thought–action repertoires, prompting them to pursue a wider range of thought and actions than is typical . . . these can build a variety of personal resources

. . . physical, social . . . intellectual . . . and psychological." In short, existing evidence provides strong grounds for concluding that positive affect is associated with, or may actually generate, a wide range of favorable outcomes. Further, this appears to be true for both state positive affect (i.e., positive affect produced by discrete events) and dispositional positive affect (i.e., stable tendencies to experience positive moods and emotions across time and situations).

The overall picture provided by research evidence is not entirely consistent, however. Although most evidence suggests that the effects of positive affect are indeed beneficial, some findings are inconsistent with this overall pattern (Judge and Ilies, 2004). For example, previous research has reported that high levels of positive affect increase susceptibility to cognitive errors that can potentially interfere with effective decision making (Isen, 2000) and can reduce performance on many tasks, especially ones involving critical reasoning and logic (Melton, 1995). Similarly, research by Zhou and George (2007) indicates that high levels of positive affect may not always facilitate creativity. Positive affect increases the volume of creative ideas, but, when intense, can actually interfere with careful evaluation of such ideas, especially in the absence of offsetting negative affect. In addition, high levels of positive affect have been found to reduce attention to negative information—especially information that contradicts currently held beliefs and attitudes (Forgas and George, 2001). Clearly, ignoring negative input can be a very dangerous tendency for entrepreneurs. Finally, high levels of positive affect—especially forms of positive affect that are high in both positive valence and activation (e.g., enthusiasm, excitement) have been found to encourage impulsiveness—the tendency to act without adequate thought, abruptly, and with little or no regard for potential negative consequences (DeYoung, 2010). To the extent positive affect encourages such behavior, it can have negative implications for entrepreneurs and their new ventures, which generally have limited resources and cannot easily recover from the detrimental effects of rash actions or hasty decisions by their founders (Khaire, 2010).

In short, evidence concerning the impact of positive affect offers something of a mixed picture: most findings indicate that it is related to important benefits, but some suggest that positive affect—especially at very high levels—may also have an important "downside." One interpretation of this somewhat mixed pattern of evidence is this: perhaps positive affect does indeed have beneficial effects on cognition, behavior, task performance, and many other outcomes, but only up to a point. In other words, there are discrete limits to these benefits and, beyond some measurable point, benefits decline and may, in fact, be replaced by detrimental effects (see Figure 4.1). In short, where positive affect is concerned, there can be "too much of a good thing"—a point beyond

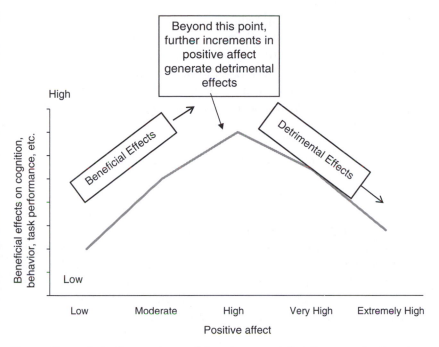

Note: Research findings and several theories suggest that there may be discrete limits to the beneficial effects of positive affect. Up to a point, rising levels of positive affect generate mainly positive effects, but beyond some discrete point these benefits decrease and may be replaced by detrimental outcomes.

Figure 4.1   *Positive affect: Are there limits to its benefits?*

which benefits decline and are replaced by processes that generate negative outcomes.

This interpretation is consistent not only with empirical evidence, but also with suggestions offered by major theories concerning the influence of affect (e.g., optimum level of affect theory; Oishi, Diener, Choi, Kim-Prieto, and Choi, 2007; broaden-and-build theory; Fredrickson and Losada, 2005). These theories converge in suggesting that there may be limits to the beneficial effects of positive affect so that, overall, the relationship between such affect and performance on many different tasks is curvilinear in nature, and takes the form of an inverted letter *U*: beneficial effects increase up to an inflection point, and then decline or totally vanish. Current theories of self-regulation—the processes through which individuals direct or guide their own thinking and actions so as to achieve important goals (Baumeister and Alquist, 2009)—suggest that high levels of positive affect may have negative implications for these important processes, ones to which we'll return in detail in Chapter 5. Specifically, very high levels of positive affect can interfere with individuals' capacity to regulate their own thoughts and actions, and that in turn can have detrimental effects on their capacity to meet important goals or standards.

Finally, in their insightful analysis of entrepreneurial passion (a topic we'll consider in detail in the next section), Cardon et al. (2009) note that high levels of such passion can sometimes reduce individuals' capacity to persist in their efforts to reach important goals. As Cardon et al. note (p. 520): "passion that is too positive or intense can limit an entrepreneur's creative problem solving . . . because the entrepreneur is resistant to exploring alternative options, fearing that doing so may dilute . . . their intense positive experience." Findings of research by Vallerand et al. (2003) offer support for this view. These authors found that "obsessive passion" led to rigid persistence in the task at hand—a tendency that limits individuals' ability to develop novel or creative solutions.

Given that entrepreneurs tend, as a group, to be very high in positive affect (higher, in fact, than any other tested group; Baron, Tang, and Hmieleski, 2011), the possibility of a curvilinear relationship between positive affect and many outcomes has important implications for entrepreneurship. In fact, very high levels of positive affect (levels that might well be described as excessive) may be one of many factors that interfere with their success. Some evidence for this conclusion is provided by a recent study by Baron et al. (2011)—one that was reviewed briefly in Chapter 1. That study reported that, up to a discrete level, entrepreneurs' positive affect was positively related to their new venture's growth in sales and innovativeness. Beyond an inflection point, however, actual declines in these measures occurred. In sum, entrepreneurs' high levels of enthusiasm, confidence, and optimism may serve both as a source of personal strength and a source of potential danger. Unless entrepreneurs can restrain their own tendencies to be "upbeat," they run the risk that their strong tendencies to experience positive affect can interfere with their own effectiveness. A key task for entrepreneurs, then, is that of learning to effectively restrain or manage these feelings. We'll comment further on this issue in a later discussion of emotional intelligence and emotion regulation.

At this point, it's crucial to add that, while high levels of positive affect can potentially exert detrimental effects in a wide range of business contexts (e.g., job interviews, performance appraisals), they may be especially relevant for entrepreneurs. First, as noted above, entrepreneurs are, as a group, extremely high in positive affect (Baron et al., 2011). Second, "too much of a good thing" effects (detrimental outcomes deriving from excessive positive affect) are, according to several theories of affect, most likely to occur at very high levels of such affect. Third, these theories also suggest that any downturn in performance at high levels of dispositional positive affect is also more likely to occur in very challenging environments (Fredrickson and Losada, 2005; Oishi, Diener, and Lucas, 2007)—precisely the kind that entrepreneurs often face. Fourth, entrepreneurs often function in situations that are complex and uncertain, and that offer few guides for their behavior. It is in such contexts that individual characteristics and preferences are most likely to influence cognition and behavior strongly (Hambrick, 2007; Kaplan et al., 2009). Finally, most new ventures are very small in size. Research on organizational culture (Schneider, Ehrhart, and Macey, 2010) suggests that the impact of founding entrepreneurs is often maximum when their firms are small (Staw, 1991). For this reason, any detrimental effects of high levels of positive affect on entrepreneurs' perception, motivation, or self-regulation may be magnified because they are reflected in the organizations' developing culture, and therefore influence many aspects of their operations.

For all these reasons, entrepreneurs and the new ventures they lead may be at particular risk of experiencing the detrimental effects of very high levels of dispositional positive affect. A summary of the benefits and potential costs of high levels of positive affect is presented in Table 4.1. Although these predictions have not yet been fully tested, they fit well both with existing theory and with a large body of empirical evidence concerning the effects of positive affect (e.g., Lyubomirsky et al., 2005).

Before we conclude this discussion, it is worth nothing that curvilinear relationships between individual characteristics (e.g., key aspects of personality) and task performance have recently been reported in several studies (Le et al., 2011). Further, and most directly relevant, in a recent paper entitled "Too much of a good thing" Grant and Schwartz (2011, p. 62) have called attention to the fact that a great deal of evidence supports the view that "there is no such thing as an unmitigated good. All positive traits, states, and experiences have costs that at high levels may begin to outweigh their benefits, creating the nonmonotonicity of an inverted U." Overall, then, there appear to be strong grounds for suggesting that a wide range of personal characteristics are related in a curvilinear rather than a linear manner to task performance and other aspects of work-related behavior. This offers further support for the view that entrepreneurs' high levels of positive affect may truly be the kind of "mixed blessing" to which Grant and Schwartz (2011) refer. Being "upbeat" is indeed often a plus; but there appear to be clear limits to its benefits, and that is a point entrepreneurs should keep in mind as they attempt to achieve their dreams.

Entrepreneurial passion: doing what you love and loving what you do

There is a widespread belief that entrepreneurs are a "breed apart"—that they are different, in important ways, from most other persons. If they really are,

Table 4.1   *The potential benefits and costs of positive affect for basic psychological processes*

Psychological processes	Benefits (up to moderately high levels of dispositional positive affect)	Costs (beyond moderately high levels of dispositional positive affect)
Cognition	Enhanced cognitive flexibility. Adoption of efficient decision-making strategies. Augmented use of heuristics that can reduce cognitive effort.	Increased susceptibility to cognitive errors. Increased reliance on heuristic thought. Biased recall of information from memory. Reduced attention to and processing of negative information.
Perception	Openness to an expanded range of opportunities. Willingness to consider multiple diverse sources of information. Balanced recognition of positive and negative information.	Tendency to overvalue ideas and opportunities. Tendency to overlook details and focus on broader perspective. Reduced ability to recognize patterns and structural alignments.
Motivation	Increased energy. Greater confidence to take action. Decreased level of self-consciousness.	Reduced effort on current tasks. Choice of inappropriate or unattainable long-term goals. Reduced tendency to develop patterns of behavior demonstrating increased flexibility and resiliency.
Self-regulation	Improved ability to cope with stress and adversity. Willingness to adapt to environmental changes. Enhanced ability to switch between divergent and convergent modes of thinking.	Reduced capacity to monitor own actions. Reduced attention to own limitations and situational constraints. Increased impulsivity. Reduced tendency to delay gratification.

Note: As shown here, positive affect can enhance various aspects of cognition, perception, motivation and self-regulation, but can—at very high levels—have negative effects for all these processes.

Source: Based on data from Baron, Tang, and Hmieleski (2011).

then what makes them unique? We'll consider this issue in detail in Chapter 5, but it is clear that one characteristic widely viewed as making entrepreneurs "special" is their passion—their intense positive feelings about, and commitment to, their activities as entrepreneurs (e.g., Vallerand et al., 2003). As Donald Trump, a well-known entrepreneur and media star (!), once put it: "Without passion, you don't have energy; without energy, you have nothing." So, in his view, passion is one of the "secret ingredients"—and perhaps the most important one—that make entrepreneurs unique.

Is that view accurate? In order to answer, it is first essential to figure out precisely what we mean by the term *entrepreneurial passion*. That basic task has been addressed in a very careful and insightful way by Cardon et al.

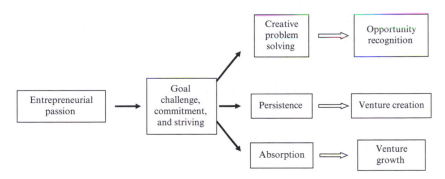

Note: Entrepreneurial passion influences the goals entrepreneurs set, and their creative problem solving, persistence, and absorption in their new ventures. These processes, in turn, strongly influence key entrepreneurial outcomes: opportunity recognition, venture creation, and venture growth.

Source: Based on suggestions by Cardon, Wincent, Singh, and Drnovsek (2009).

Figure 4.2   *Potential effects of entrepreneurial passion on key outcomes sought by entrepreneurs*

(2009). They define entrepreneurial passion as the "consciously accessible intense positive feelings experienced [by entrepreneurs] through engagement in entrepreneurial activities associated with roles that are meaningful and salient to the self-identity of the entrepreneur." In other words, entrepreneurial passion involves both a powerful emotional component (intense positive feelings) and important cognitive aspects involving entrepreneurs' self-identity. The identities involved refer to several roles entrepreneurs play: *inventor*—someone who formulates ideas for something new; *founder*—someone who actually launches a new venture or takes other steps to convert these ideas into something real; and *developer*—someone who works long and hard to make these efforts successful.

Cardon et al. (2009) also suggest ways in which such passion finds expression in entrepreneurs' overt actions. On the one hand, the positive feelings entrepreneurs experience about their ideas and new ventures lead them to set challenging goals, to be deeply committed to them, and to work diligently to attain them. This, in turn, encourages the entrepreneurs to engage in vigorous efforts to deal with and resolve problems related to their entrepreneurial activities, to persist in these activities, and to be deeply and continuously absorbed in them. The overall result is that entrepreneurial passion, through these intervening processes, influences important outcomes ranging from opportunity recognition to efforts to attain high levels of growth and profitability. The overall process is illustrated in Figure 4.2, which summarizes the complex ways in which entrepreneurial passion influences key outcomes sought by entrepreneurs.

The framework offered by Cardon et al. (2009) provides a basis for conducting research designed to examine the nature and impact of entrepreneurial passion—for obtaining actual evidence on the nature of this variable and its effects. While such research is only just beginning, one study has already addressed an intriguing and important issue related to passion: Does entrepreneurs' passion influence their success in obtaining support (financial, human) for their ideas? Since entrepreneurial passion involves high levels of enthusiasm, and enthusiasm often does "sell," it seems reasonable to expect that this would be the case: the higher the level of passion shown by entrepreneurs when making their "pitches" to venture capitalists or others for financial support, the more likely they would be to obtain this support. To investigate this issue, Chen, Yao, and Kotha (2009) conducted two studies. In the first, an ingenious laboratory experiment, executive MBA students watched business plan presentations by professional actors, who were trained to show either low or high levels of passion and low or high levels of preparation in their "pitches." Participants were told to play the role of venture capitalists and, after watching the presentations, reported on whether they would or would not make an investment in the new venture. They also completed a questionnaire designed to measure the presenters' passion and preparation. Items dealing with passion focused primarily on outward, observable signs of inner feelings and emotions: the extent to which the presenters showed energetic body movements, rich body language, animated facial expressions, and obvious enthusiasm. Items dealing with preparedness involved the content of the presentations, such as the extent to which it was thoughtful and coherent and the extent to which the arguments presented were strong and cogent. When these ratings of passion and preparation were related to the participants' investment decisions, results were clear: the higher the ratings of preparedness, the greater the likelihood that the participants (i.e., the executive MBA students) would invest in the company. In contrast, outward signs of passion by the presenters were not significantly related to these decisions.

To extend these findings, the researchers then performed a second study in which the participants were venture capitalists who watched presentations from actual business plan competitions and rated these presentations in terms of both passion and preparedness. After watching the presentations, they also indicated whether or not they intended to invest in these new ventures. Results were identical to those of the first study: once again entrepreneurs' preparedness was related to their likelihood of obtaining funding, while their passion was not.

At first blush, these findings seem to suggest that, at least in terms of obtaining external financial support, entrepreneurs' passion is not as crucial as has often been assumed. Being well prepared may, in fact, be more important. However, as noted by the researchers, passion may be important in many other ways—for instance, in helping entrepreneurs maintain their commitment even in the face of major setbacks. Further, it may be that this is yet one more instance of the "too much of a good thing" phenomenon described earlier. Up to a point, outward signs of passion may indeed help persuade venture capitalists and others to offer support for a new venture. However, beyond some point (and that point may have been reached or exceeded in this research), very high levels of passion may be perceived as signs of insincerity or as efforts to introduce irrelevant and distracting elements into the situation (e.g., by attempting to dazzle the audience with presentation that is so smooth and so eloquent that they lose sight of important business considerations). Such effects have been observed in other contexts—for instance, during job interviews, when applicants can indeed easily "overdo it" in their efforts to make a good impression on interviewers (e.g., Baron, 1986). Of course, pending the completion of further research, no firm conclusions about this or other possible interpretations can be reached. But, at present, there appear to be grounds for caution in terms of viewing entrepreneurial passion as a very central factor in entrepreneurs' success. However, it should be emphasized that outward, visible signs of passion are only a measure of this internal state: high levels of passion may in fact increase persistence and aid in opportunity recognition, as suggested by Cardon et al. (2009). In any case, please stay tuned for further developments: many researchers are currently gathering evidence concerning the potential role of passion in key aspects of entrepreneurship, and the results of such research will almost certainly help to clarify the role of this key factor in many aspects of entrepreneurship.

How entrepreneurs cope with failure—and rebound to try again

Despite entrepreneurs' passion, enthusiasm, and high levels of optimism, things don't always turn out as they hope. The new ventures they found often fail and, when entrepreneurship occurs in other contexts (e.g., within large companies or in various professions), their ideas for something new and better may meet with strong resistance and be rejected. It is a sad fact of life that many people resist change, and entrepreneurs encounter this problem often. Given entrepreneurs' deep and powerful commitment to their ideas and visions, the result is that they often experience truly bitter disappointment as a result of business failure or rejection of their ideas. This is far from surprising; after all, they invest substantial portions of their time and energy in efforts to pursue their dreams, and if the dreams evaporate they may take with them large portions of the entrepreneurs' self-esteem, reputations, and personal wealth. Unfortunately, a high probability of failure is a basic fact of life for entrepreneurs. This reality, in turn, raises an important question: How do they cope with these devastating setbacks when they occur, and bounce back to try again? That many actually do is suggested by the fact that a large proportion of successful entrepreneurs experience initial failure, and only succeed after one or sometimes several disappointing experiences. As Steve Jobs of Apple Computer once put it: "I'm convinced that about half of what separates the successful entrepreneurs from the non-successful ones is pure perseverance." And this amazingly successful entrepreneur truly needed the ability to persevere, because when he was 30, Apple's board of directors actually fired him because they wanted to take the company in a very different direction. Jobs, of course, did not give up: instead, he founded additional companies (NeXT, a major software company, and Pixar, which produced animated films). His perseverance paid off: ultimately he was rehired by Apple and led the company to unprecedented levels of success until his death in 2011.

How, then, do entrepreneurs attempt to cope with failure? What factors influence the extent to which they benefit from such adversity and actually become better able to succeed as a result of these early defeats? Insights into these intriguing issues are provided by a growing body of evidence and theory concerning what is known as *grief recovery* among entrepreneurs (e.g., Shepherd, 2003, 2009; Shepherd et al., 2009). Basically, this work suggests that, after experiencing the failure of their businesses, entrepreneurs—like other persons—engage in several different tactics for coping with the intense negative feelings (grief) they experience.

One such strategy involves what is known as *loss-oriented tactics—* ones in which they confront the loss, reflecting on why it may have occurred, and in general try to make sense of these negative events. Another involves *restoration-oriented tactics—*ones involving efforts to restore more positive moods or feelings through distraction or other techniques that shift attention away from the loss and the negative feelings it generates. A third approach involves *transition-oriented tactics—*ones that shift from loss-oriented processes to restoration-oriented processes and back again. In other words, entrepreneurs using transition-oriented tactics adopt a flexible approach to using both of these basic procedures so as to obtain maximum benefits from both. Loss-oriented tactics encourage sense making and learning from the painful experience of failure, while restoration-oriented tactics reduce the likelihood of depression and despair which can sometimes develop if attention is focused too intently on the pain of major failures.

According to a model proposed by Shepherd (2009), the length of time required to recover from failure-generated grief is reduced by certain steps: scanning the environment for possible causes of the failure, carefully interpreting this information, and seeking to learn from these efforts. In short, cognitive mechanisms play a key role in determining how quickly—and how effectively—entrepreneurs recover from the intense negative emotions they experience as a result of failure. Once again, then, the continuous and intimate interplay between affect and cognition comes into focus.

Although failure is sometimes sudden and unexpected, there are many instances in which entrepreneurs can "see it coming" for a long time. They realize that their businesses are in trouble and that they may be unable to save them no matter how hard they try. From a purely economic point of view, it makes sense—in such situations—to cut one's losses and close the company as soon as it becomes clear that it probably cannot survive. That strategy would allow entrepreneurs to conserve financial resources and energy, so that they can try again. Yet, in many cases, entrepreneurs do not follow this strategy. Instead, they persist until the truly bitter end and keep their companies afloat until it is literally impossible to do so. Why? One possibility is that they are trapped in what is known as *sunk costs*—the powerful tendency to stick to initial decisions and courses of action even if these are clearly failing. This phenomenon occurs in many contexts, and it may be a powerful force among entrepreneurs. In fact, given their powerful commitment to their ideas and companies, the impact of sunk costs may be especially powerful among entrepreneurs: they may be even more reluctant than other persons to admit that their initial decisions and strategies were wrong.

On the other hand, however, the tendency among entrepreneurs to keep their companies afloat despite a very high certainty of failure may result from a very different mechanism. Specifically, entrepreneurs who proceed down this path may do so because it allows them to benefit from a period of anticipatory grief—one in which they can come to terms with the emotional costs of business failure by preparing for it. Such psychological gains may more than make up for the increased financial costs involved. Once again, though, the relationship between these variables may be curvilinear in nature: up to a point, the longer entrepreneurs delay in closing their businesses, the better able they may be to deal with the emotional consequences of these events when they do finally occur. Beyond some point, though, their actual losses are so great that these benefits are totally offset (Shepherd et al., 2009). Only further research can provide information on the possible occurrence of such effects, but given the frequency of failure among entrepreneurs it is a topic well worthy of further study.

Is confidence a plus? Why highly confident entrepreneurs are more likely to bounce back from failure

After experiencing business failure, some entrepreneurs try again, while others do not. Why? Clearly, there is no simple answer to this question.

The magnitude of the financial losses experienced, the damage to personal reputations, the impact of failure on personal relationships and many other factors almost certainly play a role. For instance, an entrepreneur who has resigned from a secure and well-paid position or lost a large portion of her or his personal fortune is less likely to found another venture than one whose losses are small and who has been able to retain her or his current employment. One factor that may be especially important in this situation, however, is the entrepreneurs' level of personal confidence. Although overconfidence can—and often does—get entrepreneurs (and others) into serious problems (e.g., they badly underestimate the amount of resources they will need; Hayward, Shepherd, and Griffin, 2006), there are strong grounds for predicting that high levels of confidence can be beneficial from the point of view of coping with failure and rebounding to try again.

Strong feelings of confidence are closely related to positive affect and, as noted earlier, the tendency to experience such feelings and moods often and in many situations confers important benefits. In particular, one influential theory concerning the benefits of positive affect—the broaden-and-build framework proposed by Fredrickson (1998, 2001), briefly mentioned above—suggests that positive affect expands the scope of individuals' attention, cognition, and action (Fredrickson and Branigan, 2005). In other words, when individuals experience positive affect, they tend to notice more in a given situation, think about a wider range of factors and possibilities, and consider a broader range of actions than when positive affect is absent. These broadened perspectives (or "mindsets," as Fredrickson terms them) then assist individuals in building a wide array of personal resources, both intellectual (e.g., increased knowledge and intellectual complexity) and psychological (e.g., enhanced resilience, optimism, and creativity; Fredrickson, Tugade, Waugh, and Larkin, 2003). These resources then contribute to their performance of many cognitive tasks (e.g., problem solving, decision making). Moreover, these enhanced resources, once acquired, are durable, and persist long beyond the fleeting emotional states that generate their original acquisition. Thus they increase individuals' capacity to adapt to and function effectively in a wide range of situations.

Hayward, Forster, Sarasvathy, and Fredrickson (2010) have recently proposed that high levels of confidence among founding entrepreneurs facilitate positive emotions and expectations, which in turn strengthen their capacity to rebound from failure and found additional ventures. In short, high levels of confidence, and the high degrees of positive affect with which they are associated, help entrepreneurs to develop an array of skills that contribute to their resilience and allow them to recover from failure when it occurs (see Figure 4.3).

Although direct evidence for these proposals is not yet available, they

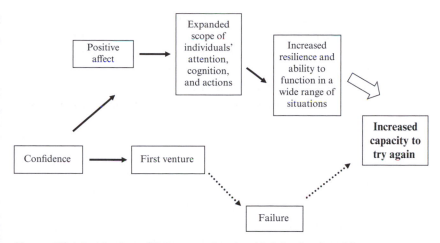

Note: High levels of confidence are related to high levels of positive affect. These, in turn, encourage the development of skills that can enhance entrepreneurs' capacity to try again after major setbacks.

Source: Based on suggestions by Hayward, Forster, Sarasvathy, and Fredrickson (2010).

Figure 4.3   *High levels of confidence: a key ingredient in repeat entrepreneurship*

are consistent with a very large body of findings concerning the benefits of positive affect, and with many studies offering support for Fredrickson's broaden-and-build framework. In short, although excessive levels of confidence (what is sometimes known as *hubris*) can have important costs, as long as confidence is not extreme it can be a very important "plus" where entrepreneurs' capacity to recover from failure is concerned.

Emotional intelligence: a key attribute for entrepreneurs?

Before concluding this discussion of the role of affect (emotions, moods, feelings) in entrepreneurship, it is, perhaps, useful to comment briefly on emotional intelligence and why it may be especially valuable for entrepreneurs. *Emotional intelligence*, a term first popularized by Goleman (1995), refers to a cluster of capacities or skills relating to the "feeling side of life," including the ability (1) to accurately perceive emotions in oneself and others (i.e., to know what we and other persons are feeling at any given point in time), (2) to use emotions to facilitate cognitive activities such as thinking and problem solving, (3) to understand emotions and relationships among them, and perhaps most crucial (4) to manage emotions in both ourselves and others (Salovey and Grewal, 2005).

There are several reasons why emotional intelligence—and especially the capacity to manage one's own emotions and influence those of others—may be especially useful for entrepreneurs. First, as noted previously, entrepreneurs tend to be exceptionally high in positive affect; although this is often an asset, it can, at very high levels, become a liability, so it is crucial that entrepreneurs be aware of their own high levels of positive affect and possess the capacity to restrain them (Baron, Hmieleski, and Henry, in press). Second, unless entrepreneurs can both accurately assess others' emotions and influence them, they may be unable to generate the enthusiasm needed to secure support and commitment for their activities. Third, in order to persevere, entrepreneurs must be able to cope effectively with the intense negative feelings generated by business failure. Finally, accurate understanding of others' emotions and feelings is often crucial to developing effective relationships with them, and for establishing large and high-quality social networks. While all these skills are useful in a wide range of contexts, they may be especially crucial for entrepreneurs, given the uncertain and often chaotic environments in which they function. Generating change—which is, in essence, what entrepreneurs try to do—is always difficult and often risky, so a high degree of competence with respect to the feeling side of life (which is what high levels of emotional intelligence involve) can be an important advantage in such contexts. Fortunately, this cluster of skills can be learned—individuals can enhance their abilities to accurately recognize emotions (their own and others'), to put emotions to good use (e.g., use them to maximize their own performance of various tasks), and to manage them effectively (e.g., Grewal, Brackett, and Salovey, 2006). To the extent entrepreneurs accomplish these tasks, this may be yet another way in which they can actively tip the odds of success considerably in their favor.

Summary of key points

Cognition is a central part of our existence, but so too is the "feeling side of life"—emotions, moods, and feelings. In fact, there are several grounds for suggesting that this aspect of life is especially relevant and important for entrepreneurs. *Affect* is a general term that refers to emotions and moods. Affect varies along two basic dimensions: activation (low–high) and valence (negative–positive). Cognition and affect interact continuously and intimately, so that affect strongly influences many aspects of thought and thought, in turn, strongly influences affect.

The tendency to experience positive affect is related to important benefits, such as improved performance on a wide range of cognitive and work-related tasks, increased career success, formation of more extensive and higher-quality personal relationships, and even better personal and psychological health. However, there may be discrete limits to these benefits, so that beyond some point further increments in positive affect fail to produce beneficial outcomes and may actually generate detrimental ones. Such effects may be especially likely to occur among entrepreneurs, who are very high in positive affect, and function in very challenging environments which offer little guidance and few restraints on their behavior—thus maximizing the potential impact of individual preferences or dispositions.

Entrepreneurs are often deeply committed to their ideas and efforts to create something new and useful. This is sometimes referred to as *entrepreneurial passion*, which can be defined as intense positive feelings experienced by engagement in entrepreneurial activities associated with roles that are meaningful and salient to the entrepreneur self-identity (e.g., inventor, founder, developer). Although entrepreneurial passion may contribute strongly to entrepreneurs' motivation and capacity to persevere in the face of even strong adversity, it does not seem to increase venture capitalists' willingness to provide entrepreneurs with financial support.

Despite their best efforts and high levels of passion and enthusiasm, entrepreneurs often fail. They attempt to deal with such setbacks, and the intense negative emotions the setbacks generate, in several ways. One involves continuing to operate their companies even when failure seems certain; this provides them with an opportunity to experience anticipatory grief, reactions that help them prepare cognitively and emotionally for the failures that will soon follow. High levels of confidence on the part of entrepreneurs may help them to cope with failure because they are related to high levels of positive affect, which in turn help entrepreneurs to acquire skills that provide the resilience they need to bounce back from such debacles. Emotional intelligence—which involves being able to accurately perceive emotions in oneself and others, to use emotions to facilitate cognitive activities such as thinking and problem solving, to understand emotions and relationships among them, and to manage emotions in both ourselves and others—may be especially valuable for entrepreneurs. This is so because high levels of emotional intelligence help entrepreneurs to establish effective relationships with others, to generate enthusiasm in others, and to build large and high-quality social networks. These advantages may help entrepreneurs tip the odds of success—which are usually strongly against them—considerably in their favor.

Bibliography

Ashby, F.G., Isen, A.M., and Turken, A.U. (1999). A neuropsychological theory of positive affect and its influence on cognition. *Psychological Review*, *106*, 529–550.

Baas, M., De Dreu, C.K.W., and Nijstad, B.A. (2008). A meta-analysis of 25 years of mood–creativity research: hedonic tone, activation, or regulatory focus? *Psychological Bulletin, 134,* 779–806.

Baron, R.A. (1986). Self-presentation in job interviews: When there can be "too much of a good thing." *Journal of Applied Social Psychology, 16,* 16–28.

Baron, R.A. (2008). The role of affect in the entrepreneurial process. *Academy of Management Review, 33,* 328–340.

Baron, R.A., and Branscombe, N. (2012). *Social psychology,* 13th edition. Boston, MA: Allyn & Bacon.

Baron, R.A., and Markman, G.D. (2003). Beyond social capital: The role of entrepreneurs' social competence in their financial success. *Journal of Business Venturing, 18,* 41–60.

Baron, R.A., and Tang, J. (2009). Entrepreneurs' social skills and new venture performance: Mediating mechanisms and cultural generality. *Journal of Management, 35,* 282–306.

Baron, R.A., Hmieleski, K.M., and Henry, R.A. (in press). Entrepreneurs' dispositional positive affect: The potential benefits—and potential costs—of being "up." *Journal of Business Venturing.*

Baron, R.A., Tang, J., and Hmieleski, K.M. (2011). Entrepreneurs' dispositional positive affect and firm performance: When there can be "too much of a good thing." *Strategic Entrepreneurship Journal, 5,* 101–119.

Baum, J.R., and Locke, E.A. (2005). The relationship of entrepreneurial traits, skill, and motivation to subsequent venture growth. *Journal of Applied Psychology, 89,* 587–598.

Baum, J.R., Locke, E.A., and Smith, K.G. (2001). A multidimensional model of venture growth. *Academy of Management Journal, 44,* 292–303.

Baumeister, R.F., and Alquist, J.L. (2009). Self-regulation as a limited resource: Strength model of control and depletion. In J.P. Forgas, R.F. Baumeister, and D.M. Tice (eds), *Psychology of self-regulation: Cognitive, affective, and motivational processes* (pp. 21–35). New York: Taylor & Francis.

Baumeister, R.F., Zell, A.L., and Tice, D.M. (2007). How emotions facilitate and impair self-regulation. In J.J. Gross (Ed.), *Handbook of emotion regulation* (pp. 408–426). New York: Guilford Press.

Cardon, M.S., Wincent, J., Singh, J., and Drnovsek, M. (2009). The nature and experience of entrepreneurial passion. *Academy of Management Review, 34,* 511–532.

Chen, X.P., Yao, X., and Kotha, S. (2009). Entrepreneur passion and preparedness in business plan presentations: A persuasion analysis of venture capitalists' funding decisions. *Academy of Management Journal, 52,* 199–214.

Ciavarella, M.A., Buchholtz, A.K., Riordan, C.M., Gatewood, R.D., and Stokes, G.S. (2004). The big five and venture success: Is there a linkage? *Journal of Business Venturing*, *19*, 465–483.

Cohen, J.D. (2005). The vulcanization of the human brain: A neural perspective on interactions between cognition and emotion. *Journal of Economic Perspectives*, *19*, 3–24.

DeYoung, C.G. (2010). Impulsivity as a personality trait. In K.D. Vohs and R.F. Baumeister (eds), *Handbook of self-regulation: Research, theory, and applications* (pp. 485–502). New York: Guilford Press.

Feldman-Barrett, L., and Gross, J.J. (2001). Emotion representation and regulation: A process model of emotional intelligence. In T.J. Mayne and G.A. Bonnano (eds), *Emotions: Current issues and future directions* (pp. 286–310). New York: Guilford Press.

Feldman-Barrett, L., and Russell, J.A. (1999). The structure of current affect: Controversies and emerging consensus. *Current Directions in Psychological Science*, *8*, 10–14.

Foo, M.D. (2011). Emotions and entrepreneurial opportunity evaluation. *Entrepreneurship Theory and Practice*, *35*, 375–393.

Foo, M.D., Uy, M.A., and Baron, R.A. (2009). How do feelings influence effort? An empirical study of entrepreneurs' affect and venture effort. *Journal of Applied Psychology*, *94*, 1086–1094.

Forgas, J.P. (2000). *Feeling and thinking: Affective influences on social cognition*. New York: Cambridge University Press.

Forgas, J.P., and George, J.M. (2001). Affective influences on judgments and behavior in organizations: An information processing perspective. *Organizational Behavior and Human Decision Processes*, *86*(1), 3–34.

Fredrickson, B.L. (1998). What good are positive emotions? *Review of General Psychology*, *2*, 300–319.

Fredrickson, B.L. (2001). The role of positive emotions in positive psychology: The broaden-and-build theory of positive emotions. *American Psychologist*, *56*, 218–226.

Fredrickson, B.L., and Branigan, C.A. (2005). Positive emotions broaden the scope of attention and thought–action repertoires. *Cognition and Emotion*, *19*, 313–332.

Fredrickson, B.L., and Losada, M.F. (2005). Positive affect and complex dynamics of human flourishing. *American Psychologist*, *60*, 678–686.

Fredrickson, B.L., Tugade, M., Waugh, C.E., and Larkin, G. (2003). What good are positive emotions in crises? A prospective study of resilience and emotions following the terrorist attacks on the United States on September 11th, 2001. *Journal of Personality and Social Psychology*, *84*, 365–376.

Frijda, N.H. (1993). Moods, emotion episodes, and emotions. In M. Lewis and J.M. Haviland (eds), *Handbook of emotions* (pp. 381–403). New York: Guilford Press.

Goleman, D. (1995). *Emotional intelligence*. New York: Bantam.

Grant, A., and Schwartz, B. (2011). Too much of a good thing: The challenge and opportunity of the inverted U. *Perspectives on Psychological Science, 6*, 61–76.

Grewal, D., Brackett, M., and Salovey, P. (2006). Emotional intelligence and the self-regulation of affect. In D.K. Snyder, J. Simpson, and J. Hughes (eds), *Emotion regulation in couples and families: Pathways to dysfunction and health* (pp. 37–55). Washington, DC: American Psychological Association.

Hambrick, D.C. (2007). Upper echelons theory: An update. *Academy of Management Review, 32*, 334–343.

Hayward, M.L., Forster, W.R., Sarasvathy, S.D., and Fredrickson, B.L. (2010). Beyond hubris: How highly confident entrepreneurs rebound to venture again. *Journal of Business Venturing, 25*, 569–578.

Hayward, M.L., Shepherd, D.A., and Griffin, D.W. (2006). A hubris theory of entrepreneurship. *Management Science, 2*, 160–172.

Hmieleski, K.M., and Baron, R.A. (2009). Entrepreneurs' optimism and new venture performance: A social cognitive perspective. *Academy of Management Journal, 52*, 473–488.

Isen, A.M. (2000). Positive affect and decision making. In M. Lewis and J.M. Haviland-Jones (eds), *Handbook of emotions*, 2nd edition (pp. 417–435). New York: Guilford Press.

Isen, A.M., and Labroo, A.A. (2003). Some ways in which positive affect facilitates decision making and judgment. In S. Schneider and J. Shanteau (eds), *Emerging perspectives on judgment and decision research* (pp. 365–393). New York: Cambridge University Press.

Judge, T.A., and Ilies, R. (2004). Is positiveness in organizations always desirable? *Academy of Management Executive, 18*(4), 151–155.

Kaplan, S., Bradley, J.C., Luchman, J.N., and Haynes, D. (2009). On the role of positive and negative affectivity in job performance: A meta-analytic investigation. *Journal of Applied Psychology, 94*, 162–176.

Khaire, M. (2010). Young and no money? Never mind: The material impact of social resources on new venture growth. *Organization Science, 21*(1), 168–185.

Le, H., Oh, I.S., Robbins, S.B., Ilies, R., Holland, E., and Westrick, P. (2011). Too much of a good thing: Curvilinear relationships between personality traits and job performance. *Journal of Applied Psychology, 96*, 113–133.

Lyubomirsky, S., King, L., and Diener, E. (2005). Benefits of frequent positive affect. *Psychological Bulletin, 131*, 803–855.

McClure, S.M., Laibson, D.I., Lowenstein, G., and Cohen, J.D. (2004).

Separate neural systems value immediate and delayed monetary rewards. *Science*, *306*, 503–507.

Melton, R.J. (1995). The role of positive affect in syllogism performance. *Personality and Social Psychology Bulletin*, *21*, 788–794.

Oishi, S., Diener, E., and Lucas, R.E. (2007). The optimum level of well-being: Can people be too happy? *Perspectives on Psychological Science*, *2*, 346–360.

Oishi, S., Diener, E., Choi, D.W., Kim-Prieto, C., and Choi, I. (2007). The dynamics of daily events and well-being across cultures: When less is more. *Journal of Personality and Social Psychology*, *93*, 685–698.

Salovey, P., and Grewal, D. (2005). The science of emotional intelligence. *Current Directions in Psychological Science*, *14*, 281–284.

Sanfey, A.G., Rilling, J.K., Aronson, J.A., Nystrom, L.E., and Cohen, J.D. (2003). The neural basis of economic decisionmaking in the ultimatum game. *Science*, *300*, 1755–1757.

Schneider, B., Ehrhart, M.G., and Macey, W.H. (2010). Perspectives on organizational climate and culture. In S. Zedek (ed.), *Handbook of industrial and organizational psychology*, Vol. 1 (pp. 373–414). Washington, DC: American Psychological Association.

Shepherd, D.A. (2003). Learning from business failure: Propositions of grief recovery for the self-employed. *Academy of Management Review*, *28*, 318–328.

Shepherd, D.A. (2009). Grief recovery from the loss of a family business: A multi- and meso-level theory. *Journal of Business Venturing*, *24*, 81–97.

Shepherd, D.A., Wiklund, J., and Haynie, J.M. (2009). Moving forward: Balancing the financial and emotional costs of business failure. *Journal of Business Venturing*, *24*, 134–148.

Staw, B.M. (1991). Dressing up like an organization: When psychological theories can explain organizational action. *Journal of Management*, *17*, 805–819.

Vallerand, R.J., Blanchard, C., Mageau, G.A., Koestner, R., Ratelle, C., Léonard, M., Gagné, M., and Marsolais, J. (2003). Les passions de l'âme: On obsessive and harmonious passion. *Journal of Personality and Social Psychology*, *85*, 756–767.

Weiss, H.M., and Cropanzano, R. (1996). Affective events theory: A theoretical discussion of the structure, causes and consequences of affective experiences at work. *Research in Organizational Behavior*, *18*, 1–74.

Zhou, J., and George, J.M. (2007). Dual tuning in a supportive context: Joint contributions of positive mood, negative mood, and supervisory behaviors to employee creativity. *Academy of Management Journal*, *50*, 605–622.

5 Ingredients of entrepreneurial success: characteristics, skills, networks . . . and self-regulation

• •

Chapter outline

Entrepreneurs: Are they really different, and if so why?
Entrepreneurs: *How* are they different? Personal characteristics that set them apart
  Self-efficacy: belief in our ability to "do it"
  Risk: Are entrepreneurs really risk takers?
  Key aspects of personality: the "big five" dimensions
  Other characteristics shown by entrepreneurs
What's needed to succeed? The key roles of social networks, social capital, and social competence
  Social networks and social capital: key ingredients in entrepreneurs' success
  Social and political skills: beyond social capital
The crucial role of self-regulatory skills: persistence, focus, and knowing what you know—and don't!

> An entrepreneur tends to bite off a little more than he can chew hoping he'll quickly learn how to chew it. (Roy Ash, co-founder of Litton Industries)

> High expectations are the key to everything. (Sam Walton)

Entrepreneurs: Are they really different, and if so why?

At the start of this book, we noted that at present the word *entrepreneur* has tremendous allure; in fact, it is, in some circles, downright "sexy." Telling someone that you are an "entrepreneur" is much more likely to grip their attention and engage their interest than telling them that you are a manager, dentist, salesperson, or (unbelievable as it may be!) professor. Why? One reason is that many people seem to believe that entrepreneurs are a "breed apart"—they are different, in important ways, from most other persons. Having met and interacted with hundreds of entrepreneurs, I find this conclusion very appealing: as the quotations above suggest, entrepreneurs *do* seem to be different, and in many ways, from most other persons.

But even assuming this is true, that entrepreneurs *are* different in some respects, does that mean that they are unique by nature—that these differences are, as some researchers have actually suggested, "in their genes" (Nicolaou and Shane, 2009)? Perhaps, but it is also possible—and perhaps more plausible—that differences between entrepreneurs and other groups are largely the result of the same basic processes that lead to important differences between people in many different fields or occupations. For instance, consider emergency room physicians. Are they different from other persons—or even from other doctors? Absolutely. But why? Similarly, consider biologists who spend their lives in the field, observing chimpanzees or gorillas. Are they different from other persons or other biologists? Again, almost certainly they are. On a more mundane level, what about people who choose to spend their careers working in government agencies? Or ones who sell insurance? Or individuals who become bakers, rising very early every day to make bread and cakes? Certainly, the individuals in each of these occupational groups are different from those in others, but the key question is: "What is the basis for these differences?" A large body of evidence in the fields of human resource management and industrial/organizational psychology indicates that the differences stem primarily from the operation of what is known as the *attraction–selection–attrition (ASA) model* of occupational choice (Schneider, 2001).

According to this model, individuals are attracted to a particular career or choose to work for a particular organization because their personal characteristics, skills, or goals are closely aligned with the work or activities in that field or organization. (That is the attraction component.) Among these persons, only some successfully navigate the selection process—for instance, only some are hired by the organization of their choice or gain admission to specific training programs, such as medical school. (That is the selection component.) And then, among these persons, only some find that they are actually suited for the field, organization, or job they have chosen; those who are remain in it, while those who are not leave. (That is the attrition component.) Ultimately, then, the individuals in any field constitute a highly selected group: persons who were attracted to it in the first place, were successful in gaining entrance to it, and then chose to remain in it.

Applying this model to entrepreneurs suggests that, if they are indeed different from other persons, this is not at all surprising, because (1) only some persons are attracted to the role of entrepreneur, (2) only some actually become entrepreneurs (e.g., only some decide to attempt to convert their ideas and dreams to reality), and (3) only some find that they are actually suited for this role. For example, individuals attracted to the role of entrepreneur may be ones who strongly value autonomy—they want very much to be their own bosses. Among these persons, however, only some are able to take all the complex steps necessary to start a new company or act entrepreneurially in some other context—only some actually become entrepreneurs. And, among this group, only some find that they actually function well as their own bosses—in the absence of anyone to tell them what to do, when to do it, and how.

In short, the ASA process operates, effectively, as a series of filters, with smaller and increasingly selected groups of persons passing through each stage—a process summarized by the phrase "Many are called but only few are chosen." Overall, this process of attraction–selection–attrition virtually ensures that people in different jobs, occupations, or roles differ in many ways.

So, if we return to the questions with which we began (Are entrepreneurs actually different from other persons? And if so why?), the answers provided by decades of research on the ASA model (e.g., Schneider, Kristof, Goldstein, and Smith, 1997) are: (1) "Yes, they are different," and (2) "They are different because of the same basic processes that almost guarantee that people in any given field are different, in various ways, from those in other fields." Entrepreneurs, like emergency room physicians, field biologists, or government employees, possess certain skills, characteristics, and interests—ones that suit them for their particular occupations or careers. By extension, repeat entrepreneurs—individuals who launch several new companies or engage in entrepreneurial activities several times—would be expected to be even more distinct, as a group, since they are even more highly selected (e.g., Baron and Ensley, 2006). An overview of this process is presented in Figure 5.1, which illustrates why, according to the ASA model, entrepreneurs would indeed be expected to be "different" from other groups.

Having addressed this basic and crucial issue, we'll now proceed to consider two additional questions. First, *how* are entrepreneurs different—what characteristics set them apart from other groups (e.g., managers in well-established companies)? A large body of research has addressed this question, and we'll summarize that evidence here. While the question "How are entrepreneurs different?" is interesting and important, however, greater attention will then be focused on a related issue—one that is, in several respects, even more central: What factors—and especially what skills (learned capacities) and capabilities—influence entrepreneurs' success? This question is a central one for the field of entrepreneurship, because identifying these skills and capabilities is a crucial initial step in helping entrepreneurs to develop them—and thus increase the likelihood that they will be successful in creating something truly new and useful, and in making it available to others.

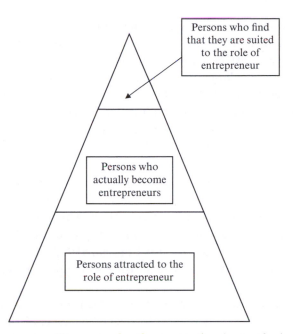

Note: Entrepreneurs, like persons in other occupational or professional groups, are as a group highly selected. Only some are attracted to this role, only some of these persons actually become entrepreneurs, and only some of those find that they are suited to this role and remain in it.

Figure 5.1 *Why entrepreneurs are different from other groups: the attraction–selection–attrition model*

Entrepreneurs: *How* are they different? Personal characteristics that set them apart

Ideas for something new and potentially useful are far from rare; in fact, as Richard Branson, founder of Virgin Enterprises, put it, "Business opportunities are like buses; there's always another one coming." That may be an exaggeration, but what is definitely not an exaggeration is the fact that very few people act on their ideas—they don't actually pursue the business opportunities they recognize. This suggests that there certainly *is* something different about entrepreneurs, the individuals who *do* take action. Initial efforts to identify these differences, however, yielded disappointing results. Just as researchers in the field of leadership initially failed in their efforts to identify a small set of characteristics that distinguish leaders from other persons or effective leaders from ineffective ones, researchers in entrepreneurship generally drew a blank in their efforts to formulate a short list of characteristics that differentiated entrepreneurs from other groups, for example managers in large corporations (e.g.,

Shaver and Scott, 1991). In fact, so disappointing were the findings of early studies focused on this issue that some researchers reached the conclusion that variables relating to the characteristics of individual entrepreneurs were largely irrelevant (e.g., Gartner, 1989). Gradually, however, it became apparent that the early research failed largely because of faulty methods rather than because of the fact that entrepreneurs are not different in any way from other persons. Early studies often failed to focus on variables that, for specific theoretical reasons, would be expected to differentiate entrepreneurs from other persons. Rather, they launched what were, in a sense, "fishing expeditions" to see if entrepreneurs differed from other persons in any measurable ways. That would be equivalent to drilling for oil at random, rather than in places where geological evidence indicates it should be found. In addition, early research often compared entrepreneurs and other groups using measures that were not reliable or valid (i.e., it was unclear that these measures actually measured what they claimed to assess).

When these flaws were corrected in subsequent research, interesting findings did emerge. We have already touched on some of these results in earlier discussions. For instance, as we noted in previous chapters, entrepreneurs are significantly higher than other persons in optimism, positive affect (Baron, Tang, and Hmieleski, 2011), and the tendency to search for connections between seemingly unrelated events (e.g., Tang, Kacmar, and Busenitz, in press). Here is a brief summary of some of the key findings of careful research designed to identify other important ways in which entrepreneurs do indeed differ from other persons.

Self-efficacy: belief in our ability to "do it"

Individuals differ greatly with respect to what is known as *self-efficacy*— the belief that they can accomplish whatever they set out to accomplish (Bandura, 1997). It seems reasonable to predict that entrepreneurs will be high on this dimension—higher, perhaps, than most other groups. If they did not believe in their own capacity to achieve what they set out to accomplish, they would—perhaps—never begin! In fact, many studies have confirmed this general suggestion (Zhao, Seibert, and Hills, 2005). Overall, entrepreneurs are indeed higher in self-efficacy than other groups. More specifically, research findings indicate that there is a positive relationship between self-efficacy and both the tendency actually to start new ventures (Markman, Balkin, and Baron, 2002; Zhao et al., 2005) and achieving financial success through such activities. In addition, other findings (Zhao et al., 2005) indicate that self-efficacy fully mediates (i.e., underlies) the impact of several other variables on entrepreneurial intentions (see Chapter 2). For instance, previous entrepreneurial experience is related to self-efficacy, and self-efficacy, in turn, is related to the tendency to engage in entrepreneurship. In short, entrepreneurs tend to be very high in the belief that they can "do it"—that they can accomplish whatever they set out to accomplish.

Risk: are entrepreneurs really risk takers?

Entrepreneurs themselves often suggest that they are "risk takers." For instance, as Victor Kiam, owner of Remington Razors, once put it: "Entrepreneurs are risk takers, willing to roll the dice with their money or reputation on the line in support of an idea or enterprise." And some research findings seemed, initially, to confirm this view (e.g., Simon, Houghton, and Aquino, 2000). Overall, however, results have been somewhat mixed. In fact, two extensive and careful meta-analyses (statistical overviews of existing evidence; Miner and Raju, 2004; Stewart and Roth, 2001) reached very different conclusions concerning risk taking by entrepreneurs. One (Stewart and Roth, 2001) concluded that entrepreneurs are indeed more accepting of risk than other persons, while the other (Miner and Raju, 2004) reached precisely the opposite conclusion. While many differences between the methods used in the two reviews may account for these contrasting conclusions, another explanation is as follows: perhaps the propensity to accept risk changes over different phases of new venture creation. In the early stages (when a new venture or other entrepreneurial activity is new or perhaps has not even begun), acceptance of relatively high levels of risk is virtually required; unwillingness to accept risk during this phase would stop the process in its tracks. With failure rates for new ventures in the range of 80–85 percent during the first three years, entrepreneurs must be willing to take a chance or they would never get started (e.g., Ariely, 2009).

On the other hand, during later phases of the process, conserving and stretching existing resources often becomes crucial, with the result that entrepreneurs (and certainly successful ones) may strive actively to limit or manage risk. So, to repeat the initial question: Are entrepreneurs really risk takers? The answer depends on how and when we measure risk, and appears to vary greatly over the course of entrepreneurial activity.

Key aspects of personality: the "big five" dimensions

At one time, the term *personality* had a very negative connotation in the field of entrepreneurship. While researchers agreed that people do indeed differ from each other in a large number of ways, there was little agreement about which of these dimensions was most important and most relevant to entrepreneurship, and it was felt that "personality" was such a complex and poorly defined concept that it could not usefully be applied to entrepreneurs.

This situation changed when attention was shifted to a well-established framework for understanding such differences known, generally, as "the big five dimensions" of personality (Barrick and Mount, 1991). These dimensions reflect what appear to be very basic aspects of individual behavior—ones that are highly reliable and very stable over time, and can be readily observed and measured. These dimensions (which we briefly considered in Chapter 2 in a discussion of entrepreneurial intentions) are—at the high end of each dimension—as follows:

1   *conscientiousness*—the tendency to be high in achievement, work motivation, organization, planning, self-control, and responsibility;
2   *openness to experience*—the tendency to be high in curiosity, imagination, creativity, and seeking out new ideas;
3   *extraversion*—the tendency to be outgoing, warm, friendly, and energetic;
4   *agreeableness*—the tendency to be trusting, cooperative, and altruistic in one's dealing with others;
5   *emotional stability*—tendencies to be calm, stable, even-tempered, and hardy (i.e., resilient) in the face of high levels of stress.

These dimensions have been shown to be related to a wide range of important outcomes, ranging from job performance (Barrick and Mount, 1991) to the size and quality of individuals' social networks. That they do indeed reflect very basic aspects of human behavior is indicated by the fact that, when strangers meet for a few minutes and then rate each other on these dimensions, the ratings they provide correlate very highly with those given by individuals who know them very well—close relatives, spouses, and co-workers (Mount, Barrick, and Strauss, 1994). In short, where people stand on several of these dimensions is readily apparent even to casual observers in very brief face-to-face encounters. This may be one reason why "speed dating" works, at least part of the time: participants can form relatively accurate impressions of each other's personality in just a few minutes (Baron and Branscombe, 2012). Research findings indicate that several of these dimensions—conscientiousness, openness to experience, and emotional stability—are significantly linked to becoming an entrepreneur (Zhao and Seibert, 2006). Specifically, entrepreneurs are higher than other groups (e.g., managers) on all three of these dimensions than other persons. However, findings are mixed with respect to extraversion: although some results indicate that entrepreneurs are higher in extraversion than other persons (e.g., Zhao, Seibert, and Lumpkin, 2010), other research results do not confirm this relationship.

Are these very basic dimensions of personality related to entrepreneurs' success—for instance, the survival of their new ventures? Research findings indicate that conscientiousness is positively related to firm survival, but in contrast at least one study has reported a negative relationship between openness to experience and this measure, and no significant links between the other three dimensions (agreeableness, extraversion, and emotional stability) and this measure of success (Ciavarella, Buchholtz, Riordan, Gatewood, and Stokes, 2004). We will return to the factors that play a role in entrepreneurs' success in a later discussion, but note that some aspects of personality—especially conscientiousness—do seem to be related to such success.

Overall, it appears that entrepreneurs do indeed differ from other persons with respect to certain aspects of personality—aspects related to central dimensions of human behavior and, moreover, ones that can be measured reliably. Thus, the suggestion that personality—which essentially refers to stable preferences and tendencies shown by individuals across many situations and over time—is irrelevant to entrepreneurship appears to have been premature and based more on faulty research than actual fact.

Other characteristics shown by entrepreneurs

Other evidence indicates that entrepreneurs are also higher in the need for autonomy—the desire to act independently, free from external constraint (Cromie, 2000; Rauch and Frese, 2005). In addition, entrepreneurs are higher in the need for achievement—the desire to excel in terms of meeting standards of excellence (e.g., Stewart and Roth, 2007).

Still other differences between entrepreneurs and other groups relate to cognition (e.g., Mitchell et al., 2007). For example, entrepreneurs have been found to demonstrate weaker tendencies to engage in counterfactual thinking (imagining what might have been) than other persons (Baron, 2000). Apparently, their strong preference for focusing on the future deters them from looking back and imagining circumstances that would have generated different outcomes than those they actually experienced. This is something of a two-edged sword. On the one hand, it reduces the amount of time and effort invested in mere speculation—a potential gain. On the other hand, it reduces entrepreneurs' tendency to imagine ways in which their performance might have been improved, and that, in turn, can impair experiential learning (e.g., Roese and Olson, 1997).

Overall, this brief review is intended to be representative rather than exhaustive in nature. Even taking this fact into account, however, it seems

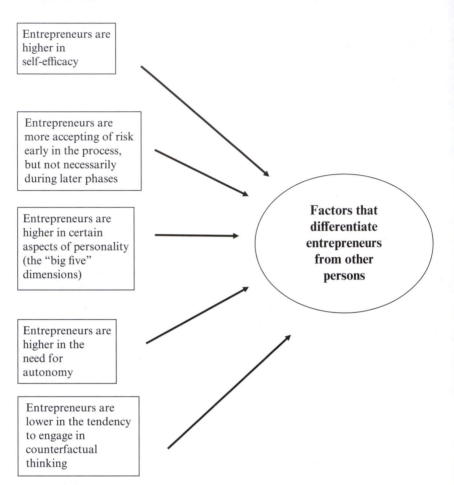

Entrepreneurs are higher in self-efficacy

Entrepreneurs are more accepting of risk early in the process, but not necessarily during later phases

Entrepreneurs are higher in certain aspects of personality (the "big five" dimensions)

Entrepreneurs are higher in the need for autonomy

Entrepreneurs are lower in the tendency to engage in counterfactual thinking

Factors that differentiate entrepreneurs from other persons

Note: As shown here, entrepreneurs do indeed appear to differ from other persons or groups (e.g., managers) in several ways.

Figure 5.2   *What makes entrepreneurs "special" or different? A summary of key findings*

clear that entrepreneurs do indeed differ in several discrete ways from persons who choose other career paths (see Figure 5.2 for a summary). Further, some of these differences—especially self-efficacy and the "big five" dimensions of conscientiousness, are related to entrepreneurs' success (e.g., Zhao et al., 2005). We will now expand on this point by considering a question that is, in some respects, one of the most central addressed by entrepreneurship research: What, precisely, is required for entrepreneurial success? What knowledge, skills, and additional capacities do entrepreneurs need to attain the outcomes they seek? Put somewhat differently, what factors distinguish highly successful entrepreneurs from ones who achieve less positive outcomes?

What's needed to succeed? The key roles of social networks, social capital, and social competence

Being an entrepreneur is, by definition, a very demanding role. Trying to do something really new is fraught with difficulties—many of them unanticipated. The environments faced by entrepreneurs are frequently unpredictable, chaotic, and marked by rapid change. Further, since entrepreneurs are often breaking new ground, there are often no firm guidelines or established practices for them to follow. Rather, as many entrepreneurs report, they must "make it up as they go along."

These basic facts raise an intriguing—and central—question for the field of entrepreneurship: What are the key ingredients that entrepreneurs need in order to succeed? Efforts to address this question have offered many useful insights, so here we will describe some of the key findings of this research.

Social networks and social capital: key ingredients in entrepreneurs' success

A basic fact of life for most entrepreneurs is this: they simply *can't* do it alone. It is one thing to have a brilliant idea for something new and useful, but quite another actually to convert that idea into useful reality; doing so usually involves many kinds of help (financial, information, support) from other persons. A key factor in entrepreneurs' success, therefore, is ensuring that such help can be attained. This, in turn, often involves building high-quality, extensive social networks (e.g., Aldrich and Kim, 2007) and then using these networks to obtain important benefits. These benefits are known as *social capital*, and are often a key factor in entrepreneurs' success.

Social capital has been defined in several different ways, but in general refers to (1) the ability of individuals to extract benefits from their social relationships with others, (2) these benefits themselves (Nahapiet and Ghoshal, 1998; Portes, 1998), or (3) the structure of individuals' social networks and their location in the larger social structure of the domain (e.g., industry) in which the entrepreneurs are functioning (see, e.g., Aarstad, Haugland, and Greve, 2009). Overall, then, social capital refers to, and derives from, the social ties entrepreneurs have with others and the benefits they can obtain from these ties (Putnam, 2000). To put it succinctly, entrepreneurs with high levels of social capital (based on extensive and high-quality social networks) can readily obtain information and guidance when they need it; entrepreneurs lacking in social capital do not have such resources at their disposal. Here's an example of social capital in operation.

Do you recall the television program *Pawn Stars* described briefly in Chapter 2? During that program, potential customers bring a wide variety of items, many of them rare or unusual, to the store for sale. For instance, in one show, a customer brought in a diving helmet that appeared to be one of the earliest ever made. The owners of the store knew very little about this kind of equipment, so they could not, by themselves, judge its authenticity or value. But their social network included someone who was truly expert in this respect, and with his help the owners were able to determine that the helmet was in fact real. Here's the key point: no matter what unusual items appear in their shop, the owners seem to know someone who can help them separate the genuine, valuable items from the counterfeit, worthless ones. In short, they have a large social network which provides them with a high degree of social capital: the people in their network are very willing to help them when the need arises, and being able to draw on their expertise is of great benefit to the owners—who, in a sense, run a very entrepreneurial business.

In more general terms, social capital provides entrepreneurs with increased access to both tangible and intangible resources. Tangible benefits include financial resources and enhanced access to potentially valuable information. Intangible benefits include support, advice, and encouragement from others, as well as increased cooperation and trust from them. While the benefits provided by these latter (intangible) resources are somewhat difficult to measure in economic terms, they are often highly valuable to the persons who obtain them. Thus social capital is an important asset for entrepreneurs—one that provides major benefits.

The social ties on which social capital rests exist within social networks (Aldrich and Kim, 2007), and are often divided into two major types: close or strong ties, for example the strong, intimate bonds that exist between members of a nuclear family or very close friends, and loose or weak ties—social linkages of the type that occur outside families or intimate friendships, for example links between persons who happen to work together or do business on a fairly regular basis (e.g., Adler and Kwon, 2002; Putnam, 2000). Social ties can occur at either the individual level, between specific persons, or at a group or organizational level. In both cases, they often serve as the basis for trust—confidence by one or more persons in the motives and predictability of one or more others.

Close (strong) ties are often viewed as leading to, or at least being associated with, what is known as *bonding social capital*—they generate relationships between individuals that are based on mutual trust. Examples can be seen in the high levels of mutual trust and concern that often exist between the founders of a new venture. Loose or weak ties, in contrast, lead to (or are associated with) *bridging social capital*—they are useful in providing individuals with information that would otherwise be difficult or costly for them to obtain. (The term *bridging* refers to the fact that, in such instances, social capital serves as a bridge or connection for external networks and, by doing so, facilitates the flow of information between them.) An example would be the information individuals or organizations acquire from membership in business networks or trade associations. Over time, loose ties sometimes develop into strong ones, in which case they would lead to relationships based on mutual trust. Since social capital offers important benefits, and derives—to a large extent—from social networks, it is clear that one important ingredient in entrepreneurs' success is their capacity to build, and then reap benefits from, extensive, high-quality social networks. But how do entrepreneurs construct strong social networks—ones that provide them with high levels of social capital? One answer involves the extent to which they possess skills that help them to get along well with others, and to develop strong, mutually beneficial relationships with them—what are known as *social and political skills* (e.g., Ferris, Davidson, and Perrewé, 2005).

Social and political skills: beyond social capital

The social networks entrepreneurs develop are an important resource for them; these networks, and the social capital they generate, often assist them in performing important tasks ranging from locating and then hiring key employees to securing access to many kinds of valuable information (Shane, 2003). In a sense, then, social capital can be viewed as being a necessary condition for entrepreneurial success: without high levels of social capital, entrepreneurs are unable to gain access to potential investors, customers, and employees, because—to put it simply—they lack the contacts and reputation necessary for doing so. Social capital, however, is not a sufficient condition for entrepreneurial success. Why? Because, once access to venture capitalists, potential customers, and potential employees has been achieved, something else must happen: the entrepreneurs must win the confidence, trust, and support of these people. Doing so involves entrepreneurs' social competence—their social and political skills. Do the prospective employees agree to join the company? Do venture capitalists provide needed funding? These and other outcomes depend on the nature of the interactions entrepreneurs have with these people (face to face or even electronic), and this, in turn, is strongly shaped by the entrepreneurs' social and political skills.

These two terms—*social skills* and *political skills*—are closely related, but derive from different research traditions. The term *social skills* was developed in the field of social psychology to refer to proficiencies that help people get along well with others (e.g., Kotsou, Nelis, Grégoire, and Mikolajczak, 2011). The term *political skills*, in contrast, derives from literature in several fields of management, and refers to individuals' ability to effectively understand others at work and to use such knowledge to influence others to act in ways that enhance personal and/or organizational objectives (e.g., Ferris et al., 2005).

Both social and political skills have been found to play an important role in key organizational processes. To mention just a few of these effects, persons high in social or political skills, compared to persons low in such skills, are more successful as job candidates (e.g., Riggio and Throckmorton, 1988), receive higher performance reviews from supervisors (e.g., Robbins and DeNisi, 1994), and attain faster promotions and higher salaries (e.g., Belliveau, O'Reilly, and Wade, 1995). Similarly, individuals high in social skills generally achieve greater success than do persons low in such skills in many different occupations (e.g., medicine, law, sales; Wayne, Liden, Graf, and Ferris, 1997), attain better results in negotiations (e.g., Lewicki, Saunders, and Barry, 2005), and often (although not always) achieve higher levels of task or job performance (e.g., Hochwarter, Witt, Treadway, and Ferris, 2006). Social skills also exert strong effects on outcomes in many contexts outside the world of work. For example, persons high in various social skills tend to have wider social networks than do persons low in social skills (e.g., Diener and Seligman, 2002). Social and political skills have even been found to influence the result of legal proceedings, with persons high in such skills attaining acquittals more often than persons low in such skills (e.g., Downs and Lyons, 1991). What, specifically, are these political and social skills? They take many different forms, but among the most important are these:

- *social perception:* the capacity to perceive others (their traits, feelings, intentions) accurately;
- *social adaptability:* the ability to adapt to a wide range of social situations, and to interact effectively with a wide range of persons;
- *expressiveness:* the tendency to show one's emotions openly, in a form others can readily perceive;
- *impression management:* the capacity to make a good first impression on others, generally through self-promotion (providing positive information about one's accomplishments or skills) or ingratiation (actions designed to induce positive feelings or reactions in the target person).

Are social or political skills relevant to entrepreneurship? Given their powerful impact in a wide range of business contexts, it seems reasonable to predict that this would be the case. In fact, there are strong grounds for suggesting that such skills might be especially important in this context. Entrepreneurs often meet and interact with a wide range of persons, many of whom are strangers. Social and political skills can be very beneficial to them in such interactions. Similarly, when presenting their "pitches" to venture capitalists, potential customers, and many other persons, entrepreneurs need excellent communication skills and high levels of persuasiveness; these, in turn, often rest, to a large extent, on social and political skills. For instance, being persuasive often requires accurate understanding of the reactions of one's audience (i.e., accuracy in social perception). Entrepreneurs also frequently face the task of generating enthusiasm for their ideas, companies, or products in others; high levels of expressiveness may be helpful in this context. Finally, it is often essential for entrepreneurs to create good first impressions on others, since they and their companies may be relatively unknown, at least initially (i.e., they have low levels of social capital).

In sum, there are several reasons why high levels of social or political skills may be especially important for entrepreneurs, and indeed a growing body of empirical findings offers support for this suggestion. In an initial study of this issue (Baron and Markman, 2003), entrepreneurs working in two different industries (cosmetics and high-tech) completed a widely used and well-validated measure of social skills (e.g., Riggio, 1986). Entrepreneurs' scores on this measure were then related to one indicator of their financial success—the income these entrepreneurs earned from their new ventures over each of several years. Results indicated that several social skills (social perception, social adaptability, and expressiveness) were significantly related to this measure of financial success. Interestingly, when people who knew the entrepreneurs well rated the entrepreneurs' social skills, these ratings were highly correlated with the entrepreneurs' self-ratings. This suggests that people are relatively accurate in assessing their own social skills.

A follow-up investigation (Baron and Tang, 2009) extended these findings by investigating the underlying (i.e., mediating) mechanisms through which entrepreneurs' social skills influence the success of their new ventures. Results indicated that entrepreneurs' effectiveness in acquiring useful information and effectiveness in obtaining essential resources both mediated the effects of their social or political skills on widely used measures of new venture performance, such as growth in sales, growth in profits, and growth in number of employees (e.g., Zahra, Neubaum, El-Hagrassey, 2002). In other words, social or political skills helped entrepreneurs to obtain information and essential resources, and these factors, in turn, contributed to their success. The study was conducted with Chinese entrepreneurs working in many different businesses; thus it expanded earlier results to a very different cultural context and to many additional industries.

To conclude: existing evidence indicates that, in acquiring essential resources for their new companies or other entrepreneurial activities, entrepreneurs draw heavily on benefits conferred by their social networks—the social capital provided by these networks. Further, their social and political skills appear to play a key role in building these networks. Overall, then, entrepreneurs who possess and effectively employ such skills tend to

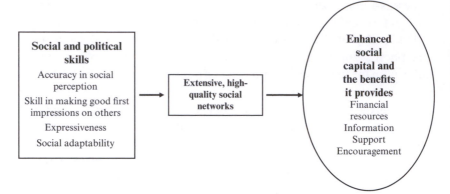

Note: Entrepreneurs high in social and political skills are often able to build extensive, high-quality social networks. These networks then provide them with important tangible (e.g., financial resources) and intangible (e.g., encouragement) benefits.

Figure 5.3   *Social and political skills, social networks, and entrepreneurs' success*

experience greater levels of success in starting new ventures than those who are lower in this respect because they are able to construct larger and higher-quality social networks, and then can draw on these networks for important tangible and intangible benefits (see Figure 5.3). In a sense, therefore, social and political skills are a key component in the entire process: they help build the networks that provide the social capital so valuable to entrepreneurs.

Fortunately, such skills can be readily acquired or strengthened (e.g., Kotsou et al., 2011). Decades of research by psychologists indicate that, with careful, guided practice, most persons can increase these skills (e.g., Kurtz and Mueser, 2008). Many courses on entrepreneurship already provide such training indirectly by requiring students to present their ideas for new products, services, or markets to other members of the class and faculty advisers or judges. Although much of the feedback provided to students focuses on the soundness of the business models they have developed, some attention is also directed to the quality of the presentations themselves. Given the powerful impact of social and political skills on success in many business contexts, greater attention to this aspect might well prove highly beneficial for entrepreneurs-in-training.

The crucial role of self-regulatory skills: persistence, focus, and knowing what you know—and don't!

Over the centuries, thoughtful persons in many fields have pondered the following question: What are the key ingredients of success? Why, in other words, do some persons in any given field excel (generally, a very small number), while most achieve only mediocrity or, even worse, actually fail? Certainly this question is highly relevant to entrepreneurship, where despite their best efforts a large proportion of entrepreneurs do not achieve their goals. Many possible solutions to this intriguing puzzle have been proposed, but among these the one that is, perhaps, most persuasive involves what are known, collectively, as *self-regulatory mechanisms*— cognitive processes through which individuals guide, direct, monitor, and evaluate their own behavior and performance in order to move toward, and ultimately attain, important goals (Forgas, Baumeister, and Tice, 2009). As Tommy Lasorda, former manager of the Los Angeles Dodgers, put it: "The difference between the impossible and possible lies in a person's determination." In other words, in his view, it is the capacities to persevere and stay focused on key goals that make the major difference between success and failure.

Research on the impact of self-regulatory processes indicates that they do, indeed, play a major role in attaining success. In fact, taken as a whole, such research (e.g., Vohs and Baumeister, 2010) suggests that, collectively, self-regulatory mechanisms are the single most important factor in this respect. Indeed, in a recent book on self-regulation, Forgas et al. (2009) note that, after more than one hundred years of systematic research, psychologists have identified only two variables that influence success across all fields of human endeavor: intelligence and self-regulation. (Recall our discussion of the many facets of intelligence in Chapter 2.)

Self-regulatory mechanisms take many different forms. One of the most important is self-control, which involves individuals' capacity to refrain from engaging in actions they would very much like to perform but should not (e.g., eating high-calorie foods), and, conversely, performing actions they would rather not perform but should (e.g., engaging in vigorous exercise, intense studying; Baumeister, Zell, and Tice, 2007). Self-control appears to be a limited resource that can be depleted: after individuals exert it with respect to one task (e.g., refraining from engaging in actions they know they should not perform), they are less able to exert such control in another, subsequent situation (e.g., Tice, 2009).

Another key aspect of self-regulation involves delay of gratification— refraining from indulging in immediately available rewards in order to obtain larger ones at a future time (Mischel, 1974, 1977, 1996; Mischel and Ayduk, 2010). The ability to delay gratification has been found to be crucial in attaining success in many fields; in fact, people who show a high capacity to delay gratification as children actually attain higher levels of success as adults than those who do not (Mischel and Ayduk, 2010).

Additional aspects of self-regulation refer to the capacity to stay focused on important tasks for long periods of time (Duckworth, Peterson,

Matthews, and Kelly, 2007), to regulate and control emotions, and to regulate one's own thinking, so that, for instance, thoughts that might interfere with performance are suppressed (e.g., ruminating endlessly about previous failures) while thoughts that increase motivation (e.g., images of ultimate success) are facilitated. Finally, self-regulation, broadly defined, also involves what is known as *metacognition*—individuals' understanding of and knowledge of their own cognition (Elfkides, 2008; Flavell, 1979). Metacognition, in turn, is often divided into several broad categories: *metacognitive knowledge*—knowledge about ourselves, other persons, tasks, and various strategies for performing them; *metacognitive experience*—individuals' awareness of what they experience when performing a task and processing information related to it; and *metacognitive skills*—deliberate use of specific tactics to control cognition.

Perhaps most relevant for entrepreneurship is one aspect of metacognitive knowledge: individuals' understanding of what they know and do not know. This idea is related to McMullen and Shepherd's (2006) suggestion that a key task for entrepreneurs is determining which opportunities they personally can, or cannot, successfully develop. Presumably, entrepreneurs who are high on this aspect of self-regulation will tend to choose more appropriate opportunities (for them) than entrepreneurs low in such self-knowledge, and will also recognize when they need, or do not need, outside help in developing opportunities they pursue.

That self-regulatory processes play an important role in performance in many different fields is well established by research findings (e.g., Forgas et al., 2009; Vohs and Baumeister, 2010). A key question, however, is this: Are they also relevant to and important for entrepreneurs? Research designed to investigate this issue has only recently begun. For instance, it has been suggested (Haynie and Shepherd, 2009; Haynie, Shepherd, Mosakowski, and Earley, 2010) that certain aspects of metacognition may play an important role in entrepreneurs' performance. Empirical evidence for the role of self-regulatory processes in entrepreneurship has recently been reported by Baron, Casper, Fox, and Hmieleski (2011). These researchers found that the capacity to focus consistently on and work persistently toward important goals (a combination known as *grit*; Duckworth et al., 2007) and self-control (e.g., Baumeister and Alquist, 2009) were related to the strategies entrepreneurs choose. One useful measure of these strategies is known as *entrepreneurial orientation (EO)*, and involves tendencies on the part of entrepreneurs to seek innovativeness (introduction of new products and services), proactiveness (seeking new opportunities), and risk taking (the propensity to take bold actions and venture into the unknown and into uncertain environments (e.g., Lumpkin and Dess, 1996). The relationship between grit and self-control, on the one hand, and entrepreneurial orientation, on the other, however, was complex. Basically, the link between grit and entrepreneurial orientation was stronger when entrepreneurs' self-control was low than when it was high. Why? No firm evidence yet exists, but one possibility is that self-control is related to the capacity to focus on actions that are consistent with important long-term goals, while refraining from actions that are incompatible with achieving these goals (Baumeister et al., 2007). The strategies represented by EO are often beneficial for new ventures, but only, perhaps, up to a point. New ventures have limited resources, and often these cannot be sufficiently "stretched" to support a focus on innovation or proactivity (identifying and developing new opportunities). Further, the costs of a strategy that accepts relatively high levels of risk may be too high for many new ventures, and so prove harmful to their survival and success. High levels of self-control may alert entrepreneurs to these potential dangers, and help them to moderate tendencies to pursue these strategies. Thus the relationship between grit and EO may be weaker when self-control (a potentially restraining influence) is high than when it is low, for these reasons. Regardless of the precise explanation for these findings, however, entrepreneurial orientation refers to important aspects of entrepreneurs' strategies for attaining success, so the results reported by Baron et al. (2011) suggest that key aspects of self-regulation do indeed play an important role in entrepreneurial activities.

It is important to note that there are several reasons for suggesting that self-regulatory processes may be especially important in the context of entrepreneurship. First, in their efforts to create something new, entrepreneurs generally lack many of the external constraints that typically guide human behavior. They have no direct supervisors, coaches, or teachers—persons who, in other contexts, might evaluate their performance, provide feedback, and advise them on how to improve. As a result, entrepreneurs must rely mainly on their own cognitive resources—on their own capacities to stay focused, persist, and perform the actions that will help them attain important goals.

Second, because they are often operating in "uncharted territory" and attempting to perform tasks they have not previously performed, entrepreneurs must rely on their own self-regulatory skills (i.e., metacognition) to understand what they know and do not know. Such knowledge can help them to make reasonable decisions about whether, and in what ways, they should proceed. If they conclude, for instance, that they do not possess the information or skills needed to pursue a specific idea, entrepreneurs would be well advised either to obtain these resources from others (e.g., through their social networks) or to shift to opportunities for which they do possess the required skills and knowledge.

Finally, as noted in Chapter 4, entrepreneurs as a group are very high in optimism and in positive affect. Although these tendencies are often beneficial, they can, as suggested previously, also generate detrimental effects (e.g., a tendency to ignore relevant, negative information, and a tendency to engage in heuristic thinking even when more systematic, careful analysis is essential; Baron, Hmieleski, and Henry, in press). Again, because entrepreneurs usually operate in situations where external factors that might restrain these tendencies are absent (e.g., they lack supervisors who might tend to restrain excessive optimism or excessive enthusiasm), they must rely on their own self-regulatory processes to hold these potentially damaging tendencies in check.

In short, entrepreneurs are, in several key respects, very much "on their own," and for this reason must depend, more than others, on their own self-regulatory mechanisms. Thus the extent to which they possess or develop such skills is a crucial factor in their ultimate success. Fortunately, procedures for developing or strengthening key aspects of self-regulation exist, and can be readily followed by persons wishing to augment such skills (e.g., Vohs and Baumeister, 2010).

Perhaps the most appropriate way to conclude this discussion is by returning to a key question posed earlier—one that has been central to the field of entrepreneurship for decades: Why are some entrepreneurs and new ventures successful, while most fail? Research on self-regulatory mechanisms suggests that at least part of the answer involves the fact that entrepreneurs differ greatly in terms of their self-regulatory skills, and that the ones high on these proficiencies gain an important advantage. As we have noted, though, strong self-regulatory mechanisms are only part of the total picture. In addition, factors such as self-efficacy, a high level of conscientiousness (i.e., being organized and reliable), well-developed and extensive social networks, and strong social and political skills play important roles. Together, this combination of skills, characteristics, and motivation (summarized in Figure 5.4) may help entrepreneurs to stay focused, to persist, and—in a key sense—to work not just hard (almost all do that), but also "smart." In short, entrepreneurial success, like success in many other fields, does not stem from one or two "special" traits, flashes of genius, or unique talents (see Chapter 2). Rather, it results from a convergence of characteristics, skills, and interests that help entrepreneurs to invest the years of hard, focused work essential for success in creating something new, useful, and better.

Summary of key points

Entrepreneurs are in fact different from other persons, but not because they are "special" to begin with. Rather, they are different because they are a highly selected group: only persons who are attracted to entrepreneurship, actually seek to engage in such activities, and find that they are indeed suited to this role continue as entrepreneurs. This same process of

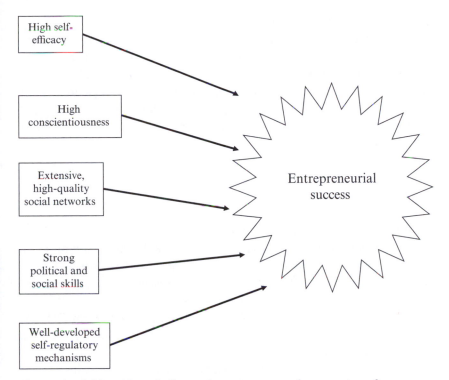

Note: Available evidence indicates that entrepreneurs' success stems from a combination of skills, characteristics, motives, and interests that together help them to work not only hard, but "smart," in their efforts to create something truly new and truly useful. The factors shown here are among the most important, but are certainly not the only ones that play a role.

Figure 5.4   *Key ingredients of entrepreneurial success*

attraction–selection–attrition applies to many other groups as well, and virtually ensures that people in different occupations or professions will differ from one another in many ways.

Entrepreneurs are different from other persons and other groups in several important ways. They are higher in self-efficacy, their perceptions of risk, certain aspects of personality, the need for autonomy, and certain aspects of cognition.

Many factors play a key role in entrepreneurs' success, but among the most important are the size and quality of their social networks, and their social and political skills. Fortunately, social and political skills can be acquired and used to build strong social networks, so these factors are, to some extent, under entrepreneurs' personal control.

Another key factor in entrepreneurs' success is self-regulatory skills—cognitive processes through which individuals guide, direct, monitor, and evaluate their own behavior and performance in order to approach, and ultimately attain, important goals. These include self-control, the capacity to remain focused on and persistently seek key goals (grit), delay of gratification, and metacognition—the understanding of one's own cognition. With respect to metacognition, entrepreneurs' understanding of what they know and do not know may be especially important. Self-regulatory skills can be learned, and efforts by entrepreneurs to build and enhance such skills may be another key step they can take to increase the likelihood of achieving the success they seek.

Bibliography

Aarstad, J., Haugland, S.A., and Greve, A. (2009). Performance spillover effects in entrepreneurial networks: Assessing a dyadic theory of social capital. *Entrepreneurship Theory and Practice*, *34*, 1003–1019.

Adler, P., and Kwon, S. (2002). Social capital: Prospects for a new concept. *Academy of Management Review*, *27*, 17–40.

Aldrich, H.E., and Kim, P.H. (2007). Small worlds, infinite possibilities? How social networks affect entrepreneurial formation and search. *Strategic Entrepreneurship Journal*, *1*, 147–166.

Ariely, D. (2009). *Predictably irrational*. New York: HarperCollins.

Bandura, A. (1997). *Self-efficacy: The exercise of control*. New York: W.H. Freeman.

Baron, R.A. (2000). Thinking about "what might have been." *Journal of Business Venturing*, *15*, 79–92.

Baron, R.A., and Branscombe, N.R. (2012). *Social psychology*, 13th edition. Boston, MA: Allyn & Bacon.

Baron, R.A., and Ensley, M.D. (2006). Opportunity recognition as the detection of meaningful patterns: Evidence from comparisons of novice and experienced entrepreneurs. *Management Science*, *52*, 1331–1344.

Baron, R.A., and Markman, G.D. (2003). Beyond social capital: The role of entrepreneurs' social competence in their financial success. *Journal of Business Venturing*, *18*, 41–60.

Baron, R.A., and Tang, J. (2009). Entrepreneurs' social skills and new venture performance: Mediating mechanisms and moderating effects of industry. *Journal of Management*, *35*, 282–306.

Baron, R.A., Casper, C., Fox, C., and Hmieleski, K.D. (2011). Entrepreneurs' self-regulatory processes and new venture strategy: Persistence, focus, and metacognitive knowledge. Paper presented at the meetings of the Academy of Management, San Antonio, TX.

Baron, R.A., Hmieleski, K.M., and Henry, R.A. (in press). Entrepreneurs' dispositional positive affect: The potential benefits—and potential costs—of being "up." *Journal of Business Venturing*.

Baron, R.A., Tang, J., and Hmieleski, K.M. (2011). Entrepreneurs' dispositional positive affect and firm performance: When there can be "too much of a good thing." *Strategic Entrepreneurship Journal*, *5*, 111–119.

Barrick, M.R., and Mount, M.K. (1991). The big five personality dimensions and job performance: A meta-analysis. *Personnel Psychology*, *44*, 1–26.

Baumeister, R.F., and Alquist, J.L. (2009). Self-regulation as a limited resource: Strength model of control and depletion. In J.P. Forgas, R.F. Baumeister, and D.M. Tice (eds), *Psychology of self-regulation: Cognitive, affective, and motivational processes* (pp. 21–35). New York: Psychology Press.

Baumeister, R., Heatherton, T.F., and Tice, D. (1994). *Losing control: How and why people fail at self-regulation*. San Diego, CA: Academic Press.

Baumeister, R.F., Vohs, K.D., and Tice, D.M. (2007). The strength model of self-control. *Current Directions in Psychological Science*, *16*, 351–355.

Baumeister, R.F., Zell, A.L., and Tice, D.M. (2007). How emotions facilitate and impair self-regulation. In J.J. Gross (ed.), *Handbook of emotion regulation* (pp. 408–426). New York: Guilford Press.

Begley, T.M., and Boyd, D.R. (1987). Psychological characteristics associated with performance in entrepreneurial firms and smaller businesses. *Journal of Business Venturing*, *3*, 79–93.

Belliveau, M.A., O'Reilly, C.A., III, and Wade, B. (1995). Social capital at the top: Effects of social similarity and status on CEO compensation. *Academy of Management Journal*, *39*, 1568–1593.

Ciavarella, M.A., Buchholtz, A.K., Riordan, C.M., Gatewood, R.D., and Stokes, G.S. (2004). The big five and venture success: Is there a linkage? *Journal of Business Venturing*, *19*, 465–483.

Cromie, S. (2000), Assessing entrepreneurial inclinations. *European Journal of Work and Organizational Psychology*, *9*, 7–30.

Diener, E., and Seligman, M.E.P. (2002). Very happy people. *Psychological Science*, *13*, 81–84.

Downs, A.C., and Lyons, P.M. (1991). Natural observations of the links between attractiveness and initial legal judgments. *Personality and Social Psychology Bulletin*, *17*, 541–547.

Duckworth, A.L., Peterson, C., Matthews, M.D., and Kelly, D.R. (2007). Grit: Perseverance and passion for long-term goals. *Journal of Personality and Social Psychology*, *92*, 1087–1101.

Elfkides, A. (2008). Metacognition: Defining its facets and levels of functioning in relation to self-regulation and co-regulation. *European Psychologist*, *13*, 277–287.

Ericsson, K.A., Charness, N., Hoffman, R., and Feltovich, P.J. (2006). *The Cambridge handbook of expertise and expert performance*. New York: Cambridge University Press.

Ferris, G.R., Davidson, S.L., and Perrewé, P.L. (2005). *Political skill at work: Impact on work effectiveness*. Mountain View, CA: Davies-Black.

Ferris, G.R., Treadway, D.C., Kolodinsky, R.W., Hochwarter, W.A., and Kacmar, C.J. (2006). Development and validation of the political skill inventory. *Journal of Management*, *31*, 126–152.

Ferris, G.R., Treadway, D.C., Perrewé, P.L., Brouer, R.L., Douglas, C., and Lux, S. (2007). Political skill in organizations. *Journal of Management*, *33*, 290–320.

Ferris, G.R., Witt, L.A., and Hochwarter, W.A. (2001). Interaction of social skills and general mental ability on job performance and salary. *Journal of Applied Psychology*, *86*, 1075–1082.

Flavell, J. (1979). Metacognition and cognitive monitoring: A new area of cognitive-developmental inquiry. *American Psychologist*, *34*, 906–911.

Forgas, J.P., Baumeister, R.F., and Tice, D.M. (2009). *The psychology of self-regulation: Cognitive, affective, and motivational processes*. New York: Psychology Press.

Gartner, W.B. (1989). Some suggestions for research on entrepreneurial traits and characteristics. *Entrepreneurship Theory and Practice*, *14*, 27–37.

Haynie, J.M., and Shepherd, D.A. (2009). A measure of adaptive cognition for entrepreneurship research. *Entrepreneurship Theory and Practice*, *33*, 695–734.

Haynie, J.M., Shepherd, D., Mosakowski, E., and Earley, P.C. (2010). A situated metacognitive model of the entrepreneurial mindset. *Journal of Business Venturing*, *25*, 217–229.

Hochwarter, W.A., Ferris, G.R., Gavin, M.B., Perrewé, P.L., Hall, A.T., and Frink, D.D. (2007). Political skill as neutralizer of felt accountability–job tension effects on job performance ratings: A longitudinal investigation. *Organizational Behavior and Human Decision Processes*, *102*, 226–239.

Hochwarter, W.A., Witt, L.A., Treadway, D.C., and Ferris, G.R. (2006). The interaction of social skill and organizational support on job performance. *Journal of Applied Psychology*, *91*, 482–489.

Kotsou, I., Nelis, D., Grégoire, J., and Mikolajczak, M. (2011). Emotional plasticity: Conditions and effects of improving emotional competence in adulthood. *Journal of Applied Psychology*, *96*, 827–839.

Kurtz, M.M., and Mueser, K.T. (2008). A meta-analysis of controlled research on social skills training for schizophrenia. *Journal of Consulting and Clinical Psychology*, *76*, 291–304.

Lewicki, R.J., Saunders, D.M., and Barry, M. (2005). *Negotiation*. New York: McGraw-Hill/Irwin.

Lumpkin, G.T., and Dess, G.G. (1996). Clarifying the entrepreneurial orientation construct and linking it to performance. *Academy of Management Journal*, *21*, 135–172.

Markman, G.D., Balkin, D.B., and Baron, R.A. (2002). Inventors and new venture formation: The effects of general self-efficacy and regretful thinking. *Entrepreneurship Theory and Practice*, Winter, 149–165.

McMullen, J.S., and Shepherd, D.A. (2006). Entrepreneurial action and the role of uncertainty in the theory of the entrepreneur. *Academy of Management Review, 31*, 132–152.

Miner, J.B., and Raju, N.S. (2004). When science divests itself of its conservative stance: The case of risk propensity differences between entrepreneurs and managers. *Journal of Applied Psychology, 89*, 3–13.

Mischel, W. (1974). Processing delay of gratification. In L. Berkowitz (ed.), *Advances in experimental social psychology*, Vol. 7 (pp. 249–292). New York: Academic Press.

Mischel, W. (1977). The interaction of person and situation. In D. Magnusson and N.S. Endler (eds), *Personality at the crossroads: Current issues in interactional psychology* (pp. 333–352). Hillsdale, NJ: Erlbaum.

Mischel, W. (1996). From good intentions to willpower. In P.M. Golwitzer and J.A. Bargh (eds), *The psychology of action: Linking cognition and motivation to behavior* (pp. 197–218). New York: Guilford Press.

Mischel, W., and Ayduk, O. (2010). Willpower in a cognitive affective processing system. In K.D. Vohs and R.F. Baumeister (eds), *Handbook of self-regulation: Research, theory, and applications* (pp. 83–105). New York: Guilford Press.

Mitchell, R.K., Busenitz, L.K., Bird, B., Gaglio, C.M., McMullen, J.S., Morse, E.A., and Smith, J.B. (2007). The central question in entrepreneurial cognition research 2007. *Entrepreneurship Theory and Practice, 31*, 1–28.

Mount, M.K., Barrick, M.R., and Strauss, J.P. (1994). Validity of observer ratings of the big five personality factors. *Journal of Applied Psychology, 79*, 272–280.

Nahapiet, J., and Ghoshal, S. (1998). Social capital, intellectual capital, and the organizational advantage. *Academy of Management Review, 23*, 242–266.

Nicolaou, N., and Shane, S. (2009). Born entrepreneurs? The genetic foundations of entrepreneurship. *Journal of Business Venturing, 23*, 1–22.

Portes, A. (1998). Social capital. *Annual Review of Sociology, 23*, 1–24.

Putnam, F. (2000). *Bowling alone: The collapse and revival of American community*. New York: Simon & Schuster.

Rauch, A., and Frese, M. (2005). Let's put the person back into entrepreneurship research: A meta-analysis on the relationships between business owners' personality and business creation and success. Unpublished manuscript.

Riggio, R.E. (1986). Assessment of basic social skills. *Journal of Personality and Social Psychology, 51*, 649–660.

Riggio, R.E., and Throckmorton, B. (1988). The relative effects of verbal and nonverbal behavior, appearance, and social skills on valuations made in hiring interviews. *Journal of Applied Psychology*, *18*, 331–348.

Robbins, T.L., and DeNisi, A.S. (1994). A closer look at interpersonal affect as a distinct influence on cognitive processing in performance evaluations. *Journal of Applied Psychology*, *79*, 341–353.

Roese, N.J., and Olson, J.M. (997). Counterfactual thinking: The intersection of affect and function. In M.P. Zanna (ed.), *Advances in experimental social psychology*, Vol. 29 (pp. 1–59). New York: Academic Press.

Schneider, B. (2001). Fits about fit. *International Review of Applied Psychology*, *50*, 141–152.

Schneider, B., Kristof, A., Goldstein, H.W., and Smith, D.B. (1997). What is this thing called fit? In N. Anderson and P. Herriott (eds), *Handbook of selection and appraisal*. London: Wiley.

Shane, S. (2003). *A general theory of entrepreneurship: The individual–opportunity nexus*. Cheltenham, UK and Northampton, MA, USA: Edward Elgar Publishing.

Shaver, K., and Scott, L. (1991). Person, process, choice: The psychology of new venture creation. *Entrepreneurship Theory and Practice*, *16*, 23–45.

Simon, M., Houghton, S.M., and Aquino, K. (2000). Cognitive biases, risk perception, and venture formation: How individuals decide to start companies. *Journal of Business Venturing*, *15*, 113–134.

Stewart, W.H., and Roth, P.L. (2001). Risk propensity differences between entrepreneurs and managers: A meta-analytic review. *Journal of Applied Psychology*, *86*, 145–153.

Stewart, W.H., and Roth, P.L. (2007). A meta-analysis of motivation differences between entrepreneurs and managers. *Journal of Small Business Management*, *45*, 401–421.

Tang, J., Kacmar, K.M., and Busenitz, L. (in press). Entrepreneurial alertness in the pursuit of new opportunities. *Journal of Business Venturing*.

Tice, D.M. (2009). How emotions affect self-regulation. In J.P. Fortas, R.F. Baumeister, and D.M. Tice (eds), *Psychology of self-regulation* (pp. 201–216). New York: Psychology Press.

Vohs, K.D., and Baumeister, R.D. (eds) (2010). *Handbook of self-regulation*, 2nd edition. New York: Guilford Press.

Wayne, S.J., Liden, R.C., Graf, I.K., and Ferris, G.R. (1997). The role of upward influence tactics in human resource decisions. *Personnel Psychology*, *50*, 979–1006.

Zahra, S.A., Neubaum, D.O., and El-Hagrassey, G.M. (2002). Competitive analysis and new venture performance: Understanding the impact of strategic uncertainty and venture origin. *Entrepreneurship Theory and Practice*, *27*, 1–28.

Zhao, H., and Seibert, S.E. (2006). The big five personality dimensions and entrepreneurial status: A meta-analytical review. *Journal of Applied Psychology*, *91*, 259–271.

Zhao, H., Seibert, S.E., and Hills, G.E. (2005). The mediating role of self-efficacy in the development of entrepreneurial intentions. *Journal of Applied Psychology*, *90*, 1265–1272.

Zhao, H., Seibert, S.E., and Lumpkin, G.T. (2010). The relationship of personality to entrepreneurial intentions and performance: A meta-analytic review. *Journal of Management*, *36*, 381–404.

PART II • THE PRACTICE OF ENTREPRENEURSHIP

6   Intellectual property: protecting your ideas

• •

Chapter outline

Intellectual property: its basic nature

Intellectual property protection based on the legal system

Copyrights: protection for the tangible expressions of ideas, but not ideas themselves

Trademarks and servicemarks: images representing companies or products

Patents: the right to exclude others from developing or using ideas or inventions

When should entrepreneurs seek legal protection for their ideas or inventions?

Intellectual property protection based on business practices and strategies

Trade secrets: gaining protection by keeping information private

The first mover advantage: the potential benefits of being first

Control of complementary assets: preventing customers from using competing products

> The patent system added the fuel of *interest* to the fire of genius.
> (Abraham Lincoln)

> A country without a patent office and good patent laws was just a crab, and couldn't travel any way but sideways or backwards. (Mark Twain)

Have you ever heard of Antonio Meucci? What about Joseph Swan? Probably these names are totally unfamiliar to you. In fact, though, they *should* be ones you know because these people are the inventors of products that truly changed the world. Antonio Meucci, *not* Alexander Graham Bell, invented the telephone; and Joseph Swan, *not* Thomas Edison, invented a practical light bulb. So why does history credit Bell and Edison with these inventions? Let's take a closer look at the circumstances that led to these outcomes, because they provide important insights concerning key aspects of the entrepreneurial process and how—and why— inventors should seek to protect their ideas and inventions.

Consider first the sad tale of Antonio Meucci. He was an Italian citizen who studied mechanical engineering in Florence. In 1830, he moved to

Cuba, where he worked on the task of using electric shocks to treat various illnesses, an idea much in vogue in medicine at the time. While carrying out this work, he discovered that sounds could be transmitted over a copper wire by electrical impulses. Recognizing a potentially important opportunity in this discovery, he moved to Staten Island, New York City, where he developed a system his wife (who was seriously ill) could use to signal him in his workshop, located in a nearby building. By 1860, he was able to stage a public demonstration of his invention (which he named the *teletrofono*) and built a working prototype. He even went so far as to file a patent for a "talking telegraph," and tried to obtain support for his invention from Western Union, the huge telegraph company. Western Union showed no interest, and in fact reported that they had "lost" the working prototype Meucci sent to them for testing. In the meantime, he ran out of funds and could not proceed. A few years later, Bell, who was familiar with Meucci's work and invention, filed for a patent on the telephone. (We'll discuss the nature of patents and the rights they confer—and do not confer—below, but for now it's simply important to note that a patent gives an inventor the exclusive right to develop and sell her or his invention for a specific period of time.) Meucci sued, but died before his case could come to court. It is a sad footnote to history that, in 2002, the United States Congress issued a resolution recognizing Meucci as the real inventor of the telephone, so his descendants did gain this satisfaction; but of course they did not share in the huge fortune Bell reaped from the telephone (see Figure 6.1). This Congressional resolution read in part:

> . . .Whereas if Meucci had been able to pay the $10 fee to maintain the caveat after 1874, no patent could have been issued to Bell; Now therefore be it Resolved that it is the sense of the House of Representative and the Senate that the life and achievements of Antonio Meucci should be recognized; and the work of Antonio Meucci in the invention of the telephone should be acknowledged. (Passed by the House and Senate in 2002 and 2003, respectively.)

Now consider the story of Joseph Swan, a British inventor who developed a light bulb based on a carbon filament several years before Edison came up with what was basically the same product. Swan filed for, and received, a British patent on his invention, and then described it in the magazine *Scientific American*. Edison knew about Swan's work, but proceeded to manufacture light bulbs anyway, and to build a system for delivering electricity to major cities. Swan sued Edison—and won!—in the British courts; as a result, Edison had to name Swan as a partner in his British electric company. But none of this stopped Edison from launching the General Electric company in the United States, or from acquiring huge wealth from exploitation of an invention which, in fact, may not have been his own.

Note: Although history credits Alexander Graham Bell with inventing the telephone, existing evidence indicates that it was actually invented by Antonio Meucci. Because he did not obtain legal protection for his invention, however, he did not share in the huge wealth reaped by Bell from this breakthrough product.

Source: Photograph courtesy of the Garibaldi-Meucci Museum, Staten Island, NY.

Figure 6.1   *Antonio Meucci: the real inventor of the telephone*

Why do we begin with these sad stories of inventors who failed to reap the benefits of their ideas? Primarily, for two reasons. First, to emphasize the fact that, although creativity and the ideas it generates lie at the heart of entrepreneurship, they are only the start of the entrepreneurial process. These ideas must be moved from the intangible (thoughts and images in the brains of specific persons, the inventors) into the realm of the tangible (real, physical objects). If they are not, the process stops, and no actual products or services follow—which means, in essence, that neither the inventors nor society reaps any benefits from these ideas, which may vanish for years or even decades until someone else "connects the dots" among technology, social trends, and other factors into the same pattern (see Chapter 3). In short, there is often a large gap between ideas and actual products or services. Entrepreneurs are, in a sense, the individuals who bridge this gap and convert the intangible into the real. Although Meucci developed a working prototype of the telephone, he was not able to secure the support needed to move forward with this device—perhaps because he never mastered English and could not describe his invention clearly or effectively. Bell, in contrast, was a masterful promoter, very successful in generating enthusiasm for the telephone—and in securing financial support for its development. Similar factors may have played a role for Joseph Swan: although he developed a working light bulb, he failed to formulate a plan for bringing electricity into homes and businesses—a basic requirement for widespread use of this invention. Edison, in contrast, focused his effort on these tasks; in addition, he was already quite famous and so had no difficulty in raising a large amount of capital and in gaining political support for bringing electricity—and electric lighting—to large cities. The result? He, not Swan, acquired huge wealth from this invention.

These two tales are also informative because they call attention to the fact that the fates suffered by Meucci and Swan can be avoided. Although ideas themselves are intangible, they can still be protected in two basic ways: legally, through copyrights, trademarks, and patents (which we'll soon describe in detail); and through other means, based largely on business practices and strategies—for instance, trade secrets or gaining the advantage of being first to develop and market a new product or service. In the remainder of this chapter, we'll examine both types of protection. In addition, we'll address the general question, "When should entrepreneurs seek protection for their ideas?" As we'll see, doing so is not always necessary, and, since it can be very costly to attain such protection (especially through the legal system), this is an important question for entrepreneurs to consider early in the process.

Intellectual property: its basic nature

Can anyone *own* an idea? At first glance, this seems like a laughable idea. If people don't share their thoughts with others, the thoughts remain their exclusive property. But, once an idea is described to other persons, how can the individual who originally had it retain possession of it? Almost by definition, she or he can't. Yet the framers of the United States Constitution recognized that the people who originate an idea should, perhaps, retain special rights in it. In fact, here's what the Constitution says (Article 1, Section 8, Clause 8): "The congress shall have the power to promote the progress of science and useful arts by securing for limited times to authors and inventors exclusive right to their respective writings and discoveries." Think for a moment about what this means: it suggests that certain creations of the human mind can be viewed as a kind of property—intellectual property—that can be protected by law, just as physical property is protected. The persons who originate these creations (writings, discoveries, or inventions) retain exclusive rights in them: no one else can use them without written, explicit permission.

Interestingly, although this view prevailed and is part of the United States Constitution, some of the founders of the United States strongly disagreed. For instance, Thomas Jefferson held the following view:

> If nature has made any one thing less susceptible than all others of exclusive property, it is the action of the thinking power called an *idea*, which an individual may exclusively possess as long as he keeps it to himself; but the moment it is divulged, it forces itself into the possession of every one, and the receiver cannot dispossess himself of it.

Jefferson, in short, agreed with what common sense suggests: once an idea is shared with others, it is no longer the property of the person who originated it. Why did most other founders of the U.S. disagree? Because they believed that there were important benefits for society that would result from granting exclusive rights (for some period of time) to the persons who formulated ideas that could, ultimately, result in useful new products, services, or means of production.

In essence, then, *intellectual property* refers to creations of the human mind—human creativity—for which legal protection can be obtained. This raises several complex questions: (1) What, specifically, can be protected? (2) What kinds of protection exist? (3) How can they be obtained? It is to these issues that we turn next.

Intellectual property protection based on the legal system

Legal systems differ from country to country, but most offer several kinds of intellectual property protection—legal protections for the products of human creativity. The most important forms of such protection are copyrights, trademarks, and—perhaps most central of all—patents. Another form, trade secrets, can be considered as a legal form of protection too, but is so different from the others that we'll consider it as part of a separate discussion of intellectual property protection based on business practices and strategies.

Copyrights: protection for the tangible expressions of ideas, but not ideas themselves

When I was in college, I played with a "combo"—a few of my friends who, for a fee, would provide live music at parties and celebrations. We were not very good and were not successful, but as a result of this experience I wrote a song. I asked my uncle, who was in the music industry, how I could protect it, and he suggested obtaining a copyright. The process was simple, and the cost low, so I went ahead and obtained a formal notice from the United States Copyright Office indicating that my song, entitled "Ice Blue Eyes," was now protected by a copyright. The copyright meant that no one could use the song without my express permission.

Songs are only one of the things for which copyrights protection can be obtained. Basically, copyright protection can be applied to anything that is original, non-functional (it doesn't *do* anything), and—most important—fixed in a tangible medium of expression. My song could be copyrighted because I wrote it down on music paper, and sent that to the Copyright Office. Other items for which copyright can be obtained include plays, pictures, photos, sculpture, computer software, rugs, and even wallpaper. Copyright cannot be obtained for furniture, however, because it is functional—it does something.

This book, as you can probably guess, is protected by copyright: it cannot be reproduced or copied without permission of the copyright holder (which in this case is the publisher). Here is a crucial point: copyrights protect the tangible expression of ideas, but not the ideas themselves. For instance, while no one can reproduce this chapter without permission, they can, if they wish, use the same organization of topics. Here's another example: in some of my other books, I use graphs that include special labels describing and calling attention to the results shown. While the specific graphs can be protected by copyright so that no one can reproduce them without the copyright holder's permission, the idea for these special labels on the graphs cannot itself be protected: other authors can use it if they wish—and occasionally some have!

What rights do copyrights confer? Basically, they stop others from reproducing the work, distributing copies of it, performing it or displaying it without the permission of the owner. Copyrights are relatively easy to obtain. An official copyright can be obtained by requesting one from the United States Copyright Office; the fees are modest—less than $100. But this is not necessary: simply placing the symbol © or the word "Copyright" on the tangible expression of the work (song, book, picture, etc.) can provide such protection. So copyrights are relatively easy to obtain, and they last a long time: the life of the author plus 90 years, or 95 years from the date of publication for "works for hire"—for instance, a book written by an author who receives royalties or other payments from a publisher. These features make copyright protection attractive, but again it's important to remember that only the tangible expression of the ideas is protected—not the ideas themselves. For instance, although the words in a book are protected and others can't copy or reproduce them, the ideas expressed in the words are not protected. In short, copyright protection is easy to obtain, but—in certain respects—not very powerful.

Trademarks and servicemarks: images representing companies or products

A second type of legal protection for intellectual property is a trademark, which refers to a word, phrase, symbol, or design that identifies the products of one person (which, in legal terms, means an individual, partnership, corporation, or association) and distinguishes these products from those of other individuals. Servicemarks identify the services of one person (again, as legally defined, which means corporations as well as individuals) from those of others. One example of a trademark is the McDonald's Golden Arches; another is Microsoft's symbol for Windows. An example of a servicemark is the symbol for Greyhound Lines, since it identifies the service provided by this company. Trademarks and servicemarks are useful to entrepreneurs because they help potential customers to clearly identify the source of a product or service, and therefore its quality. For instance, the trademark "Intel Inside" indicates to consumers that the product in question contains the "genuine article"—chips manufactured by Intel Corporation.

The value of a trademark is determined, to a large extent, by the degree to which it uniquely identifies products or services, and distinguishes them from those of other sources. The strongest trademarks are described as *arbitrary*: they have nothing directly to do with the products or services offered. For instance, the trademark for Google is arbitrary: the word "Google" has nothing directly to do with search engines, e-mail, or other services provided by this company. The symbol for Target Corporation is another; this symbol is widely recognized, but is not directly related to the products and services this chain of discount stores provides.

Somewhat less strong are trademarks or servicemarks that are suggestive of the products or services they represent. For instance, Igloo Corporation makes a line of coolers, and the word "Igloo" is suggestive of cold. Even less useful are trademarks or servicemarks that are descriptive of the products or services they represent—for instance, General Motors and IBM, since both refer directly to the products the companies provide. Least useful of all are trademarks or servicemarks that are so well known that they have become generic—they are widely used to represent a class of products or services, and have virtually become words in the vocabulary of most persons. A few examples include Scotch Tape, Kleenex, and

Arbitrary	Suggestive	Descriptive	Generic
Strongest	·····························▶		Weakest

		Examples	
Apple Computer	Igloo coolers	IBM	Xerox
McDonald's	Quicken	GM	Kleenex
Google	Nautica	TurboTax	Scotch Tape

Note: Trademarks are a word, phrase, symbol, or design that identifies the products of a company, partnership, or association, and distinguishes them from others. The more arbitrary the trademarks—that is, the less they are directly related to the products or services offered—the stronger the protection they offer. The examples above illustrate trademarks that are arbitrary, suggestive, descriptive, and generic. The strength of the trademarks declines across this dimension.

Figure 6.2   *Trademarks and servicemarks: the more arbitrary, the stronger the protection they provide*

Xerox (which is now widely used not just for Xerox Corporation, but for all copiers). (See Figure 6.2.)

Trademarks and servicemarks can be obtained in two ways: by actually using the mark or by filing an application with the U.S. Patent and Trademark Office. Actual use involves placing the appropriate symbol—®, ™, SM—on the trademark or servicemark. The right to use a particular trademark—for example, the Coca-Cola name—belongs to the first party to register or use the trademark, unless there is a conflict over its use. If there is a conflict, the courts decide who has the rights to use the trademark. In general, the courts will not allow more than one company to use the same trademark if consumers would be likely to associate the goods of one party with those of another, and as a result some trademarks become famous indeed. The costs of obtaining "official" trademark or servicemark registration are modest.

Patents: the right to exclude others from developing or using ideas or inventions

Now we come to what is, perhaps, the most important legal form of protection for ideas or inventions: patents. There is a great deal of confusion about what patents are and what they provide, so let's begin by making one point crystal clear. Patents grant the patent holder the right to exclude others from making, using, or selling an invention. They are granted by the government of a given country, and last for a particular period of time (in the United States, 20 years from the date on which a patent application is first filed). Recall that Thomas Jefferson was against the idea of patents—he felt that ideas could not be the exclusive property of the people who originated them. But, in fact, there is a strong rationale for the existence of patents: yes, the patent holder has an exclusive right to the invention and its use, but in return she or he must provide full disclosure as to how the invention works. So it is a kind of bargain: society grants the patent holder exclusive rights to the idea and inventions based on it, but only for a specific period of time, after which anyone can produce, sell, or use it. So both parties gain: society gains valuable information, and patent holders are given the exclusive opportunity to develop their inventions and ideas and profit from them.

Can all inventions be patented? Absolutely not. In the United States, and most other countries, three basic conditions must be met to obtain a patent: the invention must be useful (or at least potentially useful); it must be new—something that does not already exist; and it must be non-obvious, meaning that it should not be obvious to anyone familiar with the relevant field and existing products. If almost anyone working in a given field or industry could come up with the same idea because it is clearly suggested by existing products or services, then it cannot be patented.

A key term relating to these criteria is *prior art*, which refers to all information that has been made available to the public in any form before a given date that might be relevant to a patent's claims of originality. If an invention has been described in prior art, a patent on that invention cannot be granted. So, for instance, if an invention has been described in the press or at a convention, or discussed in a magazine article, it may not be eligible for a patent. The reasoning is: Why should society grant an exclusive right to someone for an idea or invention that is already known? Does this mean that an invention should be kept totally secret until it is patented? Yes and no. In the United States, the inventor has one year from the time information about an invention is made public to file for a patent. As long as the application is submitted during that period, the invention is still eligible for a patent.

This raises an important question: Who determines whether an invention is or is not eligible for a patent? In other words, who decides whether an invention meets the criteria of being new, non-obvious, and useful? The answer is: the patent examiner—the person who evaluates a submitted patent application. Presumably the patent examiner is someone with considerable knowledge in the field of the invention. For instance, if a patent application involves a new kind of air cleaner (as one of my own patents did), the patent examiner would presumably be someone with expertise concerning air cleaners and existing "prior art" in that field. As a result, she or he can make an informed judgment about whether the invention is really new, useful, and non-obvious. Some very famous individuals

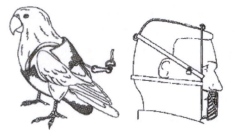

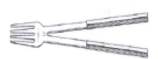

Bird diaper   Anti-eating mask   Replacement for chopsticks

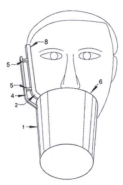

Device for curing hiccups

Note: Patent examiners decide whether a given invention meets the criteria for receiving a patent. All the inventions shown here received patents, but different people might well disagree about how useful they are!

Source: U.S. Patent and Trademark Office website, www.USPTO.gov.

Figure 6.3   *Are all these devices useful? All received patents!*

have been patent examiners during their careers—for instance, Albert Einstein—and in general the people who hold this position are very careful and knowledgeable. But, since the system involves human judgment, there is lots of room for disagreement or even error. For example, consider the devices shown in Figure 6.3. Are they all useful? Truly new? Truly non-obvious? All actually received patents, but different people might well disagree about the extent to which each meets these basic criteria.

What kind of inventions can be patented? The list includes various kinds of machines, processes (e.g., start with a set of ingredients and, through various actions, obtain various products), chemical formulas, software, drugs—virtually any new product. Among the things that can't be patented, however, are a business idea (e.g., the idea of selling fast food in a drive-through window).

Patents on most inventions qualify for what are known as *utility patents*: patents for new processes, machines, devices, and so on—something, in short, that *does* something or, at least, in which something (e.g., a process) happens. In addition, inventors can also obtain what are known as *design patents*: patents on original designs for manufactured products—the ornamental design or appearance of a functional item. For instance, the design of the classic Coca-Cola bottle is eligible for a design patent. While utility patents protect the way an invention works, design patents protect the way it looks; they are good for 14 years, rather than 20 years.

Another type of patent is for plants—*plant patents*—which protect grafted or crossbred plants. For example, Tropicana recently sued Florida orange growers who used experimental varieties of oranges that Tropicana had developed for a particular brand of premium orange juice. Because Tropicana had patented these varieties, it argued that the orange growers should be barred from using these varieties without license from Tropicana. Finally, very recently, the courts have allowed inventors to patent "business methods," such as Amazon.com's 1-Click system, which permits repeat purchasers to make purchases without reentering basic information about themselves.

How are patents obtained? I have been through the process four times, and my overall comment is: not very easily. To obtain a patent, an inventor files an application with the U.S. Patent and Trademark Office. The patent examiner assigned to the application then evaluates the invention in terms of the three basic criteria discussed earlier: newness, usefulness, and non-obviousness. The heart of a patent application is the claims. These are legal statements about what was invented. Inventors and their patent attorneys write these claims very carefully and try to make them as broad as possible for the following reason: a patent precludes other people from duplicating or using only those things stated in the claims. For example, a claim in one of my own patents (patent number 5,360,469) reads as follows:

> We claim an apparatus for enhancing the environmental quality of work and living spaces consisting essentially of (1) a portable housing, (2) a high efficiency filter mounted in such housing, (3) a means of generating airflow through the filter, (4) a means for generating sound such that . . . the noise of the motor is eliminated by this sound.

The patent examiner accepted these claims, and this gave us very strong protection, since any product that included these basic elements (e.g., a filter, a means for producing airflow, and a mechanism for generating sounds that "masked"—that is, reduced—the noise of the motor) would be in violation of our patent. If, instead, our claims had been more specific (e.g., they were restricted to only one kind of filter, one means of generating airflow, etc.), they would have been weaker. The strength of the claims in this product was one reason why my company was able to license this patent and this product to a large company, which produced it and paid us a royalty on each unit sold.

Unfortunately, obtaining a patent is a long and often expensive process: it takes an average of two years for a patent to be issued. Further, the costs are substantial: $10,000–$15,000 is not unusual, because patent attorneys are—to be frank—expensive! As a result of this fact, and because it takes on average two years for an accepted patent to be issued, many inventors first file a provisional patent application. The application for a provisional patent is a much simpler document, the costs are lower, and it does provide a record of the date on which the inventor had the idea. That is very important, because in the United States a patent can be issued only to the first person to have an idea. (In other countries, in contrast, the patent goes to the first person to file an application—even if another person created the invention earlier.) There are other ways of establishing this date, for example public disclosure of the idea and invention in a newspaper or magazine. Once that is done, however, the inventor (in the U.S.) has only one year to file a patent application, after which she or he is no longer eligible for a patent on this invention. This also applies to provisional patent applications: after one year, a regular application must be filed or the inventor loses her or his claim to the invention.

Patents can be very valuable tools for entrepreneurs, but they do involve certain disadvantages. As we noted earlier, they can be very expensive ($10,000–$15,000 is an average), and defending them can involve truly huge costs. Further, they are not always effective in preventing others from developing very similar products. Finally, the fact that they require full disclosure of the invention can make it relatively easy for others to imitate it or do what is known as *invent around* the patent.

In essence, this means coming up with a product that accomplishes the same things as the original invention, but does not violate the claims in its patent. This is much easier in some industries and with certain kinds of products than for others. For instance, consider Apple Computer's iPad. Truly, this was a breakthrough product, and sales have exceeded expectations (many millions on a single year). Certainly, Apple obtained a number of patents to protect the uniqueness of the iPad, but, as you probably know, this has not stopped many other companies from developing highly similar products. While these products differ from the iPad in various respects (e.g., they use different operating systems, or offer different features), they are providing competition for the iPad. Clearly, the companies that produce these competing products used their own technology expertise to "invent around" Apple's patents so that they could quickly manufacture and sell similar products. In high-tech industries, where progress is often amazingly rapid, this is a common situation, and it is often possible for competing firms to invent around each other's patents.

The situation is very different in the biotech industry. Here, when a new drug is developed and patented, it is very difficult to invent around it. Even a slight change in the drug's molecular structure can greatly alter its effectiveness. That's why large pharmaceutical companies reap huge profits from their patented drugs: until the patents expire, no one else can produce directly competing products. I had a first-hand experience with this fact recently, when my physician prescribed a drug whose patent had expired—it could be obtained as a generic drug; a six-month supply cost me only $50. Then the physician switched me to a time-release version of the same drug—a version that was still under patent protection. The cost? $100 for a two-week supply! Apparently, the patent protecting this drug was so strong that no one could make a competing version. In cases like this one, patents are extremely valuable to the companies or persons who hold them. We'll return to this issue in a later discussion of the questions "Should entrepreneurs seek patents or other intellectual property protection—and if so when?"

One more point about patents should also be noted: unfortunately, there is no such thing as an international patent. Patents are granted by national governments, so an inventor needs to obtain a patent in every country where she or he wants to protect an invention. This poses a major obstacle for entrepreneurs. Obtaining patents is expensive, and the need to patent in many countries means that these costs are multiplied. Second, failure to patent in a particular country means that it is legal for people in that country to imitate the invention. Since receiving a patent in the United States requires full disclosure about how the invention works, this means that, if an inventor receives a U.S. patent but does not seek patents in other countries, inventors and companies in those other countries know how the invention works but are not legally prevented from manufacturing it. Clearly, that's not a very favorable position for an inventor!

Fortunately, a mechanism that simplifies obtaining patents in many different countries does exist. It is known as the Patent Cooperation Treaty (PCT), and allows inventors to file a single application with the PCT Office. The application is then filed in a large number of countries, thus establishing a filing date in each of these countries. (Remember: in most countries the first person to file is the one who receives the patent—not the first person to come up with an idea for an invention.) The fees for this service can be very large, and there is no guarantee that each country will grant a patent. But at least the overall process is somewhat simplified.

In summary, patents can, and often do, offer important legal protection for entrepreneurs: they effectively prevent others from copying or selling the entrepreneurs' inventions. The strength of this protection depends heavily on the claims, however, and, since patents require full disclosure of how an invention actually works, they also make it possible for potential competitors to invent around the patents. Whether seeking patent protection is or is not a useful strategy for entrepreneurs, therefore, is a complex issue, and entrepreneurs should never assume that paying the costs involved is a good use of their limited financial resources. We'll return to this issue in more detail below.

When should entrepreneurs seek legal protection for their ideas or inventions?

Do you recall the inventions shown in Figure 6.3? All are interesting, but it seems clear that all are not useful, and thus would probably have limited markets at best. Yet they were all granted patents. This fact—which you may well find surprising—contains an important moral for entrepreneurs, one having to do with the question "When should entrepreneurs seek legal protection for their ideas and inventions?" Recall that obtaining a patent is a long and often costly process ($10,000–$15,000 is not at all unusual). So one basic answer to the "when" question is this: "Entrepreneurs should seek patent protection only when they have reason to believe that their product or service has economic value—when it can be the basis for a business or other activity that can actually yield tangible benefits." If an invention offers little or no chance of such outcomes, my advice would be simple: don't bother; neither the expense nor the effort involved in obtaining legal protection for the idea or invention is justified. Why, then, do so many individuals seek patents even when this basic criterion isn't met? One answer is that they are truly inventors: they love the ideas they generate, and don't really care deeply if these ideas turn into anything useful or generate tangible benefits. I had a partner who fitted this description: he loved to tinker in the laboratory, and the more ideas for new products he generated, the happier he was. Further, he felt that obtaining a patent for these ideas was almost an end in itself: it essentially "certified" his ideas as good ones, and him as a true inventor. There is nothing wrong with this approach, but it is not, in my view, a basis for entrepreneurship. That occurs only when individuals work hard and actively to convert their ideas into something real and useful. So beware of pure inventors: often they do not make successful entrepreneurs, and this can sometimes prevent the entrepreneurial process from proceeding in constructive ways.

Intellectual property protection based on business practices and strategies

Legal forms of protection for intellectual property can be highly effective. But, as we noted earlier, they are far from perfect in terms of protecting new ideas and inventions. Fortunately, however, there are other forms of protections available to entrepreneurs—forms that do not involve the services of attorneys or even, directly, regulations established by various government agencies. These additional forms are based primarily on business practices and strategies, and can be highly effective—although, again, they are far from perfect. We'll now review several of these, including trade secrets, the first mover advantage (which, it turns out, can also be a first mover *dis*advantage; e.g., Dobrev and Gotsopoulos, 2010), and complementary assets.

Trade secrets: gaining protection by keeping information private

Have you ever eaten at Kentucky Fried Chicken? If so, or even if you have merely seen their ads, you know that they use a "secret recipe" to prepare their chicken, one that cannot, supposedly, be duplicated anywhere else. Similarly, have you ever drunk Coca-Cola? If so, you may know that the recipe for this soft drink is secret: there are many imitators, but, at least according to Coca-Cola Company, none match its unique taste. When companies seek to protect their products or inventions in this way, they are using trade secrets. In a sense, this is a means for obtaining protection that is exactly the opposite to that provided by patents. Patents require inventors to disclose how their inventions work. Trade secrets, in contrast, are the sole property of the companies that own them. For this reason, trade secrets are not part of the legal system for protecting intellectual property, although they can become part of this system if they are stolen—become known to others without their owners' permission.

The biggest advantage of trade secrets is that they provide a way for entrepreneurs to protect their products or inventions without telling others how these are made (e.g., as in the formula for Coca-Cola) or work. This can be a big advantage, but it involves disadvantages too. First, to continue providing protection, a trade secret must be kept hidden. If it becomes public—for example, if it is accidentally revealed, or a disgruntled employee makes it public—it is no longer a trade secret. This is one reason why many companies insist that their employees sign non-disclosure forms, agreeing to keep trade secrets confidential; and it is why companies like Coca-Cola keep their trade secrets (e.g., the formula for "classic Coke") under lock and key, and make them available only to a small number of top people in the company. Second, in contrast to patents, trade secrets don't provide inventors with exclusive rights to their product or inventions. If a competitor discovers how the product is made or how it works, the competitor is free to use it too.

If trade secrets somehow leak out and this damages the company that owns them, it can form the basis for legal proceedings against competitors. The chances of winning in court are very low, however, unless the company that owns the secret can prove that it took reasonable steps to protect it—to keep it secret. For instance, the chemical formula for Coca-Cola is a trade secret, and only three executives in the company are allowed to see the formula, which is kept hidden in a vault in a bank in Atlanta. Only if there is clear evidence that the owner of a trade secret took adequate precautions to protect it are courts likely to take action against competitors who obtain and use the secret. The burden of proof is with the owners, not the competitors who have somehow obtained access to the key trade secrets.

The first mover advantage: the potential benefits of being first

Earlier, we noted that Apple's iPad faces competition from other companies that have, to some degree, managed to "invent around" Apple's patents for this new device. Yet, despite this fact, Apple still possesses what is known as a *first mover advantage* with respect to this product. It was the first to bring it to market, and as a result it has an important edge over its competitors, which, in a sense, are trying their best to catch up.

Is the first mover advantage real? Is it always best to be first to market with a new product, process, or service? Often it is, but not always. For instance, research findings indicate that entrepreneurs who obtain control of important resources before their competitors can do so often gain a key advantage (Lieberman and Montgomery, 1988). In the oil industry, for instance, entrepreneurs who bought the rights to drill on land where oil was likely to be located gained a major advantage over competitors, and they gained it by taking action first.

Second, being a first mover provides entrepreneurs with an advantage because it helps them to build a large customer base. For instance, when people want to buy something on the internet, they often go to Amazon. com or eBay.com first. These companies were both "first movers," and established huge customer bases before competitors could do so. That continues to give them a big advantage, even though many other competing sites now exist. Third, first movers often gain an advantage from the fact that, once their products or services are established, there may be significant costs to customers for switching to products offered by competitors. Consider the iPad once again. Millions of people now own one and are familiar with how this device operates. The products offered by competitors may be just as good in many respects, but switching to them would require customers to learn how to operate them—and that may or may not be very easy. This means that competitors who are not first movers must offer products that are clearly superior to the first ones, significantly lower in price, or both, to make it worthwhile for customers to switch.

Yet another advantage of being a first mover is that it often provides a strong reputation for the entrepreneurs or companies involved. The iPod is another example from Apple Computer—a company that has adopted "being first" with innovations as a basic business strategy. The iPod was the first MP3 player to gain huge sales, and as a result it is still, in many people's minds, the best. This perception is helped along by the fact that, even in hotels, the alarm clocks now often have a dock for the iPod—one that won't accept other MP3 players. So being first does indeed pay off handsomely in some instances.

As is true with almost any business strategy (or, in fact, almost anything!), being first has a downside, too—in fact, there is sometimes a strong first mover disadvantage, as suggested by the phrase "first to market, first to fail" (Dobrev and Gotsopoulos, 2010; Suarez and Lanzolla, 2007). Being a first mover sometimes simply shows potential competitors how to imitate an entrepreneur's products—especially if they are not protected by very strong patents. Second, in their rush to be first, some entrepreneurs bring products or services to market that are not really fully ready. Flaws become apparent to users, and this can pave the way for competitors to enter later, with better products. This sometimes happens even to very successful and experienced companies. For example, in the 1970s and 1980s, Sony Corporation—a company, like Apple, founded on the principle of being first with innovative products—launched a type of video recorder, the Betamax. It worked well, but had important limitations; for instance, it could record only two hours of material. Other companies, recognizing the huge potential market for such a product, soon developed their own video recorders using a different system—the VHS system. In a sense, they invented around Sony's patents. The VHS recorders did not perform as well as Sony's products in some ways, but were superior in the features that customers cared about most, such as length of recordings; they were also lower in price. The result? Sony's first mover advantage quickly disappeared, and its product ultimately vanished from the market. In cases like this, being first is not necessarily an advantage. In many instances, though, the entrepreneurs and companies that bring new products to market first do gain an edge, which it is often difficult for competitors to overcome.

Additional problems occur for first movers in new industries or markets, where they lack legitimacy (Dobrev and Gotsopoulos, 2010). This can lead founders to spend a large portion of their time attempting to increase the company's legitimacy—and that can interfere with their efforts to run the new venture effectively. Overall, the bottom line seems to be this: it may pay, handsomely, to be a first mover but only if (1) your product is really ready for the market—the major "bugs" have been removed; (2) costs to customers for switching from your product to ones that appear later are high; and (3) the company has, or can attain, legitimacy quickly in a new industry, where such legitimacy is often lacking.

Note: Complementary assets are assets that enable customers to use a new product. Internal combustion engines became dominant in the automobile industry because drivers could obtain fuel for them easily (the oil industry saw to that!). Can electric cars, such as those produced by Tesla Motors, succeed? Only if consumers can recharge them wherever they travel. Without such complementary assets, Tesla's products may not succeed even if they are superior in many ways and are protected by very strong patents. At present, recharging stations are rare; for instance, only three exist in the entire state of Ohio.

Source: Courtesy of Tesla Motors, Inc.

Figure 6.4   *Control of complementary assets*

Control of complementary assets: preventing customers from using competing products

At the present time, several new ventures are investing huge amounts of time, talent, and capital in efforts to develop a practical electric car. Tesla Motors is, perhaps, the one that is farthest along in this process of innovation, and it has already invested several hundred millions in developing such a vehicle—much of these funds provided by Tesla's founder, Elon Musk. (Musk is an entrepreneur who has earned hundreds of millions from previous new ventures such as PayPal.) The results are very encouraging from a technical point of view: Tesla models can travel up to 300 miles before requiring a charge, produce zero emissions, and are excellent performers (see Figure 6.4). The price is still very high (more than $100,000 for the roadster, and more than $50,000 for the sedan), but Tesla has patent protection for certain features of its power train, and it would be difficult for competitors to imitate its products. Despite this fact, however, the company faces a very key problem: it lacks control of crucial complementary assets—assets needed for the use and sales of its products. Complementary assets involve infrastructure or capabilities needed to support the commercialization and marketing of a new product—to make it possible and convenient for customers actually to use it. What complementary assets are needed for Tesla's products to be successful? Primarily, a large network of places where drivers can recharge their vehicles. Until—and unless—Tesla can gain control of these assets, it faces a very difficult task in terms of marketing its cars.

Vehicles powered by internal combustion engines, in contrast, are no longer protected by patents on the drive train—such protection generally expired long ago (recall that patents are time limited). But the continued dominance of such vehicles in the marketplace is virtually assured (at least for now) by the fact that gasoline, the fuel for vehicles powered by internal combustion engines, is available almost everywhere. In this case, then, it is not legal protections that make these products successful and prevent others from inventing practical automobiles: it is the fact that complementary assets support gasoline-powered vehicles, and are not present for other vehicles, such as Tesla's battery-powered models.

Will Tesla obtain such complementary assets? Clearly, the oil industry will be reluctant to include recharging stations in the thousands of service stations they own; that would be virtually suicidal from the point of view of their own profits. And the automobile industry, too, is not eager to see the dominant design it has used for many years (based on the internal combustion engine) replaced by something quite new: that would require huge costs of retooling and other expenses, and reduce or eliminate some of the profits from parts and service. So, although Tesla Motors offers vehicles with impressive qualities, and ones that can't be readily produced by competitors, the company will not be able to achieve a mass market until it also has control of, or at least access to, essential complementary assets. The result? Consumers will continue to buy vehicles powered by internal combustion engines (or hybrid vehicles that run partly on such engines and partly on conventional electric motors), even if they wish to "go green" and reduce dependence on fossil fuels.

In sum, there are several ways in which new ideas and products can be protected apart from those provided by copyrights, trademarks, and patents. In fact, sometimes the protection offered by trade secrets, being the first to offer a new product, and gaining control of complementary assets is considerably stronger.

Summary of key points

Creativity and the ideas it generates are the source of entrepreneurship, but, unless the persons who generate them convert these ideas into something tangible, that can be the end of the process. Entrepreneurs are, in a sense, the people who take this crucial step. When they do, they must also seek to protect their ideas and inventions from use by others. History is filled with sad stories of entrepreneurs who did not take steps to obtain protection, and so failed to benefit from their ideas. Two examples are provided by Antonio Meucci, who invented the telephone long before Alexander Graham Bell, and Joseph Swan, who invented a practical incandescent light bulb years before Thomas Edison developed the same product.

One way entrepreneurs can protect their ideas is through the legal system. Several types of protection, including copyrights, trademarks, and patents, exist. Copyrights prevent others from reproducing the work, distributing copies of it, performing it or displaying it without the permission of the copyright owner. Copyrights do not protect ideas, however, but only the tangible expression of these ideas—for instance, the words in this book, but not the ideas they present. Trademarks and servicemarks are words, phrases, symbols, and designs that identify the products or services of an individual, partnership, corporation, or association, and distinguish them from the products or services of others. Trademarks are strongest when they are arbitrary (not representative of the product or service in question, e.g., Google's trademark), and weakest when they are generic (that is, they represent an entire category of products, e.g., Scotch Tape).

Patents grant the patent holder the right to exclude others from making, using, or selling an invention. They are granted by the government of a given country and last for a particular period of time (in the United States, 20 years from the date on which a patent application is first filed). The heart of patents is the claims—legal statements about the nature of the invention. The broader these claims, the stronger the protection offered by the patent. Patents require inventors to provide full disclosure about how their inventions work, and this opens the door for others to "invent around the patent"—to make products that accomplish the same functions as the original invention, but do it in ways that do not violate the claims in the existing patent(s). This is easier in some industries (e.g., high-tech) than in others (e.g., drugs), but it is always a potential problem for patent holders. Patents are expensive to obtain, so entrepreneurs should seek them only if their inventions have real potential for generating benefits. In the United States, a patent is issued to the first person to create an idea or invention, while in most other countries it is issued to the first person to file for a patent application.

Ideas and inventions can also be protected outside the legal system through trade secrets (e.g., the formula for Coca-Cola), being a first mover, or acquiring control of, or at least providing, complementary assets—assets essential for the use and marketing of an innovative new product. For instance, manufacturers of electric vehicles (e.g., Tesla Motors) will not be able to generate substantial sales or profits, even if their cars are superior and they have strong patent protection, unless they can also control, or at least provide, essential complementary assets—for instance, a large network of places where drivers can recharge their vehicles.

Bibliography

Dobrev, S.D., and Gotsopoulos, A. (2010). Legitimacy vacuum, structural imprinting, and the first mover disadvantage. *Academy of Management Journal*, *53*, 1153–1174.

Lieberman, M., and Montgomery, C. (1988). First mover advantages. *Strategic Management Journal*, *9*, 41–58.

Short, J.C., and Payne, G.T. (2008). First movers and performance: Timing is everything. *Academy of Management Review*, *33*, 267–269.

Suarez, F.F., and Lanzolla, G. (2007). The role of environmental dynamics in building a first mover advantage theory. *Academy of Management Review*, *39*, 377–392.

7   Planning for success: where goals and creativity meet

• •

Chapter outline

Formal planning: business plans and business models
  Why write a business plan? Potential benefits—and potential costs
  Business plans: their basic parts
  Business plans: the key to success?
The importance of improvisation: making it up as you go along
  Improvisation and firm performance: the benefits of flexibility
Effectuation: using what you have to get where you want to go

> A goal without a plan is just a wish. (Antoine de Saint-Exupéry)

> Just because something doesn't do what you planned it to do doesn't mean
> it's useless. (Thomas Edison)

Even in a world where many people rely on their GPSs to get them to their destinations, few would leave home without some kind of plan. At the very least, they know where they want to go—some address, a restaurant, a business, some specific destination. So, despite the marvels of our high-tech age, planning certainly remains as a key part of life. In the field of entrepreneurship, it is often viewed as especially important. The business plan—a detailed, written plan explaining how entrepreneurs will actually convert their ideas into reality (a new, profitable business or some other kind of beneficial outcome)—has been virtually enthroned as perhaps the single most important activity entrepreneurs can perform before they launch their companies. Entire courses are devoted to this topic, and in many others students must prepare business plans, in one form or another, as part of the basic requirements. The overall message in this emphasis is clear and, to a degree, highly appropriate: planning is indeed essential for actually implementing the ideas generated by creativity. Further, careful planning is vital for obtaining the financial and human resources needed to accomplish this task. Would anyone advance large sums of money to entrepreneurs who did not have specific plans for developing their ideas into actual businesses? Probably not. And would anyone (especially individuals with high levels of talent, skill, or experience) choose to join a new venture that did not have clear and specific plans for attaining success? Again, probably not; they might be destroying their own careers. In short, planning is essential and must be part of the process of converting ideas into something new and useful. As one of the quotations above suggests, without specific plans, goals, whatever they are (e.g., the desire to obtain personal wealth, or to contribute to the welfare of society), are indeed merely wishes: they describe outcomes entrepreneurs would like to obtain, but don't indicate how they can be attained.

On the other hand, it is clear that planning isn't all there is to entrepreneurship. As John Lennon once remarked: "Life is what happens while we are busy making other plans." In fact, situations often change so rapidly and unpredictably that the plans we make are outdated before they can be implemented. This happens in many contexts other than the business world—for instance, what happened in Europe after World War I. The French military, seeking to block any future invasions from Germany, invested tremendous sums in the construction of a seemingly impregnable array of fortifications along the border between the two countries—the Maginot Line. The idea was that these fortifications would successfully prevent a German invasion such as the one that occurred in 1914. In reality, though, the forts turned out to be worse than useless: in World War II the German army, highly mobile, simply went around them, thus trapping and essentially neutralizing a large portion of the French army, which could not, therefore, assist in the rapidly evolving battle which ended in France's swift defeat. In this case, and many others, planning—although carried out by experts with painstaking precision—was indeed far from helpful (see Figure 7.1).

The same basic principle applies to entrepreneurship: although planning is indeed essential and often useful, there must also be room for improvisation—flexibility that allows for mid-course corrections and changes. Research findings indicate that many entrepreneurs engage in improvisation as standard practice, and that doing so can be very beneficial to their efforts to create successful new ventures (e.g., Hmieleski and Corbett, 2008). Similarly, growing evidence suggests that entrepreneurs often adopt an approach known as *effectuation*—a perspective that takes careful note of the fact that, although the future is unpredictable, it can be shaped by human action (e.g., Sarasvathy, 2001, 2008). This implies a kind of logic that is, in a sense, the inverse of the causal reasoning that forms the basis for science, and for traditional views of entrepreneurship. In causal logic, individuals begin with specific goals and then concentrate on ways of reaching those goals. In effectual logic, in contrast, they consider what means and resources are available to them (their own skills, talents, characteristics, knowledge, and social networks). Then, on the basis of these means or resources, they choose various goals they might be able to attain

Note: After World War I, the French military command constructed a series of supposedly impregnable forts along the border with Germany—the Maginot Line. The planning was extremely careful, and the forts were built very well, yet they failed to protect France from German invasion. The German army, highly mobile, simply went around them. So much for the value of *those* detailed plans! A parallel question has been raised about business plans: Is the detailed planning they involve actually related to subsequent success? Existing evidence paints a mixed picture.

Figure 7.1   *Is detailed planning always useful?*

by using them. In other words, they ask "Given what I have, what can I actually accomplish?" and proceed from there.

We'll consider effectuation in detail in a later section, but, to make its essential nature clear, let's consider an example of effectuation in action. Imagine an entrepreneur who has launched a gourmet restaurant, one that, like many high-end restaurants, is open only for dinner. Each day, the chef wants to include one or more special dishes on the menu—ones that are not on the regular offerings. One approach to this task would be for the chef to consult her or his file of recipes or library of cookbooks or to search for ideas for new dishes online. That would be an example of causal reasoning: the chef first chooses a goal (preparing a new, special dish) and then identifies what is needed to attain it (ingredients, cooking utensils, etc.). On the other hand, the chef could (as many do) visit the nearby wholesale markets to see what ingredients are available. On the basis of what she or he finds, the chef then proceeds to plan the day's "specials" using what is available in the market. In this case, the chef does not begin with a clear goal in mind (a particular dish), but rather develops this goal (special dishes she or he wants to prepare) on the basis of available means. Similarly, an entrepreneur applying effectuation might begin by considering what resources she or he has available, and move from there to choosing a business opportunity to develop—one for which these resources would be appropriate. We'll examine effectuation in more detail in a later section, but introduce it here because it represents an intriguing alternative to standard views of how entrepreneurship unfolds.

After these basic points, the remainder of this chapter will proceed as follows. First, business plans—what they are, why they are important, and their role in entrepreneurship—will be examined. Then attention will be shifted to improvisation, which involves the capacity to implement mid-course changes in strategy or actions in order to respond effectively to rapidly changing conditions and new opportunities (e.g., Baker, Miner, and Eesley, 2003). Finally, we'll turn once again to effectuation and its implications for traditional models of entrepreneurship, which strongly emphasize detailed business models and plans: detailed roadmaps for how a new venture or other entrepreneurial activity will create value—economic, social, or otherwise.

Formal planning: business plans and business models

At my university, and most others, some of the most exciting events that occur during the academic year involve various business plan competitions. Teams of students who have drawn on their own creativity to generate ideas for new products, services, markets, or means of production prepare formal business plans—documents describing how, in specific terms, they will convert these ideas into companies that generate value. Then teams of judges (generally highly experienced entrepreneurs and faculty members with entrepreneurial experience) evaluate these plans and select the winners. Winning is not just an honor: many of the competitions involve substantial cash prizes—funds the winning teams can use to start or grow their new ventures. Further, winning teams can advance to national competitions in which they vie with teams from many universities for even larger prizes. Overall, these are very exciting events and are a central focus of entrepreneurship faculty and the schools of management or business in which they work. Since business plans are the "entry card" for such competitions, this is one strong reason why would-be entrepreneurs invest the effort required to prepare them; and make no mistake—this effort is usually substantial, requiring many hours of highly focused work. Is gaining entry to such competitions the only potential benefit writing business plans provides? Far from it. As we'll now note, writing a business plan offers other important advantages—and, since there are few true "freebies" in life, some significant costs as well.

Why write a business plan? Potential benefits—and potential costs

Preparing a business plan involves a lot of hard work. In fact, as noted above, it usually requires many hours of careful thought, followed by the complex process of converting these ideas into a document that must follow a fairly specific format. While university professors may enjoy such activities (!), entrepreneurs generally do not. Often they are eager to get started— to launch their business and make their visions happen. And many realize that, once their new venture has been started, it will rarely follow the steps and strategies outlined in the business plan, and—moreover—preparing such a plan may not necessarily be closely related to the new venture's success, an idea supported by research findings we'll soon review.

Why, then, should entrepreneurs invest the time, energy, and effort required to generate a first-rate business plan, aside from the cash prizes it may bring in business plan competitions and the contacts with venture capitalists or other sources of financial support it may generate? Basically, the answer involves two important reasons. The first is that excellent business plans do indeed often provide a good foundation for acquiring valuable resources needed by a new venture: they help secure financial support from venture capitalists and others, and help attract excellent employees. In a sense, then, business plans are a "selling tool"—one that helps the entrepreneurs promote their ideas in ways that ultimately provide the resources needed to implement them.

Second, and perhaps of equal importance, writing a first-rate business plan helps entrepreneurs sharpen their thinking about the opportunities they wish to pursue. Writing such a plan helps them understand the many complex issues and vast array of difficulties they will face. This, in turn, assists them in formulating clearer ideas about how they will meet these challenges and create a successful new company. Again, as the quotation above suggests, having goals is important, but, unless there is some plan for actually reaching them, progress is often unlikely. Writing a business plan requires an entrepreneur to formulate such plans, so the word *plan* in the term *business plans* is very appropriate: A comprehensive business plan describes the opportunity (e.g., what needs the new product or service will meet, what markets it will have), how the product or service will be produced or delivered, what skills and abilities the founding team brings to the new venture, how the new company will be structured, how the new venture will gain a competitive advantage, what critical risks it faces, what financial resources it needs, and so on. In addition, a well-prepared business plan contains a clear and well-developed business model—a model of how the new venture will actually operate and how it will generate value (economic, social, etc.) from its activities. In short, the effort invested in preparing a first-rate business plan provides entrepreneurs with enhanced understanding of what will actually be involved in converting their ideas into something tangible. Entrepreneurs, as a group, are often highly enthusiastic about the opportunities they seek to develop, and extremely optimistic about the likelihood of success. The discipline of preparing a detailed business plan can help to moderate these tendencies—which, as noted Chapter 4, can be very, very costly.

Clearly, then, the effort of preparing a detailed business plan can be beneficial in many ways. As we'll note in detail below, however, there are clear limits to these gains. No matter how carefully written or reasoned, business plans can't really predict the unpredictable (e.g., unexpected reactions from competitors) and can't foresee every possible change that may occur in the months or years ahead—just as the French military command was unable to foresee the high levels of mobility in the new German army, and how this new and unexpected factor would undermine its carefully developed plans for the defense of the country. As a result, business plans should be viewed as "living documents," guidelines for getting started—and getting support—but ones that will almost certainly be changed as the new venture develops.

We have emphasized the benefits of writing a formal business plan, but it's important to note that there is also a downside to this activity. First, as noted above, it requires many hours of hard, concentrated work. This means that entrepreneurs engaged in preparing a business plan have less time and energy available for other activities that may also be useful to them—for instance, expanding their social networks or working on product development. Certainly, highly motivated entrepreneurs can find time (somehow!) for doing these things too, but preparing a first-rate business plan is a major undertaking, so it does involve substantial costs in terms of entrepreneurs' time and energy. Second, and perhaps more importantly, the process of preparing a business plan may encourage the development of the kind of "mental ruts" described in Chapter 2: in essence, they may lock entrepreneurs into thinking about their ideas, new products or services, potential markets, and required resources in certain ways. As we noted in Chapter 2, such cognitive rigidity can be costly: remember, for instance, that because the Inca thought of wheeled vehicles merely as toys they never used them to move large loads of heavy items. Instead, they moved these loads by placing them on wooden sleds pulled by animals—a far less efficient technique. Writing an excellent, detailed business plan, in short, may tend to reduce entrepreneurs' capacity to think "outside the box"—in this case, a mental "box" created by their own repeated thoughts. Cognitive rigidity concerning ideas, opportunities, and how to develop them may also be increased by the verbal presentations entrepreneurs must give in various courses, business competitions, and other settings. The frequent repetition of information contained in these presentations may strengthen commitment to the ideas presented, and create strong barriers against information inconsistent with these established ideas.

Partly because of this fact, there has been a recent trend to make business plans briefer, and less filled with "bells and whistles" (e.g., detailed financial projections, multicolored illustrations) than has been true in the past. Since growing evidence suggests that preparation of excellent and detailed business plans is not always closely related to later success, this seems to make good sense: Why invest countless hours in an activity that may, or may not, contribute to the new venture's survival or growth? (Evidence on this issue is presented below.)

Overall, then, is it better to start with a long, detailed business plan or a shorter and simpler one? The answer (of course!) is "It depends." In some situations, a detailed plan is necessary—for instance, when large amounts of funding are required to launch the new venture, or the market for its products or services is not immediately clear. Detailed plans are essential in such cases, because in their absence investors may be very reluctant to get involved. In other situations—for instance, when entrepreneurs will provide their own funding (an approach known as bootstrapping)—a shorter and less detailed plan is sufficient. The guiding principle, then, is always to engage in careful preparation and planning, but to make flexibility part of the process, so that the plan is seen more as a reflection of the entrepreneurs' evolving thoughts and ideas, constantly adjusted in the face of new information, than as an unalterable, rigid guide to the future of the new venture and how it will develop.

Business plans: their basic parts

Let us assume that entrepreneurs have concluded that they do need a detailed business plan, because they want to enter plan competitions and ultimately attract a large amount of funding. What information should be included? Business plans certainly vary in the scope and arrangement of their content—hardly surprising, since the ideas for new ventures are unique. But in general they must contain information on the following issues:

- What is the basic idea for the new product or service? In other words, what is the opportunity being developed?
- Why is this new product useful or appealing—and what makes it unique?
- Who will find it useful and want to buy it?
- How will the idea for the new product or service be converted into reality? What is the plan for making the product (or providing the service), for marketing it, and for dealing with existing and future competition?

- What is the business model? How will the new venture operate, and how will it generate value (economic, social, etc.)?
- Who are the entrepreneurs? Do they have the required knowledge, experience, and skills to develop this idea and to run a new company?
- How will the new venture be structured, and how will it operate once it is launched?
- If the plan is designed to raise money, how much funding is needed, what type of financing is required, how will it be used, and how will both the entrepreneurs and other persons realize a return on their investment?

This is simply a list of some of the general issues that should be addressed. Usually, they are considered in much more detail in specific sections of the plan. These sections are shown in Table 7.1, where additional explanation concerning their content and structure is provided. Among the many parts of a business plan, perhaps the most important is the executive summary—a brief overview presented at the beginning. In fact, the executive summary is so important that it merits a closer look, and attention to why it is so crucial.

Have you ever heard the phrase *elevator pitch*? It refers to efforts to present—and promote—ideas to others in a very brief format; the name *elevator pitch* refers to the fact that the presentation should be one that can be made during an elevator ride—generally two minutes or less. (Of course, elevator rides in 100-plus-story office towers can last somewhat longer, but the basic idea is clear: keep it short, simple, and to the point!) In business plans, the essence of an elevator pitch is contained in the executive summary. This part of the business plan—which should truly be brief (two to three pages at most)—provides a summary of what the new venture is all about. In essence, it offers brief answers to several of the key questions listed earlier: What is the idea behind the opportunity—the idea for the new product or service? Why is it unique? Who will find it appealing, that is, what is the potential market? What's out there right now in terms of existing products or services, and who is the competition? Can all this be accomplished in two to three pages? Absolutely. But doing so requires very careful writing. The effort invested in crafting this section to make it crystal clear, interesting, and accurate is well worthwhile, however: it represents the entrepreneurs' first, and often only, chance to generate interest among potential investors. If this section doesn't arouse their interest and curiosity so that they want to know more, they may stop reading right there, and the rest of the business plan, no matter how excellent, will be largely irrelevant. Venture capitalists often receive hundreds or even thousands of business plans each year, so they have no choice: they must use the executive summary as an initial screening device: only a few pass

Table 7.1   *Basic sections of a business plan*

Section	Description
Executive summary	Brief overview of the idea behind the opportunity—the idea for the new product or service, why it is unique, who will find it appealing, etc. No more than two to three pages.
Background, purpose, and opportunity	A section describing the idea (the opportunity) and the current state of the new venture.
Marketing	What is the potential market? How large? What is the existing competition, how will it be overcome, what will the pricing be, etc.? (Sometimes this last topic appears in a separate section, and sometimes it is included in the marketing section.)
Competition	(If not included in the marketing section.) Information on existing products and services, prices, market share, etc.
Development, production, and location	Where the product or service is right now in terms of development, how it will move toward actual production or delivery (service), where the new venture will be located, and so on. Information on operations, too, can be included in this section (how the new business will operate, whether it will seek corporate partners, etc.).
Management (the entrepreneurs)	A section describing the human capital of the new venture's founding team—their experience, skills, and knowledge—and also what human resources they will need to acquire in the months ahead. Information on current ownership of the company should be included.
Financial section	Information on the company's current financial state, projections of future needs and revenues, and other financial measures. It should also include information on the amount of funding being sought, when this is relevant, and how these funds will be used; cash flow and a breakeven analysis.
Risk factors	The various risks the new venture will face, and the steps the management team is taking to protect against them.
Harvest or exit	Investors are interested in understanding precisely how they will gain if the company is successful, so information on this important issue (e.g., when and how the company might go public) can often be very useful.
Scheduling and milestones	Information on when each phase of the new venture will be completed should be included, so that potential investors will know just when key tasks (e.g., the start of production, time to first sales, projected breakeven point) will be completed. This can be a separate section, or included in other sections, as appropriate.
Appendices	Here is where detailed financial information, and detailed résumés of the founding team should be presented. Detailed technical or scientific information can be included. These should not appear in the body of the business plan.

Note: Because the new ventures they describe are unique, business plans too are unique, but most contain the sections and information shown here.

through to receive additional scrutiny. Truly, then, starting with a strong and persuasive executive summary is a crucial task.

After the executive summary, major sections follow in an orderly arrangement. These can be organized in many different ways, but Table 7.1 offers one that is used in many traditional business plans and is quite logical. How long should a business plan be? In general, no more than 20–25 pages in the actual body of the plan (not counting appendices). An excellent business plan—one that is potentially prize winning (!)—should present basic information succinctly, clearly, and persuasively, and these characteristics should be reflected in the verbal presentations made by entrepreneurs. This is a key reason why, in preparing for such presentations, the guiding principle should be "Practice, practice, practice," so that the presentation itself is clear and cogent, and fits within whatever time limits are imposed (often these are very brief). I have attended business plan competitions where each team of entrepreneurs was given only two or three minutes to provide an overview of their ideas and business model. Some teams were ready, and completed their presentations exactly on time, or with one or two seconds to spare. Others, however, were stopped by the clock, and were unable to make key points. Needless to say, this did not impress the judges, and none of these teams won a prize.

Business plans: the key to success?

Earlier, we noted that preparing a business plan offers important benefits: in addition to opening the door to potential funding through business plan competitions and other sources (e.g., venture capitalists), writing a plan helps entrepreneurs bring their own goals and business models into sharper focus. Thinking deeply about potential markets, existing competition, and many other issues can, in short, contribute to entrepreneurs' ability to make effective strategic decisions as they proceed. These benefits, however, apply mainly to the very early phases of a new venture's existence, so another, and very crucial, question arises: "Does writing a detailed business plan also contribute to the new venture's actual success once it is launched and operating?" In other words, does the effort invested in writing such plans pay off not just in the short term (e.g., prizes in business plan competitions), but in achieving the growth and success entrepreneurs seek? This issue has sparked a heated debate in the field of entrepreneurship. On one side are strong advocates of business plans, who contend that the benefits of completing this task far outweigh any potential costs. These individuals—and this view—are definitely in the majority; virtually every program in entrepreneurship emphasizes the importance of developing excellent business plans, and all provide students with many opportunities in which to engage in this activity.

On the other side of this issue, however, are scholars who suggest that writing detailed business plans is a waste of time, at least to some extent, because they are unrelated, or only weakly related, to a new venture's ultimate success. The arguments marshaled by both sides are persuasive, so this is clearly an instance in which the subtitle of this book—*An Evidence-based Guide*—is relevant. Basically, the only way to resolve this complex issue is through careful, systematic research. How could such research proceed? One approach would be to compare new ventures that have a detailed business plan when they are launched with ones that do not, in terms of standard measures of success: growth in sales, earnings, number of employees.

In fact, that is precisely the approach taken in many recent studies, and overall the results indicate that the answer to the question "Are business plans related to new venture success?" is as complex as this question itself. For instance, consider a study conducted by Lange, Mollow, Pearlmutter, Singh, and Bygrave (2007). These researchers obtained data from 116 entrepreneurs, who indicated whether they had or did not have a detailed, written business plan when they launched their new companies. Information on the performance of these new ventures was also obtained: revenue, net income, number of employees. In addition, the entrepreneurs indicated how much financing they had obtained from external sources at the time the ventures were launched. The results were clear. First, as would be expected, new ventures that had formal business plans did receive more start-up funds from external sources than ventures that did not have such plans ($408,216 versus $196,988). That's not surprising, because venture capitalists and other sources of financing (see Chapter 8) usually want lots of information and details before they invest. More importantly, though, there was no significant relationship between whether the companies had or did not have a formal business plan and measures of their actual success (net income, revenue, number of employees). On the basis of these findings, the authors concluded that, unless entrepreneurs require a large amount of external funding, they might be better off investing the time and effort required for preparing a detailed business plan in other activities such as basic (not detailed) financial planning, attracting customers, and planning actual operations of the company. It is interesting to note that this research was conducted by faculty at Babson College—an institution famous for its entrepreneurship program and its business plan competitions!

On the other side of the equation, however, is research indicating that formal business plans *are* related to entrepreneurs' success (e.g., Burke, Fraser, and Greene, 2010). Perhaps the strongest evidence in this regard is provided by a review of all existing evidence conducted by Brinckmann, Grichnik, and Kapsa (2010). These researchers conducted a meta-analysis (a type of statistical review) of all research conducted to date on the basic question of whether formal business plans are related to new venture success. Results from 46 separate studies involving 11046 organizations were included in the review. Success was assessed by an array of standard measures—growth in sales, growth in earnings, profits, and return on investment. The companies included in the review were divided into new start-ups or more established small businesses, and additional information on a key culture-related factor—the extent to which a given culture seeks to avoid uncertainty—was obtained. Results indicated that companies that either had a written business plan or engaged in detailed processes of business planning were in fact more successful than ones that did not: they achieved higher rates of growth. However, these results were stronger for established firms than for new ventures just getting started. Further, the relationship between having a business plan and subsequent performance was weaker in cultures high in uncertainty avoidance (e.g., France, Japan) than in cultures lower on this dimension (e.g., the United States). One possible reason for this finding is that, in cultures high on uncertainty avoidance, entrepreneurs are reluctant to depart from the strategies described in their business plans, and so are less able to adapt effectively to rapidly changing conditions. In a sense, they feel "locked in" to the plans and strategies described in their business plans, and their unwillingness to depart from these can have negative effects on their growth. In contrast, greater willingness to improvise—to depart from original plans, strategies, or goals in order to respond to changing conditions—can be an important "plus" in terms of firm performance. We'll examine these effects in detail in the next section.

The finding that business plans were more strongly related to firm performance for established businesses than new ventures appears to converge with the findings of other research (e.g., Lange et al., 2007) in suggesting that, during very early stages, the time spent in developing detailed business plans may reduce entrepreneurs' capacity to engage in other tasks that may, ultimately, be more important for increasing firm performance. In other words, detailed planning under conditions of high uncertainty and ambiguous or missing information—conditions often faced by entrepreneurs—may not be highly beneficial. As Brinckmann et al. (2010) suggest, during these early phases simple, basic planning may suffice.

One more issue is worth considering: even if there is a significant link between preparation of excellent business plans and subsequent firm performance, this might not, in itself, indicate that it is the business plans themselves that contribute to such success. Rather, it might simply reflect the fact that entrepreneurs who are able to prepare effective business plans—particularly those who develop prize winning plans—are higher than those who do not in skills or characteristics that contribute to business success (e.g., conscientiousness, high levels of self-control and discipline; see Chapter 5). Further, they may be higher in verbal and presentation

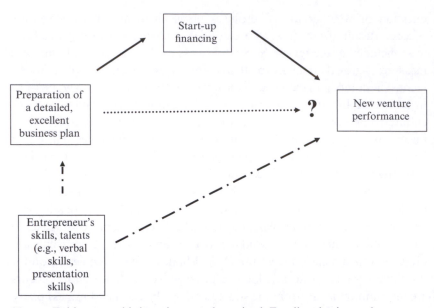

Note: Evidence on this issue is somewhat mixed. Excellent business plans certainly help entrepreneurs obtain start-up financing, but whether they contribute to long-term new venture success is still uncertain. Further, even if preparation of an excellent, prize winning business plan *is* related to new venture success, this may reflect the fact that entrepreneurs who prepare such business plans are simply higher in various talents related to business success than those who do not. So the ultimate contribution of business plans to long-term entrepreneurial success remains uncertain.

Figure 7.2   *Are business plans the key to entrepreneurial success?*

skills, higher in social skills (useful in obtaining the help they need to prepare such plans), and higher in successful intelligence (see Chapter 2). It might be these skills and characteristics, rather than the business plans themselves, that are responsible for their new venture's success (see Figure 7.2). This suggestion has not yet been examined systematically, so it should be viewed merely as an interesting possibility, one that can be investigated in future research.

Putting that idea aside for the moment, we should conclude this discussion by asking: What's the bottom line? Should entrepreneurs devote hundreds of hours to preparing detailed business plans or simply not bother? The most reasonable answer, based on current evidence, is this: yes, they should invest this effort if they absolutely require large amounts of external funding to move ahead; such support is generally not available to entrepreneurs who do not have a well-developed and persuasive business plan. But, if entrepreneurs do not require external funding, they may be better off developing less formal or detailed plans, and focusing their attention on other tasks (e.g., building their social networks, refining their products, and identifying and contacting potential customers). Doing so may also help them to adopt a flexible approach to building their new ventures—one that helps them to respond rapidly and effectively to conditions and events that cannot be predicted accurately by even the most detailed, careful planning. In fact, a growing body of evidence suggests that such an approach—which involves a high capacity to make mid-course changes and corrections, or to improvise—may be an important factor in entrepreneurs' success (e.g., Hmieleski, Corbett, and Baron, 2011). It is to this capacity that we turn next.

The importance of improvisation: making it up as you go along

Do you recall seeing the second part of this section heading? In fact, it is a phrase that has been mentioned several times in this book. And there is a good reason for its presence: in a few words, it captures a very basic and important aspect of entrepreneurship. Because they are attempting to create something new and useful that also generates value (economic, social, etc.), entrepreneurs often live and function in very chaotic and unpredictable worlds, ones filled with high levels of uncertainty. Although they may start with a detailed business plan that provides a roadmap to reaching the goals they seek, they usually discover, often almost at once, that these plans and strategies must be adjusted or, sometimes, changed entirely. The rapidly shifting environments entrepreneurs face leave little room for choice: *adjust or fail* is a basic rule of the entrepreneurial life. This suggests that entrepreneurs must be ready, willing, and able to improvise—to formulate new plans and strategies "on the fly" in response to unexpected events or trends (Baker et al., 2003; Hmieleski and Corbett, 2008).

I had first-hand experience with the importance of improvisation while running one of my own businesses (IEP Inc.). Our first product was a special kind of portable air cleaner that filtered the air, reduced noise from outside any room (office, bedroom), and, if the user wished, released pleasant fragrances into the air. It was designed to provide improved working and living conditions in small rooms—individual offices, bedrooms, dorm rooms. Our original plan was to manufacture the unit ourselves, and this was described in detail in our business plan. Early in the process, we invested in building several high-quality, working prototypes, and sent them to potential customers for testing. One—Brookstone—responded very favorably and asked us an unexpected question: How soon could we fill an initial order for 5000 units? Although we were exploring ways to manufacture our units and had received bids from several companies, we were not anywhere near to coming up with a firm date by which we could fill an order for 5000 units. Further, we had just learned that, to manufacture the product ourselves, we'd need an initial investment of more than $2 000 000. So, reluctantly, we had to tell Brookstone that it would be quite a while before we could supply a firm date or factually fill their order. Their response was simple and not at all surprising: "We can't wait that long." In a business that focuses on new products, they wanted our air cleaner now, not later.

At that point, my partner and I realized that we had to rethink the strategy outlined in our business plan. We soon came to the conclusion that we could not manufacture the units ourselves, because this would mean raising substantial amounts of capital and then waiting for the units to be produced. (The companies we had approached about manufacturing indicated that we would be at the end of the line, because the number of units involved was so small.) The air cleaner market was very "hot" at that time, and new units were coming to the market almost weekly, so we understood very clearly that we had to get our product "out there" quickly. This led us to the further conclusion that we needed to find a corporate partner—one that could manufacture the units very quickly and to which we could license our technology and patents (we had two on this particular product, and they were quite strong in terms of the claims they included; see Chapter 6). This kind of arrangement would restrict our profit potential, but it appeared to be the only logical way to proceed. That new plan succeeded, and we reached an agreement with a large company that already manufactured very similar products. As a result, our initial product was ready for sale in a few months, without a large financial investment from us. True, we received only a small royalty on units sold, and our corporate partner marketed the units to different customers than we originally had in mind, but our product was available very quickly, and we had succeeded in converting our ideas into something shoppers could find on the shelves of large stores and advertised in the pages of in-flight magazines. In short, improvisation—following a very different path than that described in our business plan—paid off handsomely for us in terms of helping us reach several of our major goals.

This kind of experience is very common for entrepreneurs; often they face the need to depart in major ways from their original plans because, to put it simply, external conditions give them no choice. In addition, such improvisation—developing new plans and strategies on the fly—is necessary for pursuing unanticipated opportunities (new markets the entrepreneurs didn't initially recognize) with unexpected problems (e.g., new competitors, new government regulations; Hmieleski and Baron, 2008; Mullins and Komisar, 2009). The capacity to improvise, therefore, is often a key one for entrepreneurs. And, in fact, willingness to improvise—to make mid-course adjustments as needed—appears to be one of the factors that play a role in the decision to become an entrepreneur. Research find-ings indicate that persons high in willingness to improvise express stronger intentions than persons lower in this tendency to become entrepreneurs (Hmieleski and Corbett, 2006). This ability to change quickly, on the fly, can be accurately measured by a brief questionnaire designed by Hmieleski and Corbett (2006). Sample items include: "When I see an opportunity, I take it"; "I think outside of the box"; and "I think well on my feet." Individuals completing the scale indicate the extent to which these items are true about themselves, and research findings indicate that it provides a useful measure of the capacity to make "mid-course corrections" very quickly.

Improvisation and firm performance: the benefits of flexibility

The comments above suggest that the willingness and capacity to impro-vise are important "pluses" for entrepreneurs. In fact, it appears that often they have no choice: as noted above, it is either improvise or fail. Research evidence indicates that the capacity to improvise is significantly related to entrepreneurs' success (e.g., Hmieleski and Corbett, 2008). However, it also appears that this is not always the case. Rather, its benefits are moderated (i.e., influenced) by several other factors, so that improvisa-tion is more of a "plus" under some conditions than others. Consider, for instance, a variable we examined in Chapter 5: self-efficacy. This refers to individuals' beliefs that they can successfully accomplish whatever they set out to accomplish—whatever tasks they undertake (e.g., Bandura, 1997). Entrepreneurs' self-efficacy has been found to be related to the success of their new ventures (De Noble, Jung, and Ehrlich, 1999), in part because entrepreneurs high in self-efficacy often show persistence: they don't give up when the going gets rough, because they believe that ultimately they will succeed (Baum and Locke, 2004).

This may be highly relevant to the benefits of improvisation, because, when they improvise, entrepreneurs are unlikely to "get it right" at first; they often need to adjust and readjust their new plans and strategies, and persevere in the face of initial setbacks. This suggests that improvisation may be more beneficial for entrepreneurs high rather than low in self-efficacy, and research findings (Hmieleski and Corbett, 2008) confirm this prediction. These researchers found that entrepreneurs' inclination to improvise (as measured by the scale mentioned above) was positively related to firm performance (sales growth) for entrepreneurs who were also high in self-efficacy, but was negatively related to firm performance for entrepreneurs who were low in self-efficacy. One possible explanation for these findings is that entrepreneurs who are low in self-efficacy lack the confidence to persevere in improvising until they find a combination of new plans, strategies, or resources that succeeds. Since they don't believe that, ultimately, they can succeed in this task, their efforts at improvisation may be hampered by these doubts, and so actually are less effective than those of persons higher in self-efficacy. Whatever the precise reasons, it is clear that improvisation does not work equally well for all entrepreneurs; rather, it is more effective in boosting firm performance for some (e.g., those high in self-efficacy) than for others.

Additional evidence (Hmieleski et al., 2011) indicates that another important characteristic of entrepreneurs, their optimism (expectations of positive outcomes), may also be relevant to the question of whether improvisation has beneficial effects on firm performance. Further, the kind of environments in which entrepreneurs operate—dynamic (changing rapidly) or stable—also plays a role. These researchers obtained information on entrepreneurs' level of optimism and their tendency to improvise, as well as information on whether their new ventures were operating in dynamic or stable environments. Results indicated that all these factors played an important role in firm performance. In dynamic environments, entrepreneurs' tendency to engage in improvisation was positively related to the performance of their firms, but only for those who were moderate rather than very high in optimism. In stable environments, in contrast, entrepreneurs' tendency to improvise was not significantly associated with the performance of their firms, and that was true regardless of entrepreneurs' level of optimism. Together, these findings indicate that the tendency to improvise can indeed be beneficial, but only in dynamic (rapidly changing) environments and only when entrepreneurs are moderate in optimism—that is, when they have realistic expectations concerning possible outcomes. (Figure 7.3 summarizes these findings.)

Effectuation: using what you have to get where you want to go

Prediction is a basic goal of science: the essential idea is that, if we understand a phenomenon sufficiently well to predict it accurately, we can then often succeed in changing it, at least to some degree. Traditional business plans take this goal of accurate prediction very seriously. They devote a great deal of attention to projections concerning many key issues: how quickly a new product or service can be brought into existence and at what cost, who will want to purchase and use it once it exists, and—perhaps most importantly—the magnitude of the value (financial or social) that will be generated. Attempting to make such predictions is a reasonable task; after all, there would be little reason to proceed with development of an opportunity without having *some* expectations concerning these issues. Further, without predictions concerning the costs of developing a new product or service, or the nature and size of potential markets for it,

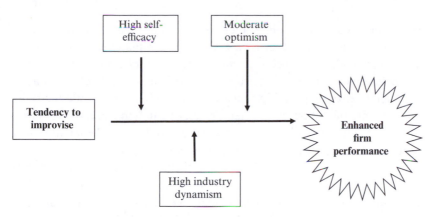

Note: Current evidence indicates that entrepreneurs' willingness to improvise can be positively related to the success of their new ventures, but only when (1) the entrepreneurs are high in self-efficacy, (2) the new ventures operate in dynamic rather than stable environments, and (3) the entrepreneurs are moderate rather than very high in optimism.

Source: Based on data from Hmieleski, Corbett, and Baron (2011).

Figure 7.3   *Is improvisation related to firm performance? Only under some conditions*

it would be impossible to estimate the scope of the financial and human resources required to move ahead.

But prediction is often a difficult task, especially in situations where knowledge is incomplete, a large number of variables are at work, and in fact a complete list of all relevant variables doesn't even exist. As Albert Einstein put it when referring to one aspect of physics: "Occurrences in this domain are beyond the reach of exact prediction because of the variety of factors in operation, not because of any lack of order in nature." In other words, there are many situations that are so complex that accurate prediction in them is difficult if not impossible to attain.

Entrepreneurship often involves such situations. So many variables are at work that accurate predictions about even such central issues as the cost of converting ideas into tangible products, the reactions of potential customers to them, or the reactions of competitors (e.g., what will they do to protect their own businesses?) are almost impossible to make. Yet they are included in business plans because potential investors generally—and reasonably—insist on their presence.

This is the traditional approach, and a key foundation for business plans, but is it the only one? In recent years, a very different perspective on entrepreneurship known as *effectuation* has emerged (e.g., Sarasvathy, 2001, 2008). This approach, which we described briefly early in this chapter, starts with the suggestion that, no matter what entrepreneurs say in their detailed business plans, they simply cannot make accurate predictions about many important issues. There are so many unknowns in the equation, and change happens so rapidly, that accurate prediction is virtually impossible. Taking note of this fact, proponents of effectuation as an approach to entrepreneurship suggest that entrepreneurs should focus not on predicting the future but, rather, on creating it—on using the resources they have at their disposal to shape future outcomes. What are these resources? Basically, they include the characteristics, skills, and motivation of the entrepreneurs (or founding team), their knowledge and experience, and their social networks—the people they know. In contrast to standard causal logic, in which entrepreneurs start by selecting specific goals (e.g., gaining a specified share of a market or obtaining a desired rate of growth) and attempt to identify means for reaching these goals, effectual logic (part of the effectuation perspective) suggests that entrepreneurs should consider their resources—the things they now have and can control—and, on basis of these, formulate a set of imagined ends. In other words, effectuation proposes that entrepreneurs should ask themselves the following question: "Given what I have and can control right now, what can I hope to accomplish?" Another basic idea of effectuation is that the future can be shaped by taking action, so why bother trying to predict it? Instead, make if unfold in the ways *you*, as an entrepreneur, wish.

Also central to effectuation are several other ideas. First, entrepreneurs should focus on affordable loss—what they can afford to lose, given their resources—rather than on potential profits. Second, they should form partnerships with others in order to increase the scope of their resources—and therefore the range of outcomes they generate. Perhaps most importantly of all, they should view unexpected events as opportunities that open up additional possibilities for creative use of current resources. In other words, as one old saying puts it, "If you have lemons, don't wish for oranges—make lemonade." Here's a concrete example: in 1985, Thomas Stemberg, one of the co-founders of Staples (a huge office supply company), needed a new printer ribbon. He found that no nearby stores had the ribbon he needed and, even worse, they would all soon be closed for a holiday, so he could not obtain the supply he needed for several days. This unexpected event caused him to wonder: Wouldn't other entrepreneurs or small business owners find an office supply store that operated like a supermarket (i.e., stayed open long hours and, because of small margins, could offer discounted prices even for small purchases) highly appealing? He had recently worked for a supermarket chain, so he used this experience (a resource he already possessed) to come up with the idea for a new venture—one that quickly became a major success. In short, Stemberg turned an unexpected and irritating event into an opportunity— one that soon yielded rapidly mounting profits.

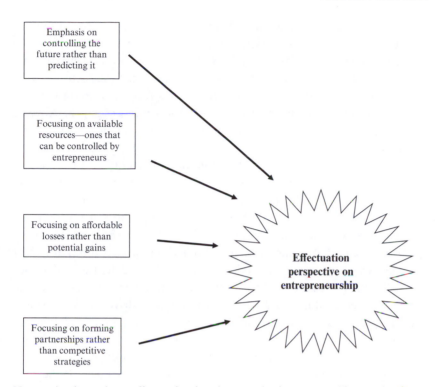

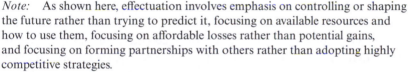

Note: As shown here, effectuation involves emphasis on controlling or shaping the future rather than trying to predict it, focusing on available resources and how to use them, focusing on affordable losses rather than potential gains, and focusing on forming partnerships with others rather than adopting highly competitive strategies.

Figure 7.4   *Key aspects of effectuation as a perspective on entrepreneurship*

The ideas of effectuation (summarized in Figure 7.4) are certainly appealing, and together suggest a very different approach to turning creativity and the ideas it generates into something new and useful. Instead of choosing specific goals and then attempting to gather the resources needed to reach them, entrepreneurs can, instead, imagine many different uses of their resources—what they have now—and take action to pursue these, remaining flexible, along the way, so as to maximize their outcomes. The key question concerning effectuation, however, is this: "Do entrepreneurs actually operate in this manner, and do they really use effectual rather than causal logic?" While the traditional model described in earlier sections of this chapter (identify an opportunity, estimate the resources needed to develop it, obtain them, and launch the new venture) remains dominant, a growing body of evidence indicates that the entrepreneurial process does indeed often reflect key aspects of effectuation (e.g., Wiltbank, Dew, Read, and Sarasvathy, 2006). For instance, in one investigation (Dew,

Read, Sarasvathy, and Wiltbank, 2009) the researchers reasoned that, as entrepreneurs become more experienced in entrepreneurial activities such as starting new companies, they will gradually shift toward using effectuation as a basis for their decisions. In other words, they will focus more on means-driven rather than goal-driven actions, on affordable loss rather than potential gains, on forming partnerships, and on leveraging unexpected events rather than avoiding them through careful, detailed planning. To investigate these predictions, Dew et al. (2009) asked two groups—highly experienced entrepreneurs (who had founded on average 7.3 companies) and novice entrepreneurs (graduate students in business administration, most of whom had not yet started a new venture)—to answer a series of questions about how they would develop an imaginary new product (a computer game focused on entrepreneurship). As they thought about each question, the entrepreneurs described their thoughts out loud, and their comments were recorded and coded in terms of the extent to which they reflected either causal logic or effectual logic (for instance, the extent to which they reflected means-driven rather than goal-driven action, focused on affordable losses rather than gains, etc.). It was predicted that the experienced entrepreneurs would show much greater reliance on effectual logic than the novice entrepreneurs, and this prediction was confirmed. Although interpretation of these findings has been questioned on the basis of the fact that the two groups differed in many other ways aside from their experience as entrepreneurs (e.g., the experienced entrepreneurs were much older than the novice entrepreneurs; Baron, 2009), the findings do seem to suggest that entrepreneurs—especially highly experienced ones—actually do think differently from other persons, including novice entrepreneurs.

To the extent this is true—that is, to the extent that the framework proposed by effectuation is accurate—important implications follow. Specifically, it is possible that business plans, although very useful in several ways (e.g., in helping entrepreneurs clarify their own thinking about their ideas and the opportunities they want to develop), are less important in the actual process of entrepreneurship than has long been suggested. Writing such plans is certainly a key "entry card" to obtaining financial resources, but perhaps focusing on this task actually impedes rather than facilitates entrepreneurs' success by causing entrepreneurs to focus on predicting variables that, in fact, can't really be predicted instead of focusing on their own resources—what they do have and *can* control. Only time and further research will resolve this issue, but it is certainly one worth pondering, given the central role assigned to business plans—and to the detailed planning and predictions they involve—at present. Sarasvathy's (2001, 2008) central idea—that often the future can't be accurately predicted, but *can* be influenced or controlled—is certainly one of the most original to emerge in the field of entrepreneurship in recent years; and, since the field itself focuses on creativity and the ideas it generates, it is clear that effectuation is an approach worthy of careful consideration.

Summary of key points

Careful planning is essential in many activities, and it plays a key role in entrepreneurship, where it is often expressed in formal business plans—detailed, written documents that explain how ideas generated by creativity will be converted into new products or services. Careful planning is not always beneficial, however, and, because entrepreneurs often face rapidly changing environments filled with uncertainty, even excellent business plans may not provide a strong basis for predicting future events and outcomes—or the success of new ventures.

Business plans generally address several key issues: What is the nature of the opportunity? What are the potential markets for new products or services? How will they actually be produced? Who are the entrepreneurs, and what skills, knowledge, and experience relevant to the new venture do they possess? All of these questions and many others are addressed carefully in business plans. However, a key section is the executive summary, which provides a brief overview of these issues. Executive summaries are crucial because, unless they succeed in attracting the interest of venture capitalists and other potential investors, the rest of the plan may go unread.

Excellent business plans are required for entering business plan competitions, one source of financial resources for entrepreneurs. In addition, by writing them, entrepreneurs may gain a fuller understanding of many issues relating to their new ventures. Is preparation of a detailed business plan actually related to the success of new ventures? The evidence is mixed; in general it indicates that business plans are beneficial, but more so for established businesses than for newly launched ones. This suggests that the large investment of time and effort entrepreneurs invest in preparing detailed business plans might be better directed to other tasks (e.g., improving their products, building their social networks).

Research findings indicate that a propensity to engage in improvisation—formulating new plans and strategies "on the fly" in response to unexpected events or trends—is related to entrepreneurs' success. This is especially true in dynamic (rapidly changing) environments, for entrepreneurs who are moderate rather than high in optimism, and for entrepreneurs who are high in self-efficacy.

In recent years, an alternative perspective on entrepreneurship known as *effectuation* has emerged. This perspective suggests that entrepreneurs should not focus on attempting to predict the future—a task that is often virtually impossible—but on shaping or controlling it. They can do this by focusing on, and effectively using, the resources they already have, such as their own skills and characteristics, their knowledge and experience, and their social networks. In addition, they should seek to form partnerships, focus on affordable losses rather than potential gains, and view unexpected events as constituting opportunities. Some research findings indicate that entrepreneurs do in fact shift toward effectual logic and away from causal logic as they gain experience in starting and running new ventures.

References

Baker, T., Miner, A., and Eesley, D. (2003). Improvising firms: Bricolage, account giving, and improvisational competency in the founding process. *Research Policy*, *32*, 255–276.

Bandura, A. (1997). *Self-efficacy: The exercise of control*. New York: W.H. Freeman.

Baron, R.A. (2009). Effectual versus predictive logics in entrepreneurial decision making: Differences between experts and novices. Does experience in starting new ventures change the way entrepreneurs think? Perhaps, but for now, "caution" is essential. *Journal of Business Venturing*, *24*, 310–315.

Baum, J.R., and Locke, E.A. (2004). The relationship of entrepreneurial traits, skill, and motivation to subsequent venture growth. *Journal of Applied Psychology*, *83*, 587–598.

Brinckmann, J., Grichnik, D., and Kapsa, D. (2010). Should entrepreneurs plan or just storm the castle? A meta-analysis on contextual factors impacting the business planning–performance relationship in small firms. *Journal of Business Venturing*, *25*, 24–40.

Burke, A., Fraser, S., and Greene, F.J. (2010). The multiple effects of business planning on new venture performance. *Journal of Management Studies*, *47*, 391–410.

De Noble, A.F., Jung, D., and Ehrlich, S.B. (1999). Entrepreneurial self-efficacy: The development of a measure and its relationship to entrepreneurial action. In P.D. Reynolds, W.D. Bygrave, S. Manigart, C.M. Mason, G.D. Meyer, H.J. Sapienza, and K.G. Shaver (eds), *Frontiers of entrepreneurship research*. Babson Park, MA: Babson College.

Dew, N., Read, S., Sarasvathy, S.D., and Wiltbank, R. (2009). Effectual versus predictive logics in entrepreneurial decision-making: Differences between experts and novices. *Journal of Business Venturing*, *24*, 287–309.

Hmieleski, K.M., and Baron, R.A. (2008). Regulatory focus and new venture performance: A study of entrepreneurial opportunity exploitation under conditions of risk versus uncertainty. *Strategic Entrepreneurship Journal*, *2*, 285–299.

Hmieleski, K.M., and Corbett, A.C. (2006). Proclivity for improvisation as a predictor of entrepreneurial intentions. *Journal of Small Business Management*, *44*, 45–63.

Hmieleski, K.M., and Corbett, A.C. (2008). The contrasting interaction effects of improvisational behavior with entrepreneurial self-efficacy on new venture performance and entrepreneur work satisfaction. *Journal of Business Venturing*, *23*, 482–496.

Hmieleski, K.M., Corbett, A.C., and Baron, R.A. (2011). Entrepreneurs' improvisational behavior and firm performance: A study of dispositional and environmental moderators. Manuscript under review.

Lange, J.K.E., Mollow, A., Pearlmutter, M., Singh, S., and Bygrave, W.D. (2007). Pre-start-up formal business plans and post-start-up performance: A study of 116 new ventures. *Venture Capital*, *9*, 237–256.

Mullins, J., and Komisar, R. (2009). *Getting to plan B: Breaking through to a better business model*. Boston, MA: Harvard Business Press.

Sarasvathy, S. (2001). Causation and effectuation: Toward a shift from economic inevitability to entrepreneurial contingency. *Academy of Management Review*, *26*, 243–263.

Sarasvathy, S.D. (2008). *Effectuation: Elements of entrepreneurial expertise*. Cheltenham, UK and Northampton, MA, USA: Edward Elgar Publishing.

Wiltbank, R., Dew, N., Read, S., and Sarasvathy, S.D. (2006). What to do next? The case for nonpredictive strategy. *Strategic Management Journal*, *27*, 981–998.

8 Getting the support you need: financial and human

Chapter outline

Financial resources: where and how to get them
Types and sources of financial resources
Venture capitalists: how they make their decisions
Human resources: winning the support and commitment of key persons
Building a strong, and versatile, founding team: the advantages of complementarity
Beyond the founding team: attracting and retaining outstanding employees
Social influence: the fine art of getting others to say "yes"
Compliance: the underlying principles
Compliance: techniques that work

> I'd say it's been my biggest problem all my life . . . money. It takes a lot of money to make these dreams come true. (Walt Disney)

> Tell everyone what you want to do and someone will want to help you do it. (W. Clement Stone)

It is one thing to have an idea for a new product, service, or other entrepreneurial activity, but quite another to turn this idea into something tangible. In order to do so, entrepreneurs generally need to acquire resources that can be used for this purpose. While these resources take many different forms, they can generally be divided into two major categories: financial and human. Unless entrepreneurs can acquire these essential resources, their dreams for creating something new, useful, and better than what's "out there" now may remain only dreams. Financial and human resources, once successfully attained, provide entrepreneurs with the means to do more than simply imagine "what might be"—they provide the means to take overt action to make these ideas real. Although many people assume that financial resources are the most important component (as Walt Disney suggests in the first quotation above), growing evidence indicates that human resources, such as good relationships with others, are equally crucial (the view implied by the second quotation above).

In this chapter, both kinds of resources will be considered, because, in essence, both are essential. As a song from the popular film and Broadway show *Cabaret* suggests, money does indeed "make the world go round," and is a key ingredient in entrepreneurship. On the other hand, new ventures—and especially successful ones—generally grow as a result of the combined skills, talents, and efforts of the founding team and the social networks they possess or strive to develop. Further, once a new venture begins to expand, its continued success depends heavily on the quality of the people it attracts, who add their own human and social capital to that of the founding team.

Following the emphasis of these basic points, the remainder of this chapter will proceed as follows. First, we'll focus on financial resources, examining such topics as whether entrepreneurs should seek to obtain them from others or just try to move forward with their own resources—bootstrapping. (As you may recall, this is the strategy recommended by the effectuation perspective discussed in Chapters 1 and 7; Read, Song, and Smith, 2009; Sarasvathy, 2008.) This discussion will expand considerably on an earlier one concerned with business plan competitions and the resources they provide (Chapter 7), by describing additional sources of financial resources and how to utilize them. One key source of funding for entrepreneurs is venture capitalist firms—organizations that specialize in providing such support for carefully selected new ventures. The decisions they make—"support" or "do not support"—are often crucial ones for new ventures, but how, precisely, are these decision made? What are the key criteria they employ? A substantial body of research has addressed this issue, and echoes comments made in Chapters 1 and 2 to the effect that, as human beings, we don't always have clear and accurate understanding of why we make the decisions we do or act in specific ways. Venture capitalists (VCs), it appears, are no exception to this rule (e.g., Dimov and Shepherd, 2005), so they may not be able to describe the criteria they use accurately, but carefully conducted research has helped reveal what criteria they actually do use in their funding decisions (e.g., Petty and Gruber, 2011; Shepherd, Zacharakis, and Baron, 2003), and we'll examine that evidence carefully. Following that discussion, we'll turn to the human side of the equation—the human resources entrepreneurs need to effectively develop the opportunities they have identified or created. Here, the role of founder teams' human and social capital will be considered, and why complementarity rather than similarity should be the guiding principle in forming founding teams. Finally, we consider social influence, and the many tactics entrepreneurs can use to gain compliance from others—getting them to say "yes" to various requests.

Financial resources: where and how to get them

As we'll soon see, many different sources of financial support for entrepreneurs exist. Before seeking such funding, however, entrepreneurs should first address an important initial question: Do they really need it? Do they actually need financial resources from external sources? As you can readily guess, such support is not free—far from it. As we'll describe below, when entrepreneurs accept external funding they must generally give up something in return—often a large portion of the ownership (i.e., equity) of their companies. In addition, they may lose control over key decisions and day-to-day operations. Since many individuals become entrepreneurs because they strongly value autonomy (see Chapter 1), this suggests that the costs attached to external support can be substantial. How can entrepreneurs determine whether they need such funds? A good way to begin is by estimating the costs involved in moving forward. In other words, what will be needed for further product development, marketing and promotion, rent, equipment, travel, supplies, postage—the list is almost endless and varies with the kind of company (and products or services) entrepreneurs seek to provide. Forecasting such costs is a very, very tricky business and, in fact, is extremely difficult to do precisely. Unexpected costs almost always emerge, and unanticipated problems (requiring financial resources) seem to appear from nowhere. Given these uncertainties, a good rule of thumb is to estimate costs for a given period of time (e.g., the first year operations) as carefully as possible—and then *at least* triple this figure. Entrepreneurs should then compare these figures with their own personal resources. If they can cover them, by and large, external funding may not be needed. If the estimated costs far exceed personal resources, external funding becomes a necessity rather than an option. Again, no precise or definitive answer to the question "Do we need external funding?" is generally available. But, given the costs involved in seeking and accepting such support, it is one every entrepreneur should ask at the start. In a sense, this is closely related to the question "Should we prepare a detailed business plan," discussed in Chapter 7. As noted in that chapter, a detailed business plan is the entry ticket for many sources of funding: without one, these sources are simply unavailable. But, since preparing such a plan requires a great deal of time and effort, this task should be pursued only when it is clear that external financial support is essential. When I started my most recent company (IEP, Inc.), I followed the advice of a friend with lots of experience in arranging support for entrepreneurs, and did prepare a detailed business plan. But as the story unfolded and we improvised—switching plans from manufacturing our products ourselves to licensing our technology and patents to a large company—the need for external funding evaporated. Ultimately, we proceeded with our own funds, plus a small amount from friends and family. That can be a risky course, especially accepting funds from family and friends, but it worked well for us and allowed us to "bootstrap" rather than seek external funding.

Now, however, assume that entrepreneurs have considered this question clearly and reached the conclusion that substantial amounts of funding are required. Where and how do they obtain it? Those are the issues to which we turn next, and that are often at the heart of the entrepreneurial process, especially in its initial phases.

Types and sources of financial resources

Two basic types of external funding for new ventures exist: equity financing and debt financing. Equity financing involves assigning part of the equity of the new venture to the source of funding: these organizations or individuals become part-owners of the new venture. Debt financing, in contrast, involves a financial obligation to return the capital provided plus a scheduled amount of interest. New ventures tend to be financed by equity for two reasons. First, until they have generated positive cash flow, they are viewed as "bad risks" by banks and other potential lenders, so securing such loans is difficult, and the interests rates will be high. Second, debt financing at a fixed rate of interest encourages people to take risky actions because, if the new venture fails, the entrepreneur can't lose any more than the funds she or he originally put into it; as a result, downside loss is the same regardless of how much risk the entrepreneur takes. However, because the entrepreneur pays the same amount of interest on debt regardless of how well the new venture does, she or he keeps all of the returns from success. As a result, debt financing creates the incentive for taking risks.

Occasionally new ventures do obtain debt financing. When new ventures receive this type of financing early in their existence, it tends to be one of three types. The first is debt guaranteed by the entrepreneur's personal assets or earning power, as is the case when an entrepreneur uses credit cards or a home equity loan to finance her business. The second is asset-based financing. Asset-based financing is debt that is secured by the equipment that it is used to buy. Many products, like trucks, computers, and photocopiers, can be financed this way. The third is supplier credit. In many industries, suppliers offer credit to entrepreneurs to obtain inventory and equipment. For example, a restaurant supplier may provide kitchen equipment to an entrepreneur starting a new restaurant. The value of the equipment constitutes a loan, on which the supplier expects interest, just as a credit card company expects interest on the funds it advances to card holders. If the entrepreneur fails to make the required payments, the supplier retains the right to seize the equipment, which is collateral for the loan.

Entrepreneurs can draw on a wide variety of sources in seeking capital for their new businesses aside from debt. Because these sources are very different from one another, and all offer advantages and disadvantages, it is important to know what they are and when they are most useful to entrepreneurs. We turn next, therefore, to a description of the different sources of capital (i.e., financial resources) potentially available to new ventures:

- *Personal savings and credit cards.* The single most important source of capital for new ventures is the entrepreneur's own savings. Research findings indicate that approximately 70 percent of all entrepreneurs finance their new businesses with their own capital. These funds can come from personal savings, but in addition many entrepreneurs "max" their credit cards, charging items until the limits for their accounts are reached.
- *Friends and family.* Many entrepreneurs turn to their friends and family members to raise the capital that they need to finance their businesses. Consistent with the suggestion "Don't go to strangers," entrepreneurs get their support very close to home. The upside is obvious: close friends and family members will often wait more patiently for a return on their investments than persons unfamiliar with the entrepreneur. Moreover, they are often willing to accept much smaller portions of equity in the company, or much lower interest if their help takes the form of loans. But the downside, too, is obvious: if things don't work out well and friends and family see little or no return on their support, this can have negative implications for their future trust in, and relations with, the entrepreneur.
- *Business angels.* Business angels are private individuals who invest in new ventures. Typical business angels are former or current entrepreneurs themselves, so they have an "insider's" view of the process. Their investments tend to be relatively small—typically $10 000 to $200 000, and they typically invest in new ventures located near their homes, since this gives them the opportunity to work closely with the entrepreneurs or, at least, to see what's happening! Business angels typically require a lower return on their investments than, for example, venture capitalists, perhaps because they invest for many reasons aside from financial gain. For instance, they may simply enjoy helping inexperienced entrepreneurs get started, or may find being involved in new ventures stimulating—they want to stay involved in the entrepreneurial process. I have been a business angel twice, making investments in two new ventures. One failed entirely, and the other was soon purchased by a larger company in which I now hold stock. Overall, then, my own performance as a business angel has been fair to middling at best.
- *Venture capitalist firms.* Venture capitalist firms are organizations

that raise money from large institutional investors, such as university endowments and company pension funds, and then invest those funds in new ventures. Venture capital firms are generally structured as limited partnerships, often set up to last for a specific period of time (e.g., 10 years). The institutional investors or others who provide capital are limited partners and have little or no say in the venture capital firm's management. The individual venture capitalists associated with the venture capital fund make investment decisions, and are general partners; they essentially run the partnerships, just as CEOs direct the activities of corporations. At the end of the life of a venture capital fund, the venture capital firm returns the capital invested to the institutional investors plus a percentage of any profits from investing in the start-ups (usually 80 percent). The general partners keep the other 20 percent and also receive a management fee (typically 2 percent of the capital in the fund annually) for managing the investments.

In addition to providing money to new firms, venture capitalists provide many other benefits to entrepreneurs, which together are known as non-financial value added benefits. For instance, they provide legitimation—they add to the credibility and reputation of the new venture, since an investment in it indicates that the venture capitalists think well enough of the venture to "put their money where their mouths are." Many other non-financial benefits have been described by Large and Muegge (2008), and include assistance with the hiring of excellent employees (a topic discussed in detail in a later section), and outreach (introducing the top management team to potential customers, suppliers, and many others). In other words, venture capitalists help extend and strengthen entrepreneurs' own networks. Other benefits provided by venture capitalists include mentoring entrepreneurs in various ways, helping them develop effective strategies, and providing advice with respect to basic operations.

Although venture capitalists offer much to new companies, they require a lot in return. In general, they expect a large share of the equity (i.e., ownership) of the venture. This amount varies with the perceived potential of the new venture: venture capitalists will accept a smaller share if they view the new venture as having exceptionally high potential. As we'll note below in a discussion of how venture capitalists make their decisions, however, they generally invest in only a small proportion of the new ventures whose business plans they receive, so they tend to view all the ventures they support as relatively high in the potential for success.

To protect their financial investments, venture capitalists also impose a large number of restrictions on the actions of entrepreneurs. They often require entrepreneurs to issue convertible preferred stock, which allows the venture capitalist to "get out" more readily in the event that the venture fails, but to have common stock ownership if the new venture succeeds. Venture capitalists also include a large number of agreements that protect their interests in their contracts with the new ventures. For instance, entrepreneurs are often barred from purchasing assets or issuing or selling shares without the venture capitalists' permission, and some contracts involve mandatory redemption rights that require entrepreneurs to return the venture capitalists' investment any time they demand it. Finally, venture capitalists often insist on forfeiture provisions that cause entrepreneurs to lose a portion of their equity in the company if performance falls below target goals. Given the demands that venture capitalists place on entrepreneurs and venture capitalists' focus on extremely high-growth companies, it is not surprising that, as noted before, an increasing number of entrepreneurs are seeking to fund their own companies through bootstrapping and related procedures. Only those who require substantial funding seek to obtain it from venture capitalists because, although the funds they provide can be substantial, the obligations they impose can be heavy.

- *Corporations.* Many companies make investments in new companies. By making these investments, they can obtain access to new products or technology owned by the new ventures. In return, the established companies provide important marketing and manufacturing support as well as improve the new venture's credibility. For instance, a new biotech company can gain considerable recognition and prestige if it receives financial support from a major drug company. Another advantage of corporate investors is that they generally offer better terms than venture capitalists and even business angels. However, entrepreneurs should proceed with care: large corporations provide favorable financial terms, relative to other investors, because they want to obtain access to the intellectual property and products developed by new companies. In a sense, they are giving with one hand (financial support), but taking with the other—and what they take may be the most valuable assets the new venture possesses.

- *Banks.* Commercial banks provide a variety of types of capital to new businesses. First, banks provide the companies with standard commercial loans. A commercial loan is a form of financing in which the borrower pays interest on the money borrowed. Second, banks often provide new companies with lines of credit—agreements to allow entrepreneurs to draw up to a set amount of money at a particular interest rate, whenever they need it. Lines of credit are usually used to finance inventory or accounts receivable. As noted earlier, bank loans are relatively rare for new businesses because they are viewed as bad risks, at least until positive cash flow provides the funds needed to pay interest on a loan.

- *Government programs.* Federal and state governments offer a variety of programs to finance new businesses. One federal program is the Small Business Innovation Research (SBIR) Program. Under this program new businesses can receive funds from government agencies to evaluate and then develop a technical idea. The program proceeds in three phases. Phase I is a six-month period used for a feasibility study. The new venture must demonstrate that the proposed innovation is feasible and has the potential to be commercialized. During this phase, new ventures can receive from $75 000 to $100 000.

  During Phase II, the business receiving government funds is required to develop and test prototypes of the innovation(s). Because this can involve considerable expense, SBIR provides up to $750 000 during this phase, which can last as long as two years. Finally, Phase III involves moving the innovations to the marketplace. SBIR does not provide funding during this phase; rather, the new venture must find funding or financing in the private sector. The SBIR Program has assisted literally thousands of small companies and is viewed by many as a highly successful government program—one that has truly helped entrepreneurs launch new ventures. Funds provided by the SBIR are grants—they do not have to repaid, even if the new venture fails, and do not require any interest. These are important advantages, and make this program highly attractive to entrepreneurs.

  Another federal program is the 7(A) Loan Guarantee Program of the U.S. Small Business Administration, which guarantees repayment to lenders of any capital that they provide to new businesses, up to a preset limit. The U.S. Small Business Administration also provides the CAPLine Program, a system for guaranteeing loans to new and small businesses to finance inventory or accounts receivable. Lastly, small business investment companies (SBICs) are organizations that the U.S. Small Business Administration licenses and to which it lends money. These organizations make minority (less than 50 percent) investments in new companies and often provide debt capital.

In sum, there are many sources of financial assistance for entrepreneurs. They vary in the kind of support they offer and what they require in return. Venture capitalists can provide the largest amounts, but they do require a great deal in return. At the other end of the scale are government programs, which can provide somewhat limited funding, but make few demands upon entrepreneurs, especially when the funds they provide are in the form of grants (e.g., funds provided by SBIR). Ultimately, then, the decision to seek external funding and, if so, further decisions concerning

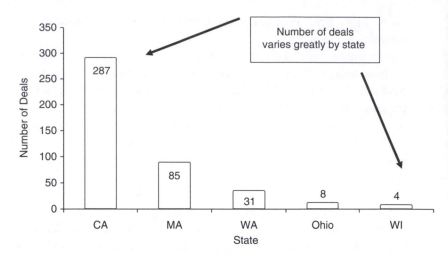

Note: As shown here, the volume of venture capital activity (number of new ventures funded) varies greatly by state. (Data are for 2010.)

Source: SSTI, Westerville, OH, website dashboard.

Figure 8.1   *Venture capital activity in various states*

how much and from what source are ones entrepreneurs must make for themselves as they proceed toward the goal of creating value out of their own creativity, skills, effort, and persistence.

Venture capitalists: how they make their decisions

Many entrepreneurs view venture capitalists as the best or at least most important source of external funding for their new ventures. If they decide to seek such funding, therefore, they often turn to venture capitalists. There are good reasons for this course of action. First, venture capitalists do indeed have "deep pockets"—the capacity to provide large amounts of capital *if they wish*. The emphasis on the last three words is intentional, because in fact venture capitalists usually fund only a small proportion of the ventures that approach them seeking financial support. This varies greatly by region, state, and country (see Figure 8.1), but in general only 1 percent of proposals receive financial support. We have already described another important reason for pursuing funding from venture capitalists: they also provide many other forms of non-financial support, from help with recruiting high-quality employees to assistance with day-to-day operations.

Given these important benefits, it is not surprising that successful venture capital firms—ones with a strong track record of supporting new ventures that have achieved great success—are deluged with business plans from entrepreneurs. A key question, then, is: How do they decide which ventures to support? This has been a topic of research in the field of entre-preneurship for many years (e.g., Fried and Hisrich, 1994; Shepherd and Zacharakis, 2005), and this work has yielded important insights into the criteria for such decisions and how they are actually made.

One way to answer this question, of course, is simply to ask VCs and other investors to describe the criteria they use in evaluating business plans and new ventures. As we noted in Chapter 1, however, as human beings we are not very good at recognizing or describing the factors that influence our decisions—especially complex decisions—or at estimating the relative importance of each of these factors.

This leaves us facing an intriguing puzzle: Is there any way to obtain a better answer—to gain accurate insight into how VCs and other inves-tors actually make their decisions? Two different methods have been used to address this question. The first, known as *policy capturing*, is based on having individuals make many decisions and then, without asking them to report on what factors influenced these decisions, identifying such factors through analysis of the actual decisions themselves. In other words, this method involves working backwards from many decisions to identify the factors that shaped them. In actual practice, the method works like this. First, factors that are believed to play a role in the decisions being studied are identified. Next, these factors are built into various cases or examples in a systematic manner. These cases are then presented to the decision makers (in this case venture capitalists), who rate the chance of success of each new venture described in the examples. Here's a concrete example. Suppose that one factor believed to affect VCs' decisions is market familiarity—the extent to which founding team members have experience in this market. The experience of the founding team would be described as *high* in some cases given to the VCs to evaluate but as *low* in others. A second factor might be the number of direct competitors for the new venture. The number of competitors would then be described as *high* in some cases given to the VCs but *low* in others. By combining several factors believed to affect VCs' decisions, many cases or examples would be generated—examples in which the key factors are varied systematically (i.e., they are high in some examples but low in others). Finally, by examining VCs' ratings of the companies in these examples, information about which factors are *actually* affecting their decisions can be obtained. For instance, if, across many dif-ferent examples, VCs rate companies in which the founding teams have a lot of market experience more highly than companies in which the found-ing teams have very little market experience, that would suggest that this factor is indeed affecting the VCs' decisions. Moreover—and this is a key point—this would be the conclusion even if the VCs themselves were not aware that this factor was influencing their decisions, that is, even if, when asked, they did not name it as playing a key role.

Procedures like these have been used in many recent studies (e.g., Shepherd et al., 2003), and the findings of such research have identified several factors that actually do play a key role in VCs' decisions. These include familiarity with the market, the leadership ability of the founding team, proprietary protection (level of protection provided because the product or service, or the process used to deliver the product or service, is unique and difficult to imitate), market growth (percentage growth over the last several years), the level of past start-up experience of the new venture team (how many other companies have they started in the past?), the number of competitors, and the relative strength of competitors assessed in terms of their market share.

One problem with such policy capturing research is that it involves specially created (i.e., hypothetical) examples. Another is that it assumes that we already know what factors might be important. If we don't, other variables that could also play a role in venture capitalists' decisions can be overlooked. To avoid such problems, a different approach involving information on actual decisions by venture capitalists over an extended period of time has been used in recent research by Petty and Gruber (2011).

These researchers were granted access to the records of a venture capitalist firm that, over an 11-year period, had considered business plans from more than 3000 new ventures (not an unusually high number for a successful venture capital company). The records contained comments by the venture capitalists about each new venture, and these were then coded into several categories: the product or service offered by the new ventures, the size and potential of the markets they hoped to enter, the management team (e.g., its experience, reputation), and the financial potential (potential return on investment, valuation). In addition, the venture capitalists' comments also included another set of factors, ones relating to the venture capital firm itself—for instance, whether the new ventures planned to operate in fields or industries on which the venture capital firm focused (e.g., retail, high-tech, etc.), whether the new venture was far enough along in its development to fund (VCs typically do not want to fund new companies that are in the very early stages of product development), the details of the deal with entrepreneurs, and so on. Results indicated that all of the factors mentioned here play a role in the VCs' actual decisions (fund, reject but leave the door open for resubmission, or reject finally), but that, contrary to previous findings, characteristics of the founding team were not as important as the product, market, potential return on investment, or "fit" of the new venture with the venture capital firm's interests and focus. Petty and Gruber (2011) suggest that the founding team may be less important in funding decisions by venture capitalists because, as one VC put it, "We have a list of experienced managers and you can always bring in a management team if needed" (Petty and Gruber, 2011, p. 180).

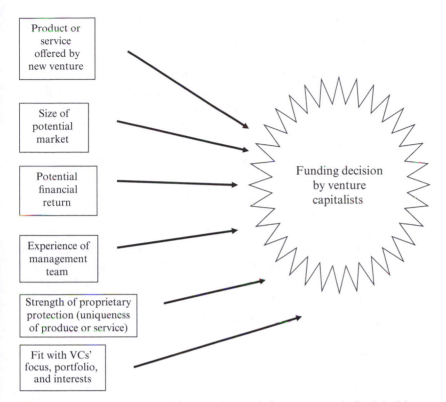

Note: As shown here, several factors play a role in venture capitalists' decisions to offer financial and non-financial support to new ventures. Additional factors also play a role, but the ones shown here appear to be among the most important.

Source: Based on the findings of many different studies.

Figure 8.2 *Factors that play an important role in venture capitalists' decisions*

Combining the two lines of research described here—policy capturing (which uses hypothetical examples) and examination of venture capitalists comments as they evaluate new ventures—suggests that many factors play a role in venture capitalists' decisions (see Figure 8.2 for a summary). Given the complexity of these decisions, the speed with which they must be made, and the large volume of business plans venture capital firms receive, this is hardly surprising. This conclusion, in turn, indicates that, if they wish to maximize their chances of success in obtaining VC funding, entrepreneurs should focus on ensuring that they—and the business models they present in their business plans—are high on these dimensions (see Figure 8.2). Success, in short, goes primarily to those best prepared to meet the stringent tests imposed by venture capitalists in their efforts to invest their funds only in new ventures with maximum chances of success.

Human resources: winning the support and commitment of key persons

No matter how good their ideas, how impressive their skills and talents, or how great their enthusiasm and motivation, entrepreneurs can almost never do it alone. Converting their ideas and the opportunities they recognize or create into functioning, profitable companies usually requires lots of help—the skills, talents, motivation, and effort of many other persons. No matter how large the financial resources entrepreneurs have or obtain, it is still people—working individually or, more often, in teams or groups—who actually move the process forward. In short, while entrepreneurs often need the financial support and other forms of help provided by venture capitalists and business angels, they also need to attract essential human resources—the people side of the equation for gaining success. We've said this before in this chapter, but it is such an important point that it bears repeating. In this section, therefore, we'll address questions such as these: What human resources are crucial? How can they be obtained? And what role do they play in new ventures' success?

Building a strong, and versatile, founding team: the advantages of complementarity

Over the years, I have known many entrepreneurs and, as noted above, few of them operated alone; the great majority worked together with several co-founders of their new venture. If you were building a "dream team" of entrepreneurs, what would it be like? One important ingredient in such an ideal team would be a broad range of skills, knowledge, talents, and interests across the various members. To the extent this was true, each member would supply something unique and valuable, and what one didn't have, another founder would provide. For instance, if one founder were highly experienced in product design, another might have strengths (knowledge, skills) relating to production, while a third could be versed in the complexities of managing financial resources. A fourth member might be expert in marketing and sales. Such a team, composed of diverse members, would, in a sense, "cover all the bases" and have a rich and deep array of human capital—resources that could contribute to the new venture's success. Such a team would show a high level of complementarity—together, their skills, knowledge, and experience would not overlap strongly; rather, each would bring something else to the table.

Is this the kind of teams I usually encounter? Far from it. Whether they are teams of students in my classes, or teams of entrepreneurs entered in important business plan competitions, they tend to show a high degree of similarity—members of the founding team tend to have similar experience, education, background, and knowledge. For instance, a typical team might consist of three engineers or three scientists, all with similar interests and background. Why? In part because teams often emerge from social networks—they develop out of the people we know well, and in general these people are ones with similar interests and background to our own. This is entirely reasonable, and does indeed offer important advantages. A large body of research indicates that people who are similar to one another in various ways tend to feel more comfortable around each other, to have better communication, and to like each other to a much greater extent than people who are not (e.g., Parker, 2009). Certainly these are important benefits, but a high degree of similarity—and overlapping skills, knowledge, and experience among founding team members—does have important implications for the founding team's human capital (its combined array of skills, knowledge, abilities, and experience) and its social capital too (the relationships founders have with others, the benefits they can obtain from these relationships, their reputations, and the extent and quality of their social networks). The more similar founding team members are, the more restricted will be their store of human capital and social capital. This is an important point, because research findings indicate a strong relationship between founding teams' human and social capital and the success of their new ventures (e.g., Ensley and Pearson, 2005).

So where does all this leave us? With the suggestion that, when entrepreneurs assemble their founding team, they should consider the basic fact that what any team of entrepreneurs needs for success is a very wide range of information, skills, aptitudes, and abilities. And this is less likely to be present when all members of the founding team are highly similar to one another in important ways than when they are more heterogeneous in their backgrounds and experience. An important guideline for entrepreneurs with respect to building their founding team, therefore, is this: try to resist the strong temptation (and it *is* strong!) to work solely with people whose background, training, and experience are highly similar to your own. Doing so will be easy and pleasant in many ways, and facilitates communication between founding team members. But it may also put a cap on the rich array of human resources the new venture needs. In essence, working with people who have what you don't have may be less fun than working with ones who are highly similar to yourself, but may, at the same time, strengthen the team's human and social capital in important ways.

Beyond the founding team: attracting and retaining outstanding employees

Where human resources are concerned, the term *founding team* is highly appropriate: the founders are indeed the foundation of these resources. As just noted, the human and social capital they bring to the new venture play a crucial role in its success. But, even if these basic resources are strong, if new ventures grow they soon need the talents, effort, and skills of additional individuals. In short, even modest growth quickly brings the founders face to face with an important question: How can they find, attract, and retain outstanding employees? Unfortunately, they soon find that this is a complex and difficult task. As a new and relatively unknown company, a new venture may appear to be a high risk for the talented, skilled persons the entrepreneurs hope to attract. Funding from venture capitalists can help by boosting the venture's legitimacy, but even then the task of finding and attracting excellent employees remains challenging. How do start-up companies overcome these difficulties? Partly through the use of their social and business networks. They draw on these networks to help them identify appropriate individuals and to assist in hiring them. This is yet another reason why it is usually crucial for entrepreneurs to build strong networks.

Networks, however, are often not enough: they may not include the kind of people a new venture wishes to attract or hire. Moreover, the tasks of finding and then recruiting new employees—difficult and time-consuming as they are—are only part of the picture. Once such persons are hired, they must be retained and motivated to do their best work. This involves developing and providing appropriate employee benefits, establishing effective performance appraisal systems, setting up compensation plans that maximize employees' motivation and commitment, providing training when needed, and dealing with the wide array of interpersonal problems that always arise when individuals work together. Entrepreneurs are generally much too busy running and building their companies to focus attention on these issues, crucial though they are, so at some point the wisest course may be to stop trying to do it themselves and, instead, decide to outsource these tasks. A large number of companies that specialize in providing such services—hiring, training, setting up compensation systems, and so on—exist, and can be retained to perform these functions. Unfortunately, research findings indicate that entrepreneurs are often reluctant to take this action (e.g., Klaas, Klimchak, Semadeni, and Holmes, 2010). They feel that the new venture cannot afford the costs, and furthermore, because of their close identification with their companies, they do not want to surrender these tasks to others. They are more likely to hire such firms when focused on strategies involving differentiation—efforts to distinguish themselves from competitors through, for example, superior customer services—and more likely to do this when they operate in highly uncertain environments. However, overall, in the earlier stages of development, when their companies are small, entrepreneurs tend to try to manage human resource-related issues themselves. Although they often seek advice from legal and accounting experts, they believe that they can deal with human resource issues without outside help. My advice is simple: don't do this! If you need help with these complex tasks, seek it: the benefits may far outweigh the costs.

Social influence: the fine art of getting others to say "yes"

In a sense, entrepreneurship involves a lot of selling. The entrepreneur who originates the idea that leads to identification of an opportunity and then, ultimately, to the launch of a new venture initially faces the task of presenting this idea to others, winning their approval of it, and persuading them to help in moving forward with its development. Along the way, entrepreneurs must often persuade other persons to provide assistance—financial or human resource based. They must, in most cases, write an organized and eloquent business plan, and make verbal presentations in which they hope to persuade venture capitalists or others to invest in their company, their idea, and themselves. Later, if the new venture grows, they face the task of "selling" the new company to prospective employees as a good place to work and risk their careers. In addition, they must somehow convince potential customers to take a chance on their products or services, even though they are a new company without an established record of reliability. So yes, indeed, entrepreneurship does involve a great deal of selling, broadly defined. In the most general sense, these efforts all involve the process of exerting social influence—efforts by one or more persons to change the behavior, attitudes, feelings, or actions of one or more others (Baron and Branscombe, 2012; Cialdini, 2008).

For entrepreneurs, the goal of such social influence is straightforward: somehow inducing others to say "yes" to their requests; and, whether they realize it or not, entrepreneurs engage in this process frequently. For this reason, some basic knowledge of the principles and techniques of social influence may be very helpful to entrepreneurs in a wide range of situations. Fortunately, a vast amount of research has focused on the nature and use of social influence; this discussion presents a brief overview of some of the key findings of this work. These, in turn, provide basic guidelines entrepreneurs can use to increase their effectiveness in getting others to say "yes."

Compliance: the underlying principles

Some years ago, Robert Cialdini, a well-known social psychologist, decided that the best way to find out about social influence—and especially the process of compliance (inducing others to comply with various requests)—was to study what he termed *compliance professionals*: people whose success (financial or otherwise) depended on their ability to get others to say "yes." Who are such persons? They include salespeople, advertisers, political lobbyists, fund-raisers, politicians, professional negotiators, and many others (including, as suggested above, entrepreneurs). Cialdini's technique for learning from these people was simple: he concealed his true identity and took jobs in various settings where gaining compliance is a way of life. In other words, he worked in advertising direct (door-to-door) sales, fund-raising, and other compliance-focused fields. On the basis of these first-hand experiences, he concluded that, although techniques for gaining compliance take many different forms, they all rest to some degree on six basic principles (Cialdini, 2008):

- *Friendship/liking.* In general, we are more willing to comply with requests from friends or other people we like than with requests from strangers or people we don't like. (Example: getting potential customers to like you can increase the chance of getting orders.)
- *Commitment/consistency.* Once we have committed ourselves to a position or action, we are more willing to comply with requests for behaviors that are consistent with this position or action than with requests that are inconsistent with it. (Getting a small order from a customer may pave the way for a larger one later, when it is requested.)
- *Scarcity.* In general, we value, and try to secure, outcomes or objects that are scarce or decreasing in availability. As a result, we are more likely to comply with requests that focus on scarcity than ones that make no reference to this issue. (Hinting to prospective employees that there are many good applicants for a job may increase their willingness to sign on immediately.)
- *Reciprocity.* We are generally more willing to comply with a request from someone who has previously provided a favor or concession to us than to someone who has not. In other words, we feel obligated to pay people back in some way for what they have done for us. (Paying a supplier ahead of schedule may increase the likelihood that the supplier will fill a special order quickly.)
- *Social validation.* We are generally more willing to comply with a request for some action if this action is consistent with what we believe persons similar to ourselves are doing (or thinking). We want to be correct, and one way to do so is to act and think like others. (Endorsement from a large company or influential person in an industry may raise the volume of a new venture's business.)
- *Authority.* In general, we are more willing to comply with requests from someone who holds legitimate authority—or simply appears to do so. (Endorsement from experts on product quality or performance may increase the volume of a new venture's business—for instance, favorable responses by customers to requests for new orders.)

According to Cialdini (2008), these basic principles underlie many techniques used by professionals—and ourselves—for gaining compliance from others. Below is a brief summary of several that have been found to be especially effective.

Compliance: techniques that work

- *Ingratiation*—getting others to like us so that they will be more willing to agree to our requests. This tactic, which is based on the first principle above (friendship/liking), can be accomplished in many ways—for example, flattery, or emphasizing points of similarity between ourselves and others. Research findings indicate that, in general, we tend to like others who are similar to ourselves more than others who are different; even very slight similarities such as having the same or a similar first name will often suffice (e.g., Burger, Messian, Patel, del Prado, and Anderson, 2004).
- *Foot-in-the-door technique.* Basically, this involves inducing target persons to agree to a small initial request ("Accept this free sample") and then making a larger request—the one desired all along ("Buy this product"). The results of many studies indicate that this tactic works—it succeeds in inducing increased compliance (e.g., Beaman, Cole, Preston, Klentz, and Steblay, 1983), apparently because of the principle of consistency: having agreed to a small request, individuals feel pressure to agree to the larger one, too, to be consistent with their previous actions. If we say "yes" to a small request, we are more likely to say "yes" to subsequent and larger ones, too, because refusing these would be inconsistent with our previous behavior.
- *The "that's-not-all" technique.* In this tactic for gaining compliance, an initial request is followed, before the target person can say "yes" or "no," by something that sweetens the deal—a small extra incentive from the persons using this tactic (e.g., a reduction in price, or "throwing in" something additional for the same price). For example, television commercials for various products frequently offer something extra to induce viewers to pick up the phone and place an order—for instance, a "free" knife or a "free" cookbook. Several studies confirm informal observations suggesting that the that's-not-all technique really works (Burger, 1986), but why? Perhaps because of the compliance principle of reciprocity: persons on the receiving end of the that's-not-all approach view the "extra" thrown in by the other side as an added benefit offered by the requester, and so feel obligated to reciprocate by agreeing to the request.
- *The deadline technique.* Department stores often use this tactic, indicating to shoppers that, after a specific date, a special sale will

end and prices will go up. They generally only imply this change in prices, because in fact often prices don't change when the "magic" date passes. But customers can't be certain, so many feel pressure to buy now in order to avoid missing out on a great deal. In the business world, the deadline technique can involve similar tactics: the suggestion that a special price or other benefit can be obtained only until a particular date.

These techniques for gaining compliance—for getting others to say "yes" to our requests or to make decisions and take actions we prefer—plus several others are summarized in Table 8.1. If used with skill and care, they can be highly effective, so familiarity with them, and skill in their application, can be very helpful to entrepreneurs in their efforts to convert their ideas into value-generating products or services. An added benefit is that they can assist entrepreneurs in recognizing, and resisting, influence from others, for as one old saying notes: "To be forewarned is often to be forearmed."

Summary of key points

To convert their ideas into reality, entrepreneurs usually need financial and human resources. They can obtain financial resources from many different sources: their own funds, friends and family, business angels, venture capitalists, corporations, banks, and government programs. All offer both advantages and disadvantages. For instance, by using their own funds, entrepreneurs can retain ownership of their companies. Friends and family and business angels generally offer better terms than venture capitalists, but they cannot generally provide large amounts of financial support. Venture capitalists have "deep pockets," but require a large share of the new venture's equity and impose many restrictions on entrepreneurs' actions.

Research using various methods (e.g., policy capturing, detailed analysis of venture capitalists' records concerning their evaluations of entrepreneurs' business plans) indicates that venture capitalists' decisions about funding new ventures are based on many factors, such as entrepreneurs' experience with a given market, the size of the potential market, the potential profitability of a new venture, and factors relating to the "fit" of the new venture with the venture capitalists' interests and portfolio of companies.

Entrepreneurs also generally need human as well as financial resources. The founding team makes an important contribution in this respect, providing human capital (the team's collective experience, knowledge, skills,

Table 8.1 *Techniques for getting others to say "yes"—and how they work*

Technique	Description	Principle on which it is based	Example
Ingratiation	Getting others to like the person seeking compliance.	Individuals are more likely to accept influence from persons they like.	The entrepreneur calls attention to similarities with a potential customer, thereby increasing the customer's liking for her or him.
Foot-in-the-door	Start with a small request, and escalate to a larger one once the first request is granted.	Consistency: individuals who have said "yes" once experience pressure to say "yes" again.	The entrepreneur offers free samples of the product; after these are accepted, she or he asks for an order.
Door-in-the-face	Start with a **very** large request and then, when this is refused, scale back to a smaller one.	Reciprocity: the requester has made a concession, so the target person feels pressure to make one too.	The entrepreneur asks for a large order; if this is declined, she or he asks for a small, token order.
That's-not-all tactic	Offer a small (trivial) extra benefit before the target person says "yes" or "no."	Reciprocity: the requester has offered something extra, so the target person feels pressure to reciprocate in some way.	The entrepreneur offers a high-quality potential employee a small extra benefit (e.g., a better office) to induce this person to join the new venture. The cost to the entrepreneur is slight, but the desirable new employee is hired.
Playing hard to get	The person seeking compliance indicates that something she or he has (product, service) is hard to obtain.	Scarcity: people tend to value things that are scarce or rare.	The entrepreneur tells a prospective employee that there are many applicants for a position in the new venture.
Deadline technique	The person seeking compliance indicates that something (product, service, etc.) will no longer be available or will be available at less advantageous terms beyond some deadline.	Scarcity.	The entrepreneur offers a "special price" to a potential customer if the customer places an order by a particular date, but only if the order is placed by that date.

Table 8.1   (continued)

Technique	Description	Principle on which it is based	Example
Low-ball technique	Very favorable terms are offered to the target person and, once she or he agrees, the terms are changed.	Consistency: many people find it hard to reverse a "yes" decision.	The entrepreneur offers a potential customer a very early delivery date for products ordered. Later, the entrepreneur indicates that this date can't be met.

Note: Individuals use many tactics to win compliance from others—to get them to agree to various requests. Whether they realize it or not, entrepreneurs often use these tactics. Increased familiarity with them can make efforts at gaining compliance more effective. These techniques must be used with considerable care, however, because they can "boomerang" and generate anger and annoyance among the persons toward whom they are directed (e.g., if entrepreneurs change a deal once it is made, customers may strongly resent this).

and interests) and social capital (team members' social networks). To maximize such human and social capital, the founding team should show a degree of complementarity rather than high similarity. In addition, as the new venture grows, it requires additional human resources. This implies finding, hiring, and retaining top-notch employees. Although entrepreneurs often try to carry out these tasks themselves, recent evidence indicates that they should, instead, outsource these tasks to companies that specialize in providing a broad range of human resource-related services: hiring, training, evaluating employees' performance, and setting up effective compensation systems.

In a key sense, entrepreneurship involves selling—efforts by entrepreneurs to exert social influence over others. An important task entrepreneurs face in this respect is gaining compliance—getting other persons to say "yes" to various requests (e.g., to place an order, come to work for this company, or provide financial and non-financial support). There are many techniques for reaching this goal, but all seem to be based on a small set of underlying principles, such as commitment (the foot-in-the-door tactic), reciprocity (the door-in-the-face procedure), and scarcity (the deadline technique). When used with skill and care, they can all be highly effective in persuading other persons to agree to specific requests. Thus entrepreneurs may benefit substantially from familiarity with them.

Bibliography

Baron, R.A., and Branscombe, N.R. (2012). *Social psychology*, 12th edition. Boston, MA: Allyn & Bacon.

Beaman, A.I., Cole, M., Preston, M., Klentz, B., and Steblay, N.M. (1983). Fifteen years of the foot-in-the-door research: A meta-analysis. *Personality and Social Psychology Bulletin, 9*, 181–186.

Burger, J.M. (1986). Increasing compliance by improving the deal: The that's-not-all technique. *Journal of Personality and Social Psychology, 51*, 277–283.

Burger, J.M., Messian, N., Patel, S., del Prado, A., and Anderson, C. (2004). What a coincidence: The effects of incidental similarity on compliance. *Personality and Social Psychology Bulletin, 30*, 35–43.

Cialdini, R.B. (2008). *Influence: Science and practice*. Boston, MA: Allyn & Bacon.

Dimov, D., and Shepherd, D.A. (2005). Human capital theory and venture capital firms: Exploring "home runs" and "strike outs." *Journal of Business Venturing, 20*, 1–21.

Ensley, M.D. and Pearson, A.W. (2005). An exploratory comparison of the behavioral dynamics of top management teams in new ventures: Cohesion, conflict, potency, and consensus. *Entrepreneurship Theory and Practice, 29*(3), 267–284.

Fried, V.H., and Hisrich, R.H. (1994). Toward a model of venture capital investment decision making. *Financial Management, 23*, 28–37.

Klaas, B.S., Klimchak, M., Semadeni, M., and Holmes, J.J. (2010). The adoption of human capital services by small and medium enterprises: A diffusion of innovation perspective. *Journal of Business Venturing, 25*, 349–360.

Large, D., and Muegge, S. (2008). Venture capitalists' non-financial value-added: An evaluation of the evidence and implications for research. *Venture Capital: An International Journal of Entrepreneurial Finance, 10*, 21–53.

Parker, S. (2009). Can cognitive biases explain venture team homophily? *Strategic Entrepreneurship Journal, 3*, 67–83.

Petty, J.S., and Gruber, M. (2011). In pursuit of the real deal: A longitudinal study of VC decision making. *Journal of Business Venturing, 26*, 172–188.

Read, S., Song, M., and Smith, W. (2009). A meta-analytic review of effectuation and venture performance. *Journal of Business Venturing, 24*, 573–587.

Sarasvathy, S.D. (2008). *Effectuation: Elements of entrepreneurial expertise*. Cheltenham, UK and Northampton, MA, USA: Edward Elgar Publishing.

Shepherd, D.A., and Zacharakis, A. (2005). Venture capital. In M. Hitt and D. Ireland (eds), *The encyclopedia of entrepreneurship* (pp. 245–246). Malden, MA: Blackwell.

Shepherd, D.A., Zacharakis, A.L., and Baron, R.A. (2003). Venture capitalists' decision processes: Evidence suggesting more experience may not always be better. *Journal of Business Venturing*, *18*, 381–401.

Zacharakis, A.L., and Shepherd, D.A. (2005). A non-additive decision-aid for venture capitalists' investment decisions. *European Journal of Operational Research*, *162*, 673–689.

PART III • ENTREPRENEURSHIP WITHOUT BOUNDARIES

9 Thinking and acting entrepreneurially: beyond new ventures

• •

Chapter outline

If you really want something, you can figure out how to make it happen. (Cher)

Imagination is more important than knowledge. (Albert Einstein)

When most people hear the word *entrepreneur* they think, immediately, of trailblazers who have an idea and develop it into a new business venture. Names such as Mark Zuckerberg, Steve Jobs, and—from earlier times— Henry Ford and Thomas Edison leap to mind. In one sense, this view of entrepreneurs, and what they do, is highly appropriate. As we have noted throughout this book, starting new business ventures is, without a doubt, the most visible, and perhaps most important, outcome of thinking and acting entrepreneurially. But, as noted in Chapter 1, it is definitely not the entire story. Individuals can, and often do, think and act entrepreneurially in other contexts. For instance, they may do so within large organizations, developing what amounts to new ventures within existing companies (e.g., Parker, 2011). Similarly, they may engage in entrepreneurial thinking and action with respect to their careers or professions, for instance the many online services operated by attorneys who offer legal advice to people seeking it—of course, for a fee! The idea for such services was a new one in the legal profession and, in a sense, transformed the practice of law by making it available to many people who, for various reasons, were reluctant or unable to consult attorneys in person.

These are just a few examples of the fact that entrepreneurial thinking and action can—and often do—occur outside the context of new ventures. In this chapter, we will focus in more detail on this topic, examining many ways that individuals use their own creativity, ingenuity, and knowledge to "break out of the ordinary" and both think and act in ways that enrich their work, careers, and lives. In other words, this chapter will explore the many ways in which the basic principles of entrepreneurial thought and action can be applied in contexts other than that of creating a new venture. Specifically, it will proceed as follows.

First, intrapreneurship—entrepreneurial activities within existing companies—will be considered. One intriguing question concerning intrapreneurship is: Why do individuals with creative ideas for something better decide to stay (remain in their companies) or to go (leave and start their own new venture)? Next, we'll turn to the relevance of entrepreneurial thinking and action to individual careers. As we'll note, major changes in the business world (e.g., the fact that few jobs are now highly secure) have created a situation in which individuals must approach their careers in different ways, which involves building their own battery of skills and identifying opportunities for furthering their careers based on them. Third, we'll examine the application of entrepreneurship in contexts that may, at first, seem surprising, but are actually natural homes for entrepreneurial thought and action: the arts and the professions (e.g., law, medicine). Perhaps most surprising of all, we'll consider the possibility that entrepreneurial thinking and action can find a home even in local governments—a context that seems, at first glance, to be an unusual home for creative thinking and innovation. Overall, the key goal is to indicate that, although the creation of new ventures is a very important context for entrepreneurship, it is definitely not the entire story.

Intrapreneurship: thinking and acting entrepreneurially within existing companies

Organizations have always faced competition, but, as the global economy has grown increasingly integrated, pressures to stay one step ahead of competitors have—with few exceptions—become more intense. While this is more true of high-tech industries, where rapid change is the normal state of affairs, it is also true of more stable industries as well. The basic message, in short, is simple: compete effectively or disappear. A good

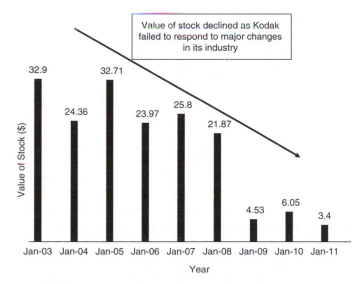

Note: As shown here, the stock value of Eastman Kodak Company has dropped sharply in recent years, largely because the company failed to anticipate, and then was slow to react to, major changes in its industry (primarily the shift from film to digital photography). The top management did not, unfortunately, think and act entrepreneurially—for instance, it did not seek to develop new, emerging opportunities through intrapreneurship.

Source: Based on public records, New York Stock Exchange.

Figure 9.1 *What happens when a company fails to compete effectively*

illustration of a famous company that failed to compete effectively is provided by Eastman Kodak Company, an old and famous company which once dominated large markets (cameras, film, film processing). For many different reasons—including its own corporate culture—Kodak underestimated the shift to digital photography, and failed to compete strongly in this rapidly expanding market when it finally did. The result? The company has piled up mounting losses, its stock has dropped sharply (see Figure 9.1), it is quickly running out of funds and, in fact, has now filed for Chapter 11 protection in order to restructure.

The intense competition faced by virtually all companies at present raises an important question: How can they best meet these challenges? While many possible answers exist (e.g., cutting costs to become "lean and mean"), one that is very compelling involves *intrapreneurship*—defined as the process of developing new products or new ventures within an existing corporation, in order to exploit new opportunities and create value (Parker, 2011; Seshadri and Tripathy, 2006). In other words, intrapreneurship involves the basic components of entrepreneurship, but within an existing organization. There are countless examples of successful intra-preneurship in many different countries, but instead of focusing on these it seems more important to examine the nature of intrapreneurship itself—what it involves and how employees can be encouraged to pursue it. It is on these issues that we focus next.

Factors that enhance—or obstruct—intrapreneurship

Why should employees of a large organization want to act entrepre-neurially—to generate creative ideas that can enhance the success of their employer? Normally, employees have what is known, not surprisingly, as an *employee mindset*: they feel that their relationship with their organiza-tion is purely an economic one: the organization compensates them, finan-cially and otherwise, for their time and effort. Given the limited scope of this relationship, they are only mildly interested in their employer's success, primarily to ensure that it will survive and continue to provide them with employment. The key task in encouraging intrapreneurship, therefore, is that of somehow generating a sense of psychological ownership among employees (e.g., Pierce, Kostova, and Dirks, 2001). In essence, they should come to feel that they are owners of the business, not simply employees of it. This sense of ownership is a key aspect of entrepreneurship, and to the extent it can be generated among employees of an existing company it can encourage a sense of commitment to the company and greatly increased willingness to help it innovate. In fact, research findings indicate that there is a strong relationship between a sense of psychological ownership among employees and innovativeness by organizations (e.g., Seshadri and Tripathy, 2006). But how, specifically, can it be encouraged? In a popular book, Prosek (2011) offers suggestions, based largely on her own experi-ence rather than systematic research, for reaching this goal and thereby turning her employees into what she terms "an army of entrepreneurs." Among the steps she recommends are these.

First, top management of the company should demonstrate authen-ticity, which implies not simply preaching the principles of entrepreneur-ship, but actually demonstrating them. According to Prosek (2011) this entails a willingness to implement creative ideas, even if this involves some risk. Second, top management should demonstrate a genuine com-mitment to people. Employees should be respected, supported, but chal-lenged, and also provided with training they need to be both effective and innovative on their jobs. Third, top management should strive to develop commitment to the business among employees. There are many ways of accomplishing this task, but a key one is to provide employees with tangible rewards for developing ideas that lead to useful innovations. In Prosek's company, in fact, these rewards are provided for the life of the

Table 9.1   *Factors described by managers as promoting or obstructing intrapreneurship*

Factors that promote intrapreneurship	Factors that block intrapreneurship
Empowering employees.	Punishing risk taking, new ideas.
Rewarding ideas and creativity.	Allowing ideas to die; no follow-through.
Free-flowing information and communication.	Failing to encourage intrapreneurship.
Management support and encouragement.	High level of organizational politics.
Developing processes for idea generation.	Poor communication.
Clearly defined organizational needs, vision, direction.	No encouragement for opportunity recognition.
Developing improved cooperation and teamwork.	Unclear mission, priorities, goals.

Note: Several factors, such as empowering employees and rewarding them for creativity and innovativeness, promote intrapreneurship. In contrast, other factors, such as unresponsiveness to new ideas by top management and preventing employees from developing a sense of personal ownership in their organizations, tend to obstruct or block intrapreneurship.

Source: Based on data reported by Eesley and Longenecker (2006).

company—for instance, a 5 percent share of all revenue deriving from the employee's idea.

Fourth, efforts to build a corporate culture that favors intrapreneurship should be continuous. This implies that the company should remain responsive to potentially useful new ideas, communicate clearly with employees, and present them with new challenges. Overall, the basic idea is develop a workforce that truly care about the company, and feel that they have an important personal investment in it. To the extent this occurs, organizations will indeed have what Prosek describes as "an army of entrepreneurs," because all employees will happily invest their creativity, ingenuity, skills, and effort in the task of building the organization's success. Whether Prosek's (2011) recommendations are actually effective remains to be seen; they have not yet been tested by systematic research, but they are certainly intriguing, and worthy of careful research designed to test their validity.

In contrast, actual research on the factors that encourage or discourage intrapreneurship has already been conducted. For instance, Eesley and Longenecker (2006) asked a large number of managers to respond to two questions: (1) What specific things do organizations do that stifle or prevent intrapreneurship? (2) What specific things can organizations do to stimulate or encourage intrapreneurship? The findings of their research are summarized in Table 9.1, but here we'll comment on several of the most important variables.

With respect to barriers to intrapreneurship—factors that prevent employees from developing a sense of personal ownership in their organization—an important factor (mentioned by 57 percent of the managers) was punishing risk taking and new ideas. Clearly, if acting entrepreneurially yields negative outcomes, employees are unlikely to behave in this manner. Another important factor (mentioned by 44 percent of the managers) was unresponsiveness to new ideas. If an employee uses his or her creativity to generate an idea for some new product, service, or ways of increasing efficiency, and the idea simply dies in the bureaucracy, the employee is unlikely to repeat such actions because, in a sense, they are simply a waste of time. In fact recent research on the factors that influence employees' decisions about remaining in their company as intrapreneurs or leaving to start their own new ventures indicates that lack of responsiveness to new ideas is one important impetus to leave (Parker, 2011).

Turning to factors that promote intrapreneurship, a culture of workforce empowerment is at the top of the list (cited by 52 percent of the managers). This means that employees are given sufficient freedom of action to pursue their ideas or create improvements. Another important factor is providing recognition and rewards for demonstrating creativity and innovativeness. This echoes Prosek's (2011) suggestions about providing employees with tangible rewards for acting like entrepreneurs. Another key factor (mentioned by 41 percent of the managers) is encouraging communication with customers and within the company. This provides useful data on current conditions, and that, in turn, is very helpful in formulating new ideas that can contribute to innovation.

In sum, existing evidence—although somewhat sparse—offers a relatively optimistic conclusion: even very large and well-established companies can develop cultures that encourage employees to freely invest their creativity, ingenuity, and skills in efforts to help their company develop new products and practices that will enhance its competitive edge. In short, size and longevity are not necessarily impediments to efficiency and innovation, a fact that is underscored by the major success of companies such as Apple Computer, Honda Motors, and General Electric. Much more important is the culture an organization builds—and maintains.

To stay or to go? The choice between intrapreneurship and entrepreneurship

When employees of a large organization have an idea for something new and useful—a new product, service, means of increasing efficiency, or whatever—they face an important decision: should they share the idea with others in the company (e.g., their supervisor) and seek to be involved in its development and implementation, or should they take their idea with them and leave to put it to use in their own new venture? In other words, they face a choice between being an intrapreneur and being an entrepreneur. This choice obviously has important implications for an employee, but it is also important for the company: if the "best and brightest"—the people most likely to have creative and potentially useful ideas—choose to leave, this can undermine the ability of the company to compete effectively and, moreover, expose it to a strong, new competitor. What factors influence this important decision? Research on this topic (e.g., Helfat and Lieberman, 2002; Klepper, 2001) has identified several factors that may play a role in this choice, including the extent to which the company in which such an individual is employed is mired in bureaucracy and rigid routines, and the extent to which the idea is linked to the human capital—skills, knowledge, talents—of the employee. However, perhaps the most revealing evidence on this issue has been provided by Parker (2011) in a study of a large sample of individuals (31 845) who responded to telephone surveys which asked them questions designed to determine if they were currently engaged in start-up activities—either entrepreneurship (new ventures) or intrapreneurship (start-up activities within existing organizations). On the basis of previous research, it was hypothesized that several factors would determine which route to implementing their new ideas would be taken by these individuals (a final sample of more than 1200). Since general human capital—individuals' knowledge, skills, and intelligence—is portable, while specific human capital—knowledge of a particular business—is not, Parker (2011) predicted that general human capital would make entrepreneurship more attractive than intrapreneurship. Similarly, he predicted that, since business-to-business opportunities (in which one business sells products or services to another) require more resources than sales to individual customers, business-to-business opportunities would be more associated with intrapreneurship than entrepreneurship. Additional hypotheses concerned the costs of developing products, and the fact that entrepreneurs are a very highly selected group (as noted in Chapter 1), so that they would be distinct from persons who engage in intrapreneurship in various ways.

Results offered support for several of the predictions. For instance, factors related to the decision to leave and become an entrepreneur related to the included general human capital (higher general human capital was linked to a greater choice of becoming an entrepreneur), the intended market of the new products or services (other companies or individual customers, with a greater focus on individual customers related to choosing entrepreneurship), and the costs of the new products (the higher these were, the more likely individuals were to choose intrapreneurship). Additional findings indicated that younger (18–24) and older (45–54) employees were more likely to choose to stay and become intrapreneurs than persons in the middle of the age distribution (e.g., 35–44), and that intrapreneurship was more common in organizations with predominantly male employees, perhaps because females in these companies were somewhat unhappy with the "male-dominated culture" this encouraged. Although full explanations for why these factors influence the choice to stay or leave, it is clear that the variables that influence this decision can be identified and, perhaps, used to select and retain employees most likely to develop their new ideas within the company that hires them.

In sum, research on intrapreneurship indicates that it can be encouraged or discouraged by conditions present in existing organizations, and that several distinct factors influence employees' decisions to develop their ideas inside their current companies or leave to start their own new venture. Since intrapreneurship has been found to make significant contributions to the innovativeness and success of existing organizations, it seems clear that efforts to facilitate its presence and impact may be one important step existing companies can take to enhance their own success in an increasingly competitive business environment.

Thinking and acting entrepreneurially about careers

I don't have many items handed down to me by my family—by and large, they favored "Get rid of it" over "Save it forever" as a philosophy of life. But I do have my grandfather's gold watch, given to him at his retirement (see Figure 9.2). The inscription on the back indicates that he worked until he was 75. At the time, that was somewhat unusual: most people worked only until they were 65 and, in fact, many retired sooner (my father, for example, retired at 59). Now, however, several trends have converged to encourage many people to emulate my grandfather and continue working into their 70s or even 80s. To name just two factors, life expectancy has risen, and a growing number of company-sponsored pension plans have failed to meet their obligations. My father experienced this situation first-hand: his pension was first decreased and then disappeared entirely—a truly devastating blow to my parents' long-term financial planning. In addition, it is now illegal in the United States and several other countries to require employees to retire at a given age, unless they have agreed to this in advance (e.g., at the time they are hired). These and other trends described below have not only increased the number of years many people work: they have also underscored the importance of thinking entrepreneurially about one's career. What does this imply? What does

Note: My grandfather received the watch I now wear with pride on his retirement in 1971. He worked until he was 75, something that was quite unusual at the time. The nature of careers has now changed greatly, and one result is that many people work into their 70s or even 80s.

Source: Courtesy of Robert A. Baron.

Figure 9.2   *My grandfather's retirement watch*

it mean to think entrepreneurially about careers? We'll now take a closer look at this issue.

How careers have changed—and why this requires approaching them entrepreneurially

In the past, many jobs were, essentially, tenured: if the individuals holding them performed at acceptable levels for several years, they rarely, if ever, got fired. As a result, the basic model most people had concerning their careers was: obtain a job with a good company, and then, by working hard, gradually (or, even better, quickly!) rise through the ranks. In a sense, there was a psychological contract between employees and their employers implying that good work and loyalty on the part of employees would be rewarded with what amounted to lifetime employment (Lester and Kickul, 2001).

In recent years, however, this informal "contract" has been altered drastically, so that "guaranteed employment" is now rare rather than common (e.g., Rousseau, 1996). Three major factors have contributed to these changes. First, the wave of restructuring and "downsizing" that began in the 1970s and accelerated in subsequent years essentially ended the guarantee of permanent employment, and left millions of individuals without jobs—often when they were in mid-career. Some then turned to entrepreneurship, and used the skills and knowledge they had acquired at work to start their own companies (e.g., Gelb, 1997). Many others, however, were forced to take jobs much less desirable than the ones they had held previously, and to adjust to sharply reduced income. Second, in an effort to reduce costs, many companies have increased their use of contracting out: hiring temporary employees to complete particular tasks. This practice, sometimes known as utilizing a "just-in-time workforce," has eliminated a large number of full-time, permanent jobs. Finally, as described in the earlier discussion of intrapreneurship, a growing number of companies are starting new ventures internally, and have also adopted a focus on projects, on which different employees work as needed. These trends have reduced the need for a permanent staff of managers, but have simultaneously increased the opportunities for persons who, in a sense, are able to generate their own jobs—to come up with ideas for new ventures or projects within their companies that receive the approval of top management. As Rosabeth Kanter, a famous management scholar, puts it (Kanter, 1989, p. 24): "In the emerging workplace, opportunity goes to those who can *create* the job, not those who inherit a predetermined set of tasks."

There is an important message in these events and trends: given that most companies no longer offer a guarantee of continuous employment, individuals must approach their careers from a different perspective. They must focus on acquiring general human capital—portable skills and knowledge they can take with them from one position to another. And they must recognize, and prepare for, the possibility that they will become entrepreneurs or intrapreneurs someday. As Kanter notes (1989, 2009), there are three distinct career paths for individuals to consider. One involves staying with a single company for many years and advancing up the ladder. This is the corpocratic career; it is centered on loyalty to the company, rather than to the task. This path is rapidly vanishing. A second is that of the professional, which is based on obtaining special, and valuable, skills and knowledge. For such persons, success is based on their personal reputation for competence, rather than their years of service or loyalty to a particular company. A good example of this kind of career path is found in Hollywood, where famous producers and stars have little or no loyalty to particular studios; rather, they move from one to another to work on particular projects. Such careers suggest that savvy individuals should strive to build their skills and reputations, and not link their hopes for success to a specific company.

Finally, a third career path is entrepreneurial. The key resource for building this career is the ability to create new products or services that create value. This does not necessarily involve starting a new venture. Some persons can remain in a given company and attain success not by moving up the hierarchy, which, in any case is becoming increasingly flat in most companies, but by increasing the size of the "territory" for which they are responsible—for instance, the size of new markets their company is trying to develop that they handle. Overall, this may be the most desirable career path in today's business world, since it provides individuals with the flexibility to work, under very favorable terms, for an organization that recognizes the value of their creative efforts, or, in contrast, to become founders of their own companies. Given the current importance of innovation to even giant companies in obtaining and holding competitive advantage and given the relative rarity of individuals who combine high levels of creativity with high levels of knowledge and excellent managerial skills, this can be a very desirable career path to pursue.

Overall, now that the psychological contract of permanent employment has all but vanished, individuals must look to their own creativity, knowledge, and skills to build the kind of challenging, rewarding careers most people want. Yes, there is more risk in such a career than in any kind of permanent position—which at present is available only in a few special places, such as universities and government agencies—but the potential rewards more than offset these costs. Moreover, under current conditions, this kind of "build my skills and knowledge" approach may ultimately yield not only challenge, but security too. If you needed yet another reason to think entrepreneurially, then, this is definitely it!

Entrepreneurship in the arts, professions, and . . . everywhere

In 1999, Jennifer Kenworth continued her art training—and sought to expand her range of skills—by taking a residency in ceramics at a pottery studio in Nevada. While there, she was approached by a local resident who asked if she could undertake a specific project: painting Elvis Presley, on the cross, on velvet. She agreed and, working from a photo of Elvis in a library book, completed the painting and sold it for $50. When she returned home to Portland, Oregon, she decided to pursue what she perceived to be a very good opportunity: paint-to-order. Whatever customers wanted, she would paint on velvet. When she displayed her work at various art shows, she began to receive orders, and opened a web page. The requests were sometimes unusual—"Paint a skeleton wearing a Dodgers cap," "Paint a monkey with a red beret." But soon she had a thriving business, and currently charges $150 for an 8-inch by 10-inch painting. Why did she take this path? "Because velvet paintings make people smile," she says, "and help them relive events in their lives."

Does Jennifer Kenworth, the artist, belong in a feature in the magazine *Entrepreneur*? That's where her work—and her company—was once featured (*Entrepreneur*, May 2011, p. 84). She certainly meets the definition of *entrepreneur* adopted in this book: she has used her own creativity, ingenuity, and skills to create something new and, to her customers at least, definitely of value. Further, she recognized an opportunity to use her skills and actively developed it. She did not, however, found a new venture in the formal sense of the term. This basic fact serves to emphasize a key point: entrepreneurial thinking and action can occur in many different contexts, including the arts—not solely in the world of business. At first glance, and to many persons, the idea that entrepreneurship can (and does) occur in the arts might seem like a contradiction in terms. But the reason behind this reaction is clear: many people associate entrepreneurial activity solely with new venture creation. As we've tried to note throughout this book, however, the basic components of entrepreneurship thrive in many other settings and many other ways. To illustrate this fact, we'll now focus on examples of entrepreneurial thinking and action in two very different professions: the law (i.e., among attorneys) and government (among urban planners, mayors, and others who shape the policies—and destinies—of cities or states).

Entrepreneurial thinking and action among professionals: attorneys as a case in point

Have you ever heard an ad for Legalzoom.com on the radio? If so, you may know that it offers legal services online. For instance, the lawyers associated with this company can provide business services (incorporation, patents, trademarks), personal services (divorce, wills, bankruptcy, power of attorney), and legal documents such as pre-nuptial agreements and real estate deed transfers. The company was founded in 2001 by four attorneys—Brian P.Y. Liu, Brian S. Lee, Edward R. Hartman (all of whom were generally unknown outside their local area), and Robert S. Shapiro (an attorney with a nationwide reputation). The first three realized that, in order to succeed, they would need to recruit a famous colleague, and once Shapiro agreed to join them they launched the company. Why did they start Legalzoom.com? Because they wanted to extend their legal knowledge and services outside their local market. Since no online service of this type existed before, the founders of Legalzoom.com were certainly thinking and acting entrepreneurially: they came up with an idea for something new and useful, recognized an online legal service as an excellent opportunity, and proceeded to develop it. The success of the company indicates that they were indeed effective in combining the role of attorney with that of entrepreneur.

This is not the only way in which attorneys have demonstrated entrepreneurial thought and action. Consider, for instance, Pre-paid Legal Services, Inc. This online company offers what amounts to insurance for legal costs. For a relatively small monthly fee ($26 per month or less for many people), Pre-paid Legal Services provides coverage for legal bills, just as health insurance provides payment of medical bills. The company was founded by Harland Stonecipher, who was involved in a head-on collision in 1969. His auto insurance covered the damage to his car, and medical insurance covered the cost of his time in the hospital, but he had no protection for the legal bills he incurred when he was sued for damages by the other party involved in the accident. He soon realized that legal bills are something for which most people are not prepared, but which often arise unexpectedly as a result of many different events and situations. Middle-class persons in particular, he reasoned, did not know attorneys, and had no conception of the costs of engaging one. This gave him the idea for legal insurance, and he founded the predecessor of Pre-paid Legal Services, Inc. in 1972. The company began with a sales force of three, who sold coverage in much the same way as for life insurance—through sales calls. In the 1980s and 1990s, the company grew rapidly, increasing its employees to almost 500 by 1999.

In the years that followed, Pre-paid Legal Services developed a presence online (as Prepaidlegal.com), and grew even faster. It currently insures more than 1.5 million members, and in 2000 made the *Forbes* list of the 200 Best Small Companies in America for the fifth time. In 2011, it was sold to a New York private equity firm for $605 million. While Harland Stonecipher himself is not an attorney, his idea for legal insurance was certainly new and useful, and has had a major impact on the lives of millions of persons, as well as on the legal profession itself.

These are not the only ways in which attorneys and others have thought and acted entrepreneurially. For instance, another company, Lawyer.com, helps individuals find an appropriate attorney—one with the specific knowledge and skills they need—in their local communities. All practicing attorneys earn their living from their profession, but what makes the ones who founded or run the companies discussed here entrepreneurs is that they identified opportunities for bringing their legal services to new markets that, in the past, did not often seek or use such services.

If attorneys—individuals working in a profession that has existed for thousands of years and that, through its powerful presence in many governments, shapes the daily lives of billions of persons—can be entrepreneurial, then it seems clear that entrepreneurship can flourish almost anywhere. But stay tuned: we will now consider yet another setting that has recently been the site of entrepreneurial thought and action that, in some ways, is even more surprising—government.

Can even governments be entrepreneurial?

In 2002, Richard Florida, a professor of economics at Carnegie Mellon University, published a book entitled *The Rise of the Creative Class*. In it, he argued that a major reason why some cities in the United States were prospering and growing while others were standing still or even declining was the existence of differences in their ability to attract what he describes as "the creative class." These are individuals who are highly educated, generally well paid for their work, and—of course!—highly creative. Florida divides this group, which he suggests is increasingly important to society, into three major categories: the "super-creative core," which consists of scientists, engineers, professors, poets, novelists, artists, actors, designers, architects, cultural figures, think-tank researchers, and others— people whose work and lives are centered around creativity; creative professionals—people who work in many different knowledge-intensive industries (e.g., financial services, high-tech companies, healthcare); and technicians who apply their knowledge to working with the physical world.

More important than the specific activities these persons perform or their particular professions, however, is their impact on the economies of the cities or regions in which they live. Because they are highly paid and seek stimulation both at work and during their leisure hours, Florida suggests that they are an important engine of growth. He notes that, because they are, a key task for cities seeking growth is that of attracting these people in substantial numbers. In other words, the cities that are successful in attracting and retaining a high "creative class" will soon prosper.

How can this be accomplished? In the past, most local governments advertised their cities as "great places for families," and focused on attracting successful married couples in their 30s and 40s—people with good jobs and high income. But Florida says this is a mistake. First, such people constitute a declining share of the adult population, so on this basis alone they can't be a pillar of growth. Second, the kind of creative people he believes encourage growth do not fit this description. Many are single, and they do not necessarily value good schools, large shopping malls, modern housing, or even low crime and clean air—the themes on which cities have focused in the past in order to encourage people to move there. On the contrary, creative people want to live in communities or regions that have high levels of cultural and ethnic diversity, are welcoming to a wide variety of lifestyles, and offer specific amenities that are valued by the creative class, such as a vibrant and varied nightlife, outdoor recreational activities (e.g., bicycle trails), and an active local street-culture (e.g., cafés, small galleries, and bistros). In other words, they desire a lifestyle that fits their values and interests and, according to Florida, will voluntarily migrate to areas that provide it. Factors traditionally viewed as important in attracting new residents—low taxes, personal safety, and good services—are far less important to the "creative class."

To test his views—which were certainly new and potentially controversial—he created an index to measure the attractiveness to "the creative class" of cities or regions. This index included such factors as the share of people from the creative class in the total workforce, the presence of high-tech industry, and the number of gay people in the population (which Florida interpreted as an index of a region's openness to different lifestyles). He found that cities varied greatly on this measure, with San Francisco, Austin, San Diego, Boston, and Seattle being high, and Memphis, Las Vegas, Buffalo, and Louisville being low. Similar differences emerged for medium-sized cities and small ones too. According to Florida, cities high on this "attractiveness to the creative class" index will attract large numbers of affluent, creative, open-minded residents, and therefore will prosper. His advice: cities and regions should stop trying to achieve growth through such actions as building sports arenas and large office parks and encouraging the number of shopping centers and "big box" stores (Wal-Mart, Home Depot, Staples, etc.). The creative class does not care about such things. Instead, cities should seek to build prosperity through providing environments attractive to the creative class. This implies that cities, regions, or states should seek to encourage diversity through legislation that supports varied lifestyles (e.g., legalizing gay marriage), offering financial support for artists and musicians, building recreational activities, and so on.

Florida is an eloquent speaker and, through personal appearances and his best-selling book, has influenced many urban policymakers and governments that have "bought into" his recommendations. Consistent with Florida's theory, they have begun to spend large amounts of money on making the changes he recommends. For instance, despite a large state budget deficit, Anita Walker, the director of cultural affairs for the state of Iowa, has declared that: "Culture is no longer a frill. It is economic fuel." To back up these words, her department is investing in hiking trails and entertainment districts throughout the state. Austin, Texas—long known for its open and tolerant environment—has embarked on a "Keep Austin Weird" program to continue to support the offbeat culture that city planners believe is essential for its continued growth. Mayors from New Zealand to Canada, too, have adopted Florida's recommendations. For instance, Glen Murray, mayor of Winnipeg, has remarked: "What kills a city are people who want only low taxes, and want cities to be about pipes, pavement, and policing."

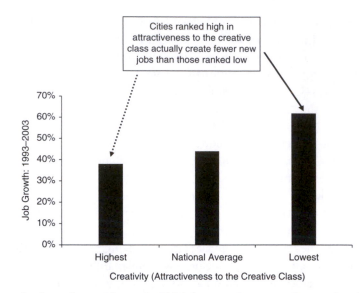

Note: As shown here, cities ranked high in attractiveness to the creative class (according to a measure developed by Richard Florida) do not grow more rapidly than ones ranked low. In fact, they create new jobs at a rate lower than the national average.

Source: Based on data from Malanga (2004).

Figure 9.3   *Does the creative class in a city or region promote economic growth?*

Florida's ideas are entrepreneurial in the sense that they introduce something new and—hopefully—useful into a context (city planning and government) that has been struggling for decades to find the road to prosperity. But here is where one of the key themes of this book—the importance of concrete, reliable data (an evidence-based approach to complex issues and questions)—comes into play. Does existing evidence support Florida's views concerning the crucial role of "the creative class" in economic growth? Given the importance of his (2002, 2006) theories, this issue seems to be deserving of a closer look.

Is the creative class really an engine of growth? Perhaps the first question that should be addressed is this: Does the presence of the creative class in an area actually result in (i.e., cause) economic growth? The second is: Even if it does, has Florida identified the key factors that brought members of the creative class to these locations in the first place? With respect to the first question, the evidence appears to be negative (e.g., Malanga, 2004). Yes, cities do indeed differ greatly in terms of the index Florida created, but—and this is crucial—these differences are not significantly related to basic measures of economic growth. For instance, one key measure of growth is the number of new jobs created. (Without new jobs, growth is unlikely or even impossible.) As Figure 9.3 shows, however, cities ranked high on Florida's creative index actually created fewer new jobs in recent years than those ranked low. I have personally lived in two cities that differ greatly in terms of Florida's index. Albany, NY, a region in which I lived for 22 years, has been in economic decline for decades. When I arrived there, in 1987, many large companies in the area employed large workforces. For instance, General Electric employed something like 20 000 people in the region. By the time I left, in 2009, this number was down to fewer than 4000. Overall, employment in the private sector declined steadily, primarily because of very high taxes—both corporate and local—and a vast array of regulations that were viewed as unfriendly to businesses located in the region. This region did have lots of engineers, scientists, and musicians, but overall the cultural environment was not especially rich. In fact, people who moved there from larger cities often described Albany as "Smallbany." So, although it is ranked high by Florida in attractiveness to "the creative class," it has not generated rapid job growth.

In contrast, Oklahoma City, where I live now, was ranked very low in Florida's index. Yet it has generated new jobs at much higher rates than the national average, and has done so for many years—long before the time Florida rated it as "unattractive" to the creative class. As for its cultural life, people who move here from other cities and regions are often "blown away" by the huge variety of music, art, restaurants, and museums, and find many attractive older neighborhoods fully intact and prospering. Another important fact to consider, and one that also argues strongly against Florida's suggestions: cities ranked high in his index of creativity (i.e., attractiveness to the creative class) are not, as a group, growing faster in population than ones ranked low. In fact, they are among the cities with the largest population declines in recent decades. New York City lost more than 500 000 people between 1990 and 2000, and San Francisco—which Florida ranks first—lost more than 200 000 during the same period.

How can Florida, a skilled and experienced economist and a professor at a prestigious university, be so wrong? According to one critic (Malanga, 2004), partly because he fell into the trap of circular reasoning. First, he focused on a select group of cities—ones that prospered during the "internet bubble" of the late 1990s (e.g., San Francisco, Boston). Then he identified what he personally thought were the key characteristics of these cities. Finally, he based his index on these factors. Given that fact, how could these cities *not* score highly in terms of "attractiveness to the creative class"? This was virtually guaranteed because Florida designed the index to measure the characteristics he believed to be important in the growth of these cities. Note: he relied on his personal views rather than empirical evidence in formulating this list. Also crucially, he did not collect data measuring basic economic indicators of growth, for instance number of new jobs created, proportion of companies in a city or region showing high growth. In other words, he did not provide data crucial in testing the validity of his views—no specific evidence that his high-ranking cities actually did grow faster than the low-ranking ones.

There is certainly no intention here of being too ultra-critical of Florida or his theories—far from it. His ideas are indeed creative, and he has stated them eloquently in several books. (His 2006 book *The Flight of the Creative Class* suggests that economic decline follows when the creative class no longer finds a city or region attractive.) But the tremendous impact of his theories has occurred in the absence of strong supporting economic data, and that means that urban policymakers and governments all over the globe may well have embarked on projects and programs that, ultimately, will do little to provide the growth they seek. It is certainly desirable to seek to attract creative individuals who will start high-growth businesses and enrich both the economy and the cultural life of a city or region: Who could argue with that? But existing evidence suggests that what attracts such people is not necessarily the factors Florida describes— bicycle paths, vibrant "street life," and social legislation favorable to many different lifestyles. Instead, it appears that familiar—and perhaps less exciting—factors such as low taxes, safe streets, good roads, and clean air and water are more important.

To conclude: novel ideas fluently presented can indeed be persuasive and bring about many changes; but, as noted in Chapter 1, they should not be accepted as fact in the absence of strong supporting data. This a key point we should all keep in mind in our quest for accurate, valid, and comprehensive knowledge about the complex process of entrepreneurship— the place where human creativity and dreams meet, and change reality. To fully understand it, we will need more than the insights, memories, and heartfelt advice of successful entrepreneurs, useful though these are; we will also need real evidence, based on carefully gathered data, and that in essence is what this book is all about.

Summary of key points

Intrapreneurship involves the process of developing new products or new ventures within an existing corporation in order to exploit new opportunities and create value. Several factors appear to enhance its occurrence—for instance, empowering employees, increasing their sense of psychological ownership in the company, and recognition of creative ideas and activity. In contrast, other factors reduce or block intrapreneurship—including unresponsiveness by top management to new ideas. When employees of a large company have an idea for something new and potentially useful, they face an important decision: Should they seek to develop the idea within their company (i.e., become intrapreneurs) or take it outside and start their own new venture (i.e., become entrepreneurs)? Noncompete agreements may prevent employees from leaving and using knowledge gained on the job to start new ventures, but, aside from this legal factor, research findings indicate that several additional factors play a role in this decision: for instance, possession of a high level of human capital encourages entrepreneurship, while the costs of developing the new product or service encourage intrapreneurship. In addition, younger and older persons are more likely to choose to stay, while those in the middle of the age distribution are more likely to leave and become entrepreneurs.

Major changes in the business world in recent years have made it essential for most people to think entrepreneurially about their careers. The number of jobs offering "guaranteed, lifetime employment" has declined greatly, which means that growing numbers of persons must expect to move from job to job and company to company, and should prepare to become entrepreneurs or intrapreneurs at various points in their careers. For this reason, an approach focused on acquiring personal skills and knowledge may be the best one.

Entrepreneurial thought and action can occur in many contexts aside from creating new ventures. In the arts, for instance, individual artists can recognize opportunities based on their own skills, and develop these in various ways. Entrepreneurial thought and action also occur in professions such as medicine and the law. Attorneys, especially, have successfully adopted an entrepreneurial perspective (mindset) in recent years. Companies such as Legalzoom.com, which provides legal services online, and Pre-paid Legal Services, Inc., which provides insurance for legal costs, are examples of how the principles of entrepreneurship can be successfully applied within an important and influential profession.

Entrepreneurial thought and action are also possible in government. One example is provided by Richard Florida's theory that cities and regions can encourage economic growth by attracting increasing numbers of what he describes as "the creative class." Presumably these high-income, active, creative people stimulate growth in many different ways. This theory suggests that cities and regions seeking growth should offer the kind of environment such people want (e.g., one that is highly diverse and tolerant of many different lifestyles). Many urban planners and city governments have accepted these views, and attempted to implement them through publicly funded projects. Unfortunately, however, research employing basic measures of economic growth, such as number of new jobs created or number of high-growth companies, has failed to support Florida's intriguing theories. In fact, cities that score high on an index of attractiveness to the creative class (e.g., San Francisco, New

York) have actually shown lower job growth than ones rated low (e.g., Oklahoma City). This suggests that, as is true in many different contexts, new urban policies should be adopted only on the basis of strong supporting evidence.

References

Eesley, D.T., and Longenecker, C.O. (2006). Gateways to intrapreneurship. *Industrial Management, 48*, 18–23.

Florida, R. (2002). *The rise of the creative class: And how it's transforming work, leisure, community, and everyday life*. New York: Perseus Books Group.

Florida, R. (2006). *The flight of the creative class*. New York: HarperCollins.

Gelb, B.D. (1997). Perceptions of "downsized" employees considering entrepreneurship. *Journal of Business and Entrepreneurship*, October.

Helfat, C.E., and Lieberman, M.B. (2002). The birth of capabilities: Market entry and the importance of pre-history. *Industrial and Corporate Change, 11*, 725–760.

Kanter, R.M. (1989). The contingent job and the post-entrepreneurial career. *Academy of Management Review, 78*(4), 22–27.

Kanter, R.M. (2009). *SuperCorp: How vanguard companies create opportunity, profits, growth, and social good*. New York: Crown.

Klepper, S. (2001). Employee start-ups in high-tech industries. *Industrial and Corporate Change, 10*, 639–674.

Lester, S.W., and Kickul, J. (2001). Psychological contracts in the 21st century: What employees value most and how well organizations are responding to these expectations. *Human Resource Planning, 24*, 10–21.

Malanga, S. (2004). The curse of the creative class. *City Journal*, Winter.

Parker, S.C. (2011). Intrapreneurship or entrepreneurship? *Journal of Business Venturing, 26*, 19–34.

Pierce, J.L., Kostova, T., and Dirks, K.T. (2001). Toward a theory of psychological ownership in organizations. *Academy of Management Review, 26*, 298–310.

Prosek, J. (2011). *Building an army of entrepreneurs*. New York: American Management Association.

Rousseau, D.M. (1996). *Psychological contracts in organizations: Understanding written and unwritten agreements*. Newbury Park, CA: Sage.

Seshadri, D.V.R., and Tripathy, A. (2006). Innovation through intrapreneurship: The road less travelled. *Vikalpa: The Journal of Decision Makers, 31*, 17–29.

Author index

Subject index